MAJOR CRITICAL ESSAYS

Bernard Shaw was born in Dublin in 1856. Essentially shy, he yet created the persona of G.B.S., the showman, satirist, controversialist, critic, pundit, wit, intellectual buffoon and dramatist. Commentators brought a new adjective into English: Shavian, a term used to embody all his brilliant qualities.

After his arrival in London in 1876 he became an active Socialist and a brilliant platform speaker. He wrote on many social aspects of the day; on *Common Sense about the War* (1914), *How to Settle the Irish Question* (1917) and *The Intelligent Woman's Guide to Socialism and Capitalism* (1928). He undertook his own education at the British Museum and consequently became keenly interested in cultural subjects. Thus his prolific output included music, art and theatre reviews, which were collected into several volumes published as *Music in London 1890–1894* (3 vols., 1931); *Pen Portraits and Reviews* (1931); and *Our Theatres in the Nineties* (3 vols., 1931). Among his five novels, *Cashel Byron's Profession* and some shorter fiction including *The Black Girl in Search of God and Some Lesser Tales* are published in Penguins.

He conducted a strong attack on the London theatre and was closely associated with the intellectual revival of British theatre. His many plays fall into several categories: his 'Plays Pleasant'; 'Plays Unpleasant'; comedies; chronicle-plays; 'metabiological Pentateuch' (*Back to Methuselah*, a series of plays) and 'political extravaganzas'. G.B.S. died in 1950.

Michael Holroyd, who was born in 1935, is half-Swedish and partly Irish. He studied science at Eton College and read literature at the Maidenhead Public Library. He has written biographies of Hugh Kingsmill, Lytton Strachey and Augustus John. He has been Chairman of the Society of Authors and of the Book Trust, and President of P.E.N. He is working on the authorized biography of Bernard Shaw, of which he has published two volumes. In 1989 he was awarded the C.B.E. for services to literature. He is married to Margaret Drabble.

Bernard Shaw

MAJOR CRITICAL ESSAYS

THE QUINTESSENCE OF IBSENISM

THE PERFECT WAGNERITE

THE SANITY OF ART

WITH AN INTRODUCTION BY MICHAEL HOLROYD

PENGUIN BOOKS

PENGUIN BOOKS

Published by the Penguin Group
Penguin Books Ltd, 27 Wrights Lane, London W8 5TZ, England
Viking Penguin, a division of Penguin Books USA Inc.
375 Hudson Street, New York, New York 10014, USA
Penguin Books Australia Ltd, Ringwood, Victoria, Australia
Penguin Books Canada Ltd, 2801 John Street, Markham, Ontario, Canada L3R 1B4
Penguin Books (NZ) Ltd, 182–190 Wairau Road, Auckland 10, New Zealand

Penguin Books Ltd, Registered Offices: Harmondsworth, Middlesex, England

First published separately in 1891, 1898 and 1895 respectively
Published in Penguin Books 1986

3 5 7 9 10 8 6 4

Printed in England by Clays Ltd, St Ives plc
Typeset in VIP Palatino

CONTENTS

CONTENTS

INTRODUCTION

Bernard Shaw was in his mid-seventies when he chose, and revised for the last time, 'The Quintessence of Ibsenism', 'The Perfect Wagnerite' and 'The Sanity of Art' to represent his *Major Critical Essays* in the Collected and Standard editions of his works. But the three essays had originally been composed between thirty and forty years earlier, when he was at the height of his powers as a polemicist and critic of the arts.

In 1876, aged not quite twenty, he had left Dublin for London determined to set himself up as 'a professional man of genius'. His upbringing in Dublin had been a torture to him; London represented hope. But after almost ten years of failure, rejection and obscurity, during which he later estimated he had earned a little under ten pounds from his own writings, the flame of his ambition had sunk low. He wrote a thousand words a day, but his five novels were turned down by every publisher in Britain and America who read them; and he could find no journalistic employment. Every opening seemed to be an accident, and waiting for accidents was a hardening process 'from which I have never quite recovered'.

In 1884, as a result of his increasing interest in socialism, he had joined the Fabian Society and was kept well-exercised writing unpaid pamphlets and making unpaid speeches. But it was not for another year that he 'slipped into paid journalism'.

This came about as a result of his friendship with William Archer, the theatre critic and translator of Ibsen. Working in the British Museum Reading Room, Archer's attention had been drawn to what appeared to be a damaged brown paper parcel in the next seat. This was Shaw. 'My interest was excited not only by his appearance,' Archer wrote, 'but by the literature to which he devoted himself day after day. It consisted of Karl Marx's *Das Kapital* in French, and a full orchestral score of Wagner's *Tristan und Isolde*.'

Before long they were introduced. 'We had many interests in common,' Archer wrote, 'and soon became intimate friends.' Troubled by the sight of his friend making tepid porridge over the gas fire in his room, Archer decided to take his affairs in hand. 'It was the easiest thing in the world to get him work, because whatever he did was brilliant,' Archer later explained. He planted him among the reviewing staff of the *Pall Mall Gazette* for which he wrote book reviews from the middle of 1885 to the end of 1888; he found him work as a music critic for the *Dramatic Review* and *The Magazine of Music*; and with much relief he handed over to him his own job as art critic on *The World*.

Over the next thirteen years, until his marriage in 1898, Shaw established himself as the most brilliant critic of music and the theatre in England. It was during these years that he wrote the three critical essays in this volume. The first was 'The Quintessence of Ibsenism'.

In the summer of 1890, rather to their dismay, the Fabians had found themselves committed to a programme of addresses under the general heading 'Socialism in Contemporary Literature'. Shaw chose Ibsen, and between May and July worked at his lecture which was delivered on 18 July at the St James's Restaurant. The minutes record that 'the effect on the packed audience was overwhelming'. Not all the Fabians were happy. 'It is very clever,' Sidney Webb reported, 'and not so bad as I feared . . . But his glorification of the Individual Will distresses me.' In fact Shaw had used Ibsen's texts to support his case for an adaptable as opposed to doctrinaire socialism, which in the immediate context meant Fabian gradualism and permeation as against the Marxist dogma and revolutionary politics of H. M. Hyndman's Social Democratic Federation.

It was probably the Parnell case that encouraged Shaw to

expand his lecture into a book. This *cause célèbre* had by November 1891 resulted in Captain O'Shea being granted a decree nisi against his wife, naming Charles Stewart Parnell, leader of the Irish Party in the House of Commons, as co-respondent. In letters to the *Star* Shaw had defended Parnell against the outcry of 'Parnell Must Go!' that sounded through the country following this flouting of domestic ideals by a public figure. On 16 December, he wrote to his fellow Fabian Sydney Olivier criticizing the opposition to Parnell from within the Fabian Society; and that same day he decided to publish *The Quintessence of Ibsenism*.

The book came out the following October, designed to purge socialism of the flattering myths and sentimentalities that, like barnacles, were already becoming encrusted over its reforming body. Shaw felt an immediate affinity with Ibsen. Archer, meeting Ibsen in Denmark in 1887, had observed that he 'is essentially a kindred spirit with Shaw – a parodist, a sort of Devil's Advocate, who goes about picking holes in every "well-known fact" '. It was this similarity, accounting for many parallels in their plays, that helped to give Shaw an instinctive insight into Ibsen's work. The joy of this essay is the feeling of Shaw's agile and ingenious mind working with such vitality on material so sympathetic to him.

The chief objection to *The Quintessence of Ibsenism* was brought by Ibsen's interpreters who charged it with being a brilliantly misconceived piece of criticism that, while helping to gain acceptance for Ibsen on the British stage, butchered him to make a Fabian holiday. Shaw tried to guard against this by prefacing his book with the warning that he is not concerned here with Ibsen as a poet and dramatist, but as a teacher; that though acutely responsive to the poetry and drama, he is not attempting to write literary criticism but an exposition of the philosophy of which, he believed, Ibsen was a leading exponent. The book also presents Shaw's credentials as someone who was carrying on Ibsen's business of 'changing the mind of Europe'.

Ibsen's name does not appear in Shaw's letters before 1889, but two years later he has appropriated him. Following productions of *The Doll's House* and *Ghosts*, the name of Ibsen had emerged from obscurity into huge contention in Britain as the playwright who was forcing a generation to revalue its ideas. The critics battled resoundingly over his reputation, and Shaw assumed the generalship of the British campaign for Ibsen as part of that same world struggle he had discovered to be at the centre of his plays. In this way Ibsen became for Shaw not simply a literary symbol but a tool in the unheroic Fabian plan to make things, not as they ought to be (that was utopianism), but as they could be made (that was socialism).

As a model for his argument, Shaw used a threefold division of humankind into philistine, idealist and (pending the word superman) realist. This division required an inversion of the terms realist and idealist in their common usage, which he cleverly justifies in terms of Ibsen's plays. He proposes a hypothetical community of one thousand people in which seven hundred are easygoing philistines, two hundred-and-ninety-nine dangerous idealists, and there is one realistic pioneer essential to the evolution of the species. The philistine, substituting 'custom for conscience', is satisfied with the social system as it is. The irony of his position is that, though he sees any interference with the social machinery as highly dangerous, the real danger comes from allowing that machinery to grow outdated. The philistine believes blindly in safety and employs the idealist to think for him, to 'idealize' his lack of thought. The idealist, though higher in the ascent of human evolution than the philistine, is a moral coward coerced by the majority into conformity. His instinct is perverted by fear and he uses all his powers of reason to obscure the truth, substituting for the human will and spirit a set of abstract ethical principles set hard within the structure of idealized public institutions, laws and creeds. Ideals, in Shavian terminology, are therefore illusions which have their origin in the fear of facts; and they become excuses

12

for doing what we do, which is always what we have done. So idealism in life is the rule of precedent, and the idealist a pedlar of fancy pictures that advertise this rule. Shaw likens these pictures to beautiful masks which the idealist puts on the unbearable faces of truth: the poetic mask of immortality on the king of terrors, death; the mask of eternal happiness on the brutalities of the sex instinct; and on his own self-murder the religious concept of self-sacrifice. But the realist, bolder than the rest, lays hold of these masks and exposes a new aspect of a disagreeable truth. So he helps to relieve us from useless sacrifice to the tyranny of ideals: for the 'destroyer of ideals, though denounced as an enemy of society, is in fact sweeping the world clear of lies'. This was the Ibsen-impulse, 'to get away from idolatry and to get to the truth regardless of shattered ideals'.

Sidney Webb's distress at his friend's 'glorification of the Individual Will' underlines the difference between a man who was by nature a collectivist and another who worked his way partly against the grain of his natural talent from individualism to collectivism. Shaw tried to accommodate Webb's objection by admitting that Ibsen was an arch-individualist who 'has not enjoyed the Fabian advantage', since socialism in his day was one of the most outrageously idealistic of all the new -isms. But the acknowledgement has a note of comedy that mocks the cultural philistinism of the Fabians. In the 1913 edition, however, Shaw added a number of passages in which he makes clear that he is enshrining the individual will, not when directed to personal ends but when working in harmony with the world-will (or Life Force as it became known). He is opposed to anarchism and to the aggrandisement of the self. Although society needs to be shocked pretty often, he believes that 'the need for freedom of evolution is the sole basis of toleration, the sole reason for not burning heretics and sending every eccentric person to the madhouse'. So the heretic of today (Galileo, Darwin, Marx and possibly Shaw himself), striving to realize future possibilities, becomes the pillar of the community tomorrow; and pretence slowly recedes.

Some of the confusion among readers of the *Quintessence* arose from Shaw's choice of one word. In the same way as 'superman', with its Nietzschean associations, was to suggest not a symbol of synthesis but a dictatorship, so the word Will indicated not 'our old friend, soul or spirit' but an assertion of power over others. In neither case did Shaw originally mean this, but the ambiguity of these words points to an impulse that was gradually to gain possession of him.

The philosophy of the *Quintessence* is pragmatism. 'Life is an adventure, not the compounding of a prescription', and we must live it according to circumstances. The golden rule, Shaw tells us, is that 'there are no golden rules'. Human conduct must 'justify itself by its effect on happiness'. By happiness he meant human welfare (a phrase he used in a similar sentence in the preface to *Getting Married*) and for the 1913 edition he changed the word 'happiness' to 'life'.

In 1938 Shaw wrote to the editor of *Nordisk Tidende*: 'I have not a word of my "Quintessence of Ibsenism" written in my early thirties, to withdraw or dilute now that I am in my early eighties.' But though he kept the same apparatus of argument, his political philosophy had begun to change even in the seven years that separated 'The Quintessence of Ibsenism' from 'The Perfect Wagnerite'. In the earlier work he divided human beings into three classes, and in the sequel he again makes a threefold division, representing the Wagnerian dwarfs, giants and gods as 'dramatizations of the three main orders of men: to wit, the instinctive, predatory, lustful, greedy people; the patient, toiling, stupid, respectful, money-worshipping people; and the intellectual, moral, talented people who devise and administer States and Churches'.

This modification (subdividing the philistines into dwarfs and giants) reflects a shift in Shaw towards a deeper pessimism that arose from his greater experience of national and local politics. Among the three categories he describes in 'The

Perfect Wagnerite', the gods now being idealists, there is no realistic deliverer of man. Shaw had begun to feel that progress in prosaic instalments simply through the permeation tactics of the Fabians was no longer inevitable. A more romantic figure than that of the civil servant and political researcher was needed to win the imagination of the philistine. This was his final answer to Sidney Webb's objection to his glorification of the Individual Will, and an observation as to how G.B.S. could popularize Webb in everyday politics. Realists must call up their own brand of idealism. The quietist should dress himself in a loud coat – a magical garment, its pockets rattling with the fool's gold of illusions that Shaw had previously derided in 'The Quintessence of Ibsenism'. Most people had to be paid in such coin. Appearance, providing it was a successful imposture like the public personality of G.B.S., was an important feature of human politics. Change the appearance of things and you were a long way to changing the reality. Acknowledging this, Shaw seems to accommodate a fourth class of human being into his philosophy. 'History shews us,' he writes, 'only one order higher than the highest of these: namely, the order of Heros.'

In fact Shaw's heroes are his realists from the 'Quintessence' in disguise: they are Wagner's blond warriors, raised into a higher order of man ready to do their work in the twentieth century. Wagner's cycle of music dramas had told a story of love lost and regained; Shaw's commentary is a retelling of the story as love lost and replaced by something else. His 'frightful and loveless' childhood in Dublin, followed by his years of poverty and social unacceptability in London, made Shaw immediately sympathetic to Wagner's tragic view of human history. He followed it breathlessly, finding not only an allegory of contemporary political dilemmas, but also an image of his own life. His sense of lovelessness makes him feel at one with all mankind in its expulsion from Eden. There is no mistaking his personal involvement. From Shaw's reading of the Ring we see Man forswearing love only when it was denied to him and made the instrument for murdering his self-respect. In his loveless desperation he either succumbs to (the giant philistines) or exploits (the dwarf philistines) the malign forces of loveless greed – those corrupt millions of Rhine Gold – on which our own sordid capitalist systems are built. These systems displace the need for human love with a love for the machinery of power. They establish their dominion over the world through the idealistic gods who enshrine them with the majesty and superstition of the Church and guard them with the terrifying powers of the law. Only one quality can explode this tyranny of religion and law, and establish in its place the unfettered action of Humanity: and that is the heroic quality of fearlessness. The redemption of mankind therefore depends upon the appearance in the world of a hero, or the spirit of heroism. Shaw agrees with Wagner on the inspiration of raising up the example of intrepid force of character; a person elevated to perfect confidence in his own impulses by an intense and joyous vitality which is above fear – someone who no longer bows to circumstance, environment, necessity, but takes his destiny in his own hands and shapes it for himself. Wagner's glorious Siegfried is a symbol of love, the original deprivation of which has been the genesis of man's tragic story. For Shaw, love was not the romantic solvent for our evils because it could have little place in the down-to-earth conflict between humanity and its gods and governments. Love belonged to heaven where Wagner transported us once the Ring changed from music drama into opera. Shaw does not try to lead us from earth to heaven but to conduct a marriage of heaven and earth, religion and politics. He was to supplant Siegfried with a succession of eccentrically common-sense figures from Julius Caesar to St Joan and to experiment with ways of substituting eugenics for eroticism, the Shavian Life Force for Wagnerian resurrection. This was the creed he was to explore in the dream sequence of *Man and Superman* – a moral commitment to progress, answering the need in

16

someone whose observation of the world was growing pessimistic.

To adapt Wagner to the Shavian temperament Shaw needed to pull him out of his antiquated heavens, place him in the contemporary socialist scene, and transpose his sultry eroticism into concentrated intellectual music. He throws the emphasis of his criticism on what he interprets as being 'at the back of Wagner's mind', translating these thoughts into the vocabulary of his own mind, and 'creatively melting them down', as Thomas Mann described the process, 'into something totally new and personal'. It is an extraordinarily lucid exposition, subtle and sustained, that used Wagner as he had previously used Ibsen to work out his philosophical position.

'The Sanity of Art' was written between the two other essays and had a curious provenance. It was composed in the form of an open letter to, and at the request of, Benjamin Tucker, the anarchist-editor of an American magazine, *Liberty*, and appeared in that paper on 27 July 1895 under the title 'A Degenerate's View of Nordau'. In Shaw's view Max Nordau was a perfect example of the idealist. His book *Entartung*, which had been translated that year with the title *Degeneration*, gave the philistines a plausible case for dismissing almost all contemporary art as an aberration or symptom of sickness. Tucker was alarmed at the great impression this work was making on the American mind. Searching round for some effective counter-attack, he invited Shaw as the 'only man in the world capable of tackling Nordau on his various fields of music, literature, painting etc' to lead it. He promised him that if he could find out the highest figure ever paid by, for example, the *Nineteenth Century*, for a single article to any writer (not excluding Gladstone), he would match it for a review of *Degeneration*. Shaw chose the form of an open letter as the best way of answering this peculiar commission. Touched by Tucker's philosophic honesty and generosity, and being convinced that he would one day find himself in prison for attacking American institutions, Shaw asked for no fee at all. Tucker printed a double number to contain Shaw's thirteen thousand words, and sent a free copy to every paper in America. He 'probably worked double shifts and ate half meals for the next two years to pay off what the adventure cost him, even with the author's work thrown in for love', Shaw speculated. But the result was that 'Nordau's book has never been heard of in an American newspaper since', Shaw claimed with a polemical flourish ten years later.

There was, however, a curious sequel to this incident. When Shaw's German translator, Siegfried Trebitsch, encouraged him to revise the essay for publication in the German newspapers in 1907, Shaw arranged for the New Age Press in London and Benjamin Tucker in New York to issue a small revised edition which he proposed to call *The Sanity of Art: an Exposure of Some Current Nonsense about Artists being Degenerates*. In the event, when the work was published on 8 February 1908, the final s was left out. The German translation, however, had been published in *März* during the previous autumn, and, despite all the previous publicity, was apparently read there for the first time by Nordau himself. 'It must not be published as something new,' Shaw had instructed Trebitsch, 'that would be unfair and discourteous to Nordau.' Nevertheless, it was new to Nordau; and also new was the preface in which Shaw described the author of *Degeneration* as 'one of those remarkable cosmopolitan Jews who go forth against modern civilization as David went against the Philistines or Charles Martel against the Saracens'. Nordau protested that this was anti-Semitic and wrote 'An Open Letter to Mr Shaw' for *Frankfurter Zeitung* complaining of Shaw's xenophobia. Of all the ripostes to his onslaught this must have been the most unlikely, and Shaw replied with yet another open letter explaining how Nordau had misunderstood one of the few sentences intended as a compliment. That Shaw certainly felt there to be nothing wrong with this sentence may be deduced from the fact that he left it

18

unchanged when revising the piece for inclusion in *Major Critical Essays*.

'You are, I notice, a little bewildered by the extraordinary suddenness and completeness of your demolition,' Shaw observed to Nordau. As a pamphleteer, he was strangely unhurtful. However damning or outrageous his statements, they were almost always penetrated by humour and targeted to destroy his adversary's opinions rather than his self-respect. Even with its revisions, which 'softened one or two expressions which now shock me as uncivil to Dr Nordau', *The Sanity of Art* was by Shavian standards a caustic piece of writing. 'I am not offering him the insult of attempting to spare his feelings,' Shaw claimed, 'I am simply trying to mend my own manners.' Yet Max Nordau's feelings could not have been too badly bruised. When, years later, he came with his daughter to London, he grew very friendly with Shaw, and conceived for him, it was said, 'a great admiration amounting to deference'.

Unlike the other two critical essays in this volume, 'The Sanity of Art' does not alter or advance Shaw's thinking. It is an example of his philosophy in action, the theory of pragmatism being put to practical use. He turns Nordau's company of incompetents, the sick, the wicked and the lunatic, into a model army of active thinkers, Ibsen and Wagner, Whistler and William Morris, and switches them back into the campaign against philistine reaction. This is a battle in the war for men's minds, conducted by a polemicist who was to tell Tolstoy that 'I am not an "Art for Art's sake" man, and would not lift my finger to produce a work of art if I thought there was nothing more than that in it.' His essay is a fine example of what Matthew Arnold had called the 'New Journalism' – the rise of literary Jacobinism led by lawless young people who began to write and print the living English language of their own day. It was as one of these new journalists that Shaw claimed in his preface to 'The Sanity of Art' that journalism could be the highest form of literature, and that all the highest literature was journalism since it arose from contemporary life. 'I also am a journalist,' he writes, 'proud of it, deliberately cutting out of my works all that is not journalism, convinced that nothing that is not journalism will live long as literature, or be of any use whilst it does live.' By journalism, Shaw does not mean that inventive craft practised by the Newspaper Man in *The Doctor's Dilemma*. Nor, by turning his back contemptuously on art for art's sake, does he intend other than to add emphasis to the potential power of the artist. For if art is to win privileges in the world of a pragmatist, it must do so by its 'solid usefulness'. 'The Sanity of Art' contains Shaw's most positive affirmation in the use of the arts. It is a statement of religious faith, a puritan's encyclical.

The claim of art to our respect must stand or fall with the validity of its pretension to cultivate and refine our senses and faculties until seeing, hearing, feeling, smelling and tasting become highly conscious and critical acts with us, protesting vehemently against the ugliness, noise, discordant speech, frowsy clothing and re-breathed air, and taking keen interest and pleasure in beauty, in music and in nature, besides making us insist, as necessary for comfort and decency, on clean, wholesome, handsome fabrics to wear, and utensils of fine material and elegant workmanship to handle. Further, art should refine our sense of character and conduct, of justice and sympathy, greatly heightening our self-knowledge, self-control, precision of action, and considerateness, and making us intolerant of baseness, cruelty, injustice, and intellectual superficiality or vulgarity. The worthy artist or craftsman is he who serves the physical and moral senses by feeding them with pictures, musical compositions, pleasant houses and gardens, good clothes and fine implements, poems, fictions, essays and dramas which call the heightened senses and ennobled faculties into pleasurable activity. The great artist is he who goes a step beyond the demand and, by supplying works of a higher beauty and a higher interest than has yet been perceived, succeeds after a brief struggle with its strangeness, in adding this fresh extension of sense to the heritage of the race.

20

Major Critical Essays is essential reading for anyone who wishes to understand the plays of Shaw's early and middle periods. It also gives us the perspective through which to see what happened in the last decades of Shaw's life when, disillusioned by the failure of the Labour Party to introduce socialism to Britain, he focused his optimism beyond the horizon and idealized the Soviet Union.

MICHAEL HOLROYD

THE QUINTESSENCE OF IBSENISM

NOW COMPLETED TO THE DEATH OF IBSEN

PREFACE TO THE THIRD EDITION

SINCE the last edition of this book was printed, war, pestilence and famine have wrecked civilization and killed a number of people of whom the first batch is calculated as not less than fifteen millions. Had the gospel of Ibsen been understood and heeded, these fifteen millions might have been alive now; for the war was a war of ideals. Liberal ideals, Feudal ideals, National ideals, Dynastic ideals, Republican ideals, Church ideals, State ideals, and Class ideals, bourgeois and proletarian, all heaped up into a gigantic pile of spiritual high explosive, and then shovelled daily into every house with the morning milk by the newspapers, needed only a bomb thrown at Sarajevo by a handful of regicide idealists to blow the centre out of Europe. Men with empty phrases in their mouths and foolish fables in their heads have seen each other, not as fellow-creatures, but as dragons and devils, and have slaughtered each other accordingly. Now that our frenzies are forgotten, our commissariats disbanded, and the soldiers they fed demobilized to starve when they cannot get employment in mending what we broke, even the iron-mouthed Ibsen, were he still alive, would perhaps spare us, disillusioned wretches as we are, the well-deserved 'I told you so'.

Not that there is any sign of the lesson being taken to heart. Our reactions from Militarist idealism into Pacifist idealism will not put an end to war: they are only a practical form of the *reculer pour mieux sauter*. We still cannot bring ourselves to criticize our ideals, because that would be a form of self-criticism. The vital force that drives men to throw away their lives and those of others in the pursuit of an imaginative impulse, reckless of its apparent effect on human welfare, is, like all natural forces, given to us in enormous excess to provide against an enormous waste. Therefore men, instead of economizing it by consecrating it to the service of their highest impulses, grasp at a phrase in a newspaper article, or in the speech of a politician on a vote-catching expedition, as an excuse for exercising it violently, just as a horse turned out to grass will gallop and kick merely to let off steam. The shallowness of the ideals of men ignorant of history is their destruction.

But I cannot spend the rest of my life drawing the moral of the war. It must suffice to say here that as war throws back civilization inevitably, leaving everything worse than it was, from razors and scissors to the characters of the men that make and sell and buy them, old abuses revive eagerly in a world that dreamed it had got rid of them for ever; old books on morals become new and topical again; and old prophets stir in their graves and are read with a new sense of the importance of their message. That is perhaps why a new edition of this book is demanded.

In spite of the temptation to illustrate it afresh by the moral collapse of the last ten years, I have left the book untouched. To change a pre-war book into a post-war book would in this case mean interpreting Ibsen in the light of a catastrophe of which he was unaware. Nobody can pretend to say what view he would have taken of it. He might have thought the demolition of three monstrous idealist empires cheap at the cost of fifteen million idealists' lives. Or he might have seen in the bourgeois republics which have superseded them a more deeply entrenched fortification of idealism at its sub-urban worst. So I have refrained from tampering with what I wrote when I, too, was as pre-war as Ibsen.

G. B. S.

1922

PREFACE: 1913

In the pages which follow I have made no attempt to tamper with the work of the bygone man of thirty-five who wrote them. I have never admitted the right of an elderly author to alter the work of a young author, even when the young author happens to be his former self. In the case of a work which is a mere exhibition of skill in conventional art, there may be some excuse for the delusion that the longer the artist works on it the nearer he will bring it to perfection. Yet even the victims of this delusion must see that there is an age limit to the process, and that though a man of forty-five may improve the workmanship of a man of thirty-five, it does not follow that a man of fifty-five can do the same.

When we come to creative art, to the living word of a man delivering a message to his own time, it is clear that any attempt to alter this later on is simply fraud and forgery. As I read the old Quintessence of Ibsenism I may find things that I see now at a different angle, or correlate with so many things then unnoted by me that they take on a different aspect. But though this may be a reason for writing another book, it is not a reason for altering an existing one. What I have written I have written, said Pilate, thinking (rightly, as it turned out) that his blunder might prove truer than its revision by the elders; and what he said after a lapse of twenty-one seconds I may very well say after a lapse of twenty-one years.

However, I should not hesitate to criticize my earlier work if I thought it likely to do any mischief that criticism can avert. But on reading it through I have no doubt that it is as much needed in its old form as ever it was. Now that Ibsen is no longer frantically abused, and is safe in the Pantheon, his message is in worse danger of being forgotten or ignored

27

than when he was in the pillory. Nobody now dreams of calling me a 'muck ferreting dog' because I think Ibsen a great teacher. I will not go so far as to say I wish they did; but I do say that the most effective way of shutting our minds against a great man's ideas is to take them for granted and admit he was great and have done with him. It really matters very little whether Ibsen was a great man or not; what does matter is his message and the need of it.

That people are still interested in the message is proved by the history of this book. It has long been out of print in England; but it has never been out of demand. In spite of the smuggling of unauthorized American editions, which I have winked at because the absence of an English reprint was my own fault (if it be a fault not to be able to do more than a dozen things at a time), the average price of copies of the original edition stood at twenty-four shillings some years ago, and is no doubt higher now. But it was not possible to reprint it without additions. When it was issued in 1891 Ibsen was still alive, and had not yet produced The Master Builder, or Little Eyolf, or John Gabriel Borkman, or When We Dead Awaken. Without an account of these four final masterpieces, a book entitled The Quintessence of Ibsenism would have been a fraud on its purchasers; and it was the difficulty of finding time to write the additional chapters on these plays, and review Ibsen's position from the point of view reached when his work ended with his death and his canonization as an admitted grand master of European literature, that has prevented me for twenty years from complying with the demand for a second edition. Also, perhaps, some relics of my old, or rather, my young conscience, which revolted against hasty work. Now that my own stream is nearer the sea, I am more inclined to encourage myself in haste and recklessness by reminding myself that *le mieux est l'ennemi du bien*, and that I had better cobble up a new edition as best I can than not supply it at all.

I have taken all possible precautions to keep the reader's

mind free from verbal confusion in following Ibsen's attack on ideals and idealism, a confusion that might have been avoided could his plays, without losing the naturalness of their dialogue, have been translated into the language of the English Bible. It is not too much to say that the works of Ibsen furnish one of the best modern keys to the prophecies of Scripture. Read the prophets, major and minor, from Isaiah to Malachi, without such a key, and you will be puzzled and bored by the almost continuous protest against and denunciation of idolatry and prostitution. Simpletons read all this passionate invective with sleepy unconcern, concluding thoughtlessly that idolatry means praying to stocks and stones instead of to brass lectern eagles and the new reredos presented by the local distiller in search of a title; and as to prostitution, they think of it as 'the social evil', and regret that the translators of the Bible used a much blunter word. But nobody who has ever heard real live men talking about graven images and traders in sex can for a moment suppose them to be the things the prophets denounced so earnestly. For idols and idolatry read ideals and idealism; for the prostitution of Piccadilly Circus read not only the prostitution of the journalist, the political lawyer, the parson selling his soul to the squire, the ambitious politician selling his soul for office, but the much more intimate and widespread idolatries and prostitutions of the private snob, the domestic tyrant and voluptuary, and the industrial adventurer. At once the prophetic warnings and curses take on meaning and proportion, and lose that air of exaggerated righteousness and tiresome conventional rant which repels readers who do not possess Ibsen's clue. I have sometimes thought of reversing the operation, and substituting in this book the words idol and idolatry for ideal and idealism; but it would be impossible without spoiling the actuality of Ibsen's criticism of society. If you call a man a rascally idealist, he is not only shocked and indignant but puzzled: in which condition you can rely on his attention. If you call him a rascally idolater, he

29

concludes calmly that you do not know that he is a member of the Church of England. I have therefore left the old wording. Save for certain adaptations made necessary by the lapse of time and the hand of death, the book stands as it did, with a few elucidations which I might have made in 1891 had I given the text a couple of extra revisions. Also, of course, the section dealing with the last four plays. The two concluding chapters are new. There is no fundamental change: above all, no dilution.

Whether this edition will change people's minds to the extent to which the first did (to my own great astonishment) I do not know. In the eighteen-nineties one jested about the revolt of the daughters, and of the wives who slammed the front door like Nora. At present the revolt has become so general that even the feeblest and oldest after-dinner jesters dare no longer keep Votes for Women on their list of stale pleasantries about mothers-in-law, rational dress, and mixed bathing. Men are waking up to the perception that in killing women's souls they have killed their own. Mr Granville-Barker's worthy father of six unmarriageable daughters in The Madras House, ruefully exclaiming, 'It seems to me I've been made a convenience of all my life', has taken away the excited attention that Nora once commanded when she said, 'I have been living all these years with a strange man.' When she meets Helmer's 'No man sacrifices his honor for a woman' with her 'Thousands of women have done that for men,' there is no longer the old impressed assent; men fiercely protest that it is not true; that, on the contrary, for every woman who has sacrificed her honor for a man's sake, ten men have sacrificed their honor for a woman's. In the plays of Gorki and Tchekov, against which all the imbecilities and outrages of the old anti-Ibsen campaign are being revived (for the Press never learns anything by experience), the men appear as more tragically sacrificed by evil social conditions and their romantic and idealistic disguises than the women. Now it may be that into this new atmosphere my book will

come with quite an old-fashioned air. As I write these lines
the terrible play with which Strindberg wreaked the revenge
of the male for A Doll's House has just been performed for the
first time in London under the title of Creditors. In that, as in
Brieux's Les Hannetons, it is the man who is the victim of
domesticity, and the woman who is the tyrant and soul
destroyer. Thus A Doll's House did not dispose of the
question: it only brought on the stage the endless recriminations of idealistic marriage. And how has Strindberg, Ibsen's
twin giant, been received? With an even idler stupidity than
Ibsen himself, because Ibsen appealed to the rising energy of
the revolt of women against idealism; but Strindberg attacks
women ruthlessly, trying to rouse men from the sloth and
sensuality of their idealized addiction to them; and as the
men, unlike the women, do not want to be roused, whilst the
women do not like to be attacked, there is no conscious
Strindberg movement to relieve the indifference, the dull
belittlement, the spiteful hostility against which the devotees
of Ibsen fought so slashingly in the nineties. But the unconscious movement is violent enough. As I write, it is only two
days since an eminent bacteriologist filled three columns of
The Times with a wild Strindbergian letter in which he
declared that women must be politically and professionally
secluded and indeed excluded, because their presence and
influence inflict on men an obsession so disabling and
dangerous that men and women can work together or legislate
together only on the same conditions as horses and mares:
that is, by the surgical destruction of the male's sex. The
Times and The Pall Mall Gazette gravely accept this outburst
as 'scientific', and heartily endorse it; though only a few
weeks have elapsed since The Times dismissed Strindberg's
play and Strindberg himself with curt superciliousness as
uninteresting and negligible. Not many years ago, a performance of a play by myself, the action of which was placed in an
imaginary Ibsen Club, in which the comedy of the bewilderment of conventional people when brought suddenly into

contact with the Ibsenist movement (both understood and misunderstood) formed the atmosphere of the piece, was criticized in terms which shewed that our critics are just as hopelessly in the rear of Ibsen as they were in 1891. The only difference was that whereas in 1891 they would have insulted Ibsen, they now accept him as a classic. But understanding of the change of mind produced by Ibsen, or notion that they live in a world which is seething with the reaction of Ibsen's ideas against the ideas of Sardou and Tom Taylor, they have none. They stare with equal unintelligence at the sieges and stormings of separate homesteads by Ibsen or Strindberg, and at the attack all along the front of refined society into which these sieges and stormings have now developed. Whether the attack is exquisite, touching, delicate, as in Tchekov's Cherry Orchard, Galsworthy's Silver Box and Granville-Barker's Anne Leete, or ruthless, with every trick of intellectual ruffianism and ribaldry, and every engine of dramatic controversy, there is the same pettish disappointment at the absence of the old conventions, the same gaping unconsciousness of the meaning and purpose of the warfare in which each play is a battle, as in the days when this book was new.

Our political journalists are even blinder than our artistic ones in this matter. The credit of our domestic ideals having been shaken to their foundations, as through a couple of earthquake shocks, by Ibsen and Strindberg (the Arch-Individualists of the nineteenth century) whilst the Socialists have been idealizing, sentimentalizing, denouncing Capitalism for sacrificing Love and Home and Domestic Happiness and Children and Duty to money greed and ambition, yet it remains a commonplace of political journalism to assume that Socialism is the deadliest enemy of the domestic ideals and Unsocialism their only hope and refuge. In the same breath the world-grasping commercial synthesis we call Capitalism, built up by generations of Scotch Rationalists and English Utilitarians, Atheists, Agnostics and Natural-Selectionists, with Malthus as the one churchman among all its prophets, is proclaimed the bulwark of the Christian Churches. We used to be told that the people that walked in darkness have seen a great light. When our people see the heavens blazing with suns, they simply keep their eyes shut, and walk on in darkness until they have led us into the pit. No matter: I am not a domestic idealist; and it pleases me to think that the Life Force may have providential aims in thus keeping my opponents off the trail.

But for all that I must not darken counsel. I therefore, without further apology, launch my old torpedo with the old charge in it, leaving to the new chapters at the end what I have to say about the change in the theatre since Ibsen set his potent leaven to work there.

AYOT ST LAWRENCE, 1912—13

PREFACE TO THE FIRST EDITION

In the spring of 1890, the Fabian Society, finding itself at a loss for a course of lectures to occupy its summer meetings, was compelled to make shift with a series of papers put forward under the general heading of Socialism in Contemporary Literature. The Fabian Essayists, strongly pressed to do 'something or other', for the most part shook their heads; but in the end Sydney Olivier consented to 'take Zola'; I consented to 'take Ibsen'; and Hubert Bland undertook to read all the Socialist novels of the day, an enterprise the desperate failure of which resulted in the most amusing paper of the series. William Morris, asked to read a paper on himself, flatly declined, but gave us one on Gothic Architecture. Stepniak also came to the rescue with a lecture on modern Russian fiction; and so the Society tided over the summer without having to close its doors, but also without having added anything whatever to the general stock of information on Socialism in Contemporary Literature. After this I cannot claim that my paper on Ibsen, which was duly read at the St James's Restaurant on the 18th July 1890, under the presidency of Mrs Annie Besant, and which was the first form of this little book, is an original work in the sense of being the result of a spontaneous internal impulse on my part. Having purposely couched it in the most provocative terms (of which traces may be found by the curious in its present state), I did not attach much importance to the somewhat lively debate that arose upon it; and I had laid it aside as a *pièce d'occasion* which had served its turn, when the production of Rosmersholm at the Vaudeville Theatre by Florence Farr, the inauguration of the Independent Theatre by Mr J. T. Grein with a performance of Ghosts, and the sensation created by the experiment of Elizabeth Robins and

Marion Lea with Hedda Gabler, started a frantic newspaper controversy, in which I could see no sign of any of the disputants having ever been forced by circumstances, as I had, to make up his mind definitely as to what Ibsen's plays meant, and to defend his view face to face with some of the keenest debaters in London. I allow due weight to the fact that Ibsen himself has not enjoyed this Fabian advantage; but I have also shewn that the existence of a discoverable and perfectly definite thesis in a poet's work by no means depends on the completeness of his own intellectual consciousness of it. At any rate, the controversialists, whether in the abusive stage, or the apologetic stage, or the hero-worshipping stage, by no means made clear what they were abusing, or apologizing for, or going into ecstasies about; and I came to the conclusion that my explanation might as well be placed in the field until a better could be found.

With this account of the origin of the book, and a reminder that it is not a critical essay on the poetic beauties of Ibsen, but simply an exposition of Ibsenism, I offer it to my readers to make what they can of.

LONDON, June 1891

THE TWO PIONEERS

THAT is, pioneers of the march to the plains of heaven (so to speak).

The second, whose eyes are in the back of his head, is the man who declares that it is wrong to do something that no one has hitherto seen any harm in.

The first, whose eyes are very longsighted and in the usual place, is the man who declares that it is right to do something hitherto regarded as infamous.

The second is treated with great respect by the army. They give him testimonials; name him the Good Man; and hate him like the devil.

The first is stoned and shrieked at by the whole army. They call him all manner of opprobrious names; grudge him his bare bread and water; and secretly adore him as their savior from utter despair.

Let me take an example from life of my pioneers. Shelley was a pioneer and nothing else: he did both first and second pioneer's work.

Now compare the effect produced by Shelley as abstinence preacher or second pioneer with that which he produced as indulgence preacher or first pioneer. For example:

SECOND PIONEER PROPOSITION: It is wrong to kill animals and eat them.

FIRST PIONEER PROPOSITION: It is not wrong to take your sister as your wife.[1]

Here the second pioneer appears as a gentle humanitarian, and the first as an unnatural corrupter of public morals and family life. So much easier is it to declare the right wrong than the wrong right in a society with a guilty conscience, to which, as to Dickens's detective, 'Any possible move is a probable move provided it's in a wrong direction.' Just as the liar's punishment is, not in the least that he is not believed, but that he cannot believe any one else; so a guilty society can more easily be persuaded that any apparently innocent act is guilty than that any apparently guilty act is innocent.

The English newspaper which best represented the guilty conscience of the middle class, was, when Ibsen's plays reached England, The Daily Telegraph. If we can find that The Daily Telegraph attacked Ibsen as The Quarterly Review used to attack Shelley, it will occur to us at once that there must be something of the first pioneer about Ibsen.

The late Clement Scott, at that time dramatic critic to The Daily Telegraph, was a sentimentally goodnatured gentleman, not then a pioneer, though he had in his time fought hard for the advance in British drama represented by the plays of Robertson. He was also an emotional, impressionable, zealous and sincere Roman Catholic. He accused Ibsen of dramatic impotence, ludicrous amateurishness, nastiness, vulgarity, egotism, coarseness, absurdity, uninteresting verbosity and 'suburbanity', declaring that he has taken ideas that would have inspired a great tragic poet, and vulgarized and debased them in dull, hateful, loathsome, horrible plays. This criticism, which occurs in a notice of the first performance of Ghosts in England, is to be found in the Daily Telegraph for the 14th March 1891, and is supplemented by a leading article which compares the play to an open drain, a loathsome sore unbandaged, a dirty act done publicly, or a lazar house with all its doors and windows open. Bestial, cynical, disgusting, poisonous, sickly, delirious, indecent, loathsome, fetid, literary carrion, crapulous stuff, clinical confessions; all these epithets are used in the article as descriptive of Ibsen's work. 'Realism,' said the writer, 'is one thing; but the nostrils of the audience must not be visibly held before a play can be stamped as true to nature. It is difficult to expose in decorous words the gross and almost putrid indecorum of this play.' As the performance of Ghosts took place on the evening of the 13th March, and the criticism appeared next morning, it is evident that Clement Scott must have gone straight from the theatre to the newspaper office, and there, in an almost hysterical condition, penned his share of this extraordinary protest. The literary workmanship bears marks of haste and disorder, which, however, only heighten the expression of the passionate horror produced in the writer by seeing Ghosts on the stage. He calls on the authorities to cancel the license of the theatre, and declares that he has been exhorted to laugh at honor, to disbelieve in love, to mock at virtue, to distrust friendship, and to deride fidelity.

If this document were at all singular, it would rank as one of the curiosities of criticism, exhibiting, as it does, the most seasoned playgoer in London thrown into convulsions by a performance which was witnessed with approval, and even with enthusiasm, by many persons of approved moral and artistic conscientiousness. But Clement Scott's criticism was hardly distinguishable in tone from dozens of others which appeared simultaneously. His opinion was the vulgar opinion. Mr Alfred Watson, critic to The Standard, the leading Tory daily paper, proposed that proceedings should be taken against the theatre under Lord Campbell's Act for the suppression of disorderly houses. Clearly Clement Scott and his editor Sir Edwin Arnold, with whom rested the final responsibility for the article which accompanied the criticism, represented a considerable party.

How then is it that Ibsen, a Norwegian playwright of European celebrity, attracted one section of the English people so strongly that they hailed him as the greatest living dramatic poet and moral teacher, whilst another section was so revolted by his works that they described him in terms which they themselves admitted to be, by the necessities of the case, all but obscene? This phenomenon, which has occurred throughout Europe whenever Ibsen's plays have been acted, as well as in America and Australia, must be exhaustively explained before the plays can be described without danger of reproducing the same confusion in the reader's own mind. Such an explanation, therefore, must be my first business.

Understand, at the outset, that the explanation will not be an explaining away. Clement Scott's judgment did not mislead him in the least as to Ibsen's meaning. Ibsen means all that most revolted his critic. For example, in Ghosts, the play in question, a clergyman and a married woman fall in love with one another. The woman proposes to abandon her husband and live with the clergyman. He recalls her to her duty, and makes her behave as a virtuous woman. She afterwards tells him that this was a crime on his part. Ibsen agrees with her, and has written the play to bring you round to his opinion. Clement Scott did not agree with her, and believed that when you are brought round to her opinion you have been morally corrupted. By this conviction he was impelled to denounce Ibsen as he did, Ibsen being equally impelled to propagate the convictions which provoked the attack. Which of the two is right cannot be decided until it is ascertained whether a society of persons holding Ibsen's opinions would be higher or lower than a society holding Clement Scott's.

There are many people who cannot conceive this as an open question. To them a denunciation of any recognized practices is an incitement to unsocial conduct; and every utterance in which an assumption of the eternal validity of these practices is not implicit is a paradox. Yet all progress involves the beating of them from that position. By way of illustration, one may rake up the case of Proudhon, who in the year 1840 carefully defined property as theft. This was thought the very maddest paradox that ever man hazarded: it seemed obvious that a society which countenanced such a proposition must speedily be reduced to the condition of a sacked city. Today schemes for the confiscation by taxation and supertaxation of mining royalties and ground rents are commonplaces of social reform; and the honesty of the relation of our big property holders to the rest of the community is challenged on all hands. It would be easy to multiply instances, though the most complete are now ineffective through the triumph of the original paradox having obliterated all memory of the opposition it first had to encounter. The point to seize is that social progress takes effect through the replacement of old institutions by new ones; and since every institution involves the recognition of the duty of conforming to it, progress must involve the repudiation of an established duty at every step. If the Englishman had not repudiated the duty of absolute obedience to his king, his political progress would have been impossible. If women had not repudiated the duty of absolute submission to their husbands, and defied public opinion as to the limits set by modesty to their education, they would never have gained the protection of the Married Women's Property Act, the municipal vote, or the power to qualify themselves as medical practitioners. If Luther had not trampled on his duty to the head of his Church and on his vow of chastity, our clergy would still have to choose between celibacy and profligacy. There is nothing new, then, in the defiance of duty by the reformer: every step of progress means a duty repudiated, and a scripture torn up. And every reformer is denounced accordingly: Luther as an apostate, Cromwell as a traitor, Mary Wollstonecraft as an unwomanly virago, Shelley as a libertine, and Ibsen as all the things enumerated in The Daily Telegraph.

This crablike progress of social evolution, in which the individual advances by seeming to go backward, continues to illude us in spite of all the lessons of history. To the pious man the newly made freethinker, suddenly renouncing supernatural revelation, and denying all obligation to believe the Bible and obey the commandments as such, appears to be claiming the right to rob and murder at large. But the freethinker soon finds reasons for not doing what he does not want to do; and these reasons seem to him to be far more binding on our conscience than the precepts of a book of which the infallibility cannot be rationally proved. The pious man is at last forced to admit – as he was in the case of the late Charles Bradlaugh, for instance – that the disciples of Voltaire and Tom Paine do not pick pockets or cut throats oftener than your even Christian: he actually is driven to doubt whether Voltaire himself (poor Voltaire, who built a church, and was the greatest philanthropist of his time!) really screamed and saw the devil on his death-bed.

This experience by no means saves the rationalist[2] from falling into the same conservatism when the time comes for his own belief to be questioned. No sooner has he triumphed over the theologian than he forthwith sets up as binding on all men the duty of acting logically with the object of securing the greatest good of the greatest number, with the result that he is presently landed in vivisection, Contagious Diseases Acts, dynamite conspiracies, and other grotesque but strictly reasonable abominations. Reason becomes Dagon, Moloch and Jehovah rolled into one. Its devotees exult in having freed themselves from the old slavery to a collection of books written by Jewish men of letters. To worship such books was, they can prove, as absurd as to worship sonatas composed by German musicians, as was done by the hero of Wagner's novelette, who sat up on his death-bed to say his creed, beginning, 'I believe in God, Mozart, and Beethoven.' The Voltairean freethinker despises such a piece of sentiment; but is it not much more sensible to worship a sonata constructed by a musician than to worship a syllogism constructed by a logician, since the sonata may encourage heroism, or at least inspire feelings of awe and devotion? This does not occur to the votary of reason; and the rationalist's freethinking soon comes to mean syllogism worship with rites of human sacrifice; for just as the rationalist's pious predecessor thought that the man who scoffed at baptism and the Bible must infallibly yield without resistance to all his criminal propensities, so the rationalist in turn becomes convinced that when a man once loses his faith in vaccination and in Herbert

Spencer's Data of Ethics, he is no longer to be trusted to keep his hands off his neighbor's person, purse or wife.

In process of time the age of reason had to go its way after the age of faith. In actual experience, the first shock to rationalism comes from the observation that though nothing can persuade women to adopt it, their impatience of reasoning no more prevents them from arriving at right conclusions than the masculine belief in it (never a very deeply rooted faith in England, by the way, whatever it may have been in France or Greece) saves men from arriving at wrong ones. When this generalization has to be modified in view of the fact that some women are beginning to try their skill at ratiocination, reason is not re-established on the throne; because the result of Woman's reasoning is that she begins to fall into all the errors which men are just learning to mistrust. The moment she sets about doing things for reasons instead of merely finding reasons for what she wants to do, there is no saying what mischief she will be at next: there being just as good reasons for burning a heretic at the stake as for rescuing a shipwrecked crew from drowning; in fact, there are better.

One of the first and most famous utterances of rationalism would have condemned it without further hearing had its full significance been seen at the time. Voltaire, taking exception to the trash of some poetaster, was met with the plea 'One must live.' 'I don't see the necessity,' replied Voltaire. The evasion was worthy of the Father of Lies himself; for Voltaire was face to face with the very necessity he was denying; must have known, consciously or not, that it is the universal postulate; would have understood, if he had lived today, that since all valid human institutions are constructed to fulfil man's will, and his will is to live even when his reason teaches him to die, logical necessity, which was the sort Voltaire meant (the other sort being visible enough) can never be a motor in human action, and is, in short, not necessity at all. But that was not brought to light in

Voltaire's time; and he died impenitent, bequeathing to his disciples that most logical of agents, the guillotine, which also 'did not see the necessity'.

In our own century the recognition of the will as distinct from the reasoning machinery began to spread. Schopenhauer was the first among the moderns[3] to appreciate the enormous practical importance of the distinction, and to make it clear to amateur metaphysicians by concrete instances. Out of his teaching came the formulation of the dilemma Voltaire had shut his eyes to. Here it is. Rationally considered, life is only worth living when its pleasures are greater than its pains. Now to a generation which has ceased to believe in heaven, and has not yet learned that the degradation by poverty of four out of every five of its number is artificial and remediable, the fact that life is not rationally worth living is obvious. It is useless to pretend that the pessimism of Koheleth, Shakespear, Dryden and Swift can be refuted if the world progresses solely by the destruction of the unfit, and yet can only maintain its civilization by manufacturing the unfit in swarms of which that appalling proportion of four to one represents but the comparatively fit survivors. Plainly then, the reasonable thing for the rationalists to do is to refuse to live. But as none of them will commit suicide in obedience to this demonstration of 'the necessity' for it, there is an end of the notion that we live for reasons instead of in fulfilment of our will to live. Thus we are landed afresh in mystery; for positive science gives no account whatever of this will to live. Positive science has dazzled us for nearly a century with its analyses of the machinery of sensation. Its researches into the nature of sound and the construction of the ear, the nature of light and the construction of the eye, its measurement of the speed of sensation, its localization of the functions of the brain, and its hints as to the possibility of producing a homunculus presently as the fruit of its chemical investigation of protoplasm have satisfied the souls of our atheists as completely as belief in divine omniscience and scriptural revelation satisfied the souls of their pious fathers. The fact remains that when Young, Helmholtz, Darwin, Haeckel, and the rest, popularized here among the literate classes by Tyndall and Huxley, and among the proletariat by the lectures of the National Secular Society, have taught you all they know, you are still as utterly at a loss to explain the fact of consciousness as you would have been in the days when you were instructed from The Child's Guide to Knowledge. Materialism, in short, only isolated the great mystery of consciousness by clearing away several petty mysteries with which we had confused it; just as Rationalism isolated the great mystery of the will to live. The isolation made both more conspicuous than before. We thought we had escaped for ever from the cloudy region of metaphysics; and we were only carried further into the heart of them.[4]

We have not yet worn off the strangeness of the position to which we have now been led. Only the other day our highest boast was that we were reasonable human beings. Today we laugh at that conceit, and see ourselves as wilful creatures. Ability to reason accurately is as desirable as ever; for by accurate reasoning only can we calculate our actions so as to do what we intend to do: that is, to fulfil our will; but faith in reason as a prime motor is no longer the criterion of the sound mind, any more than faith in the Bible is the criterion of righteous intention.

At this point, accordingly, the illusion as to the retrogressive movement of progress recurs as strongly as ever. Just as the beneficent step from theology to rationalism seems to the theologist a growth of impiety, does the step from rationalism to the recognition of the will as the prime motor strike the rationalist as a lapse of common sanity; so that to both theologist and rationalist progress at last appears alarming, threatening, hideous, because it seems to tend towards chaos. The deists Voltaire and Tom Paine were, to the divines of their day, predestined devils, tempting mankind hellward.[5] To deists and divines alike, Ferdinand Lassalle, the godless self-worshipper and man-worshipper, would have been a monster. Yet many who today echo Lassalle's demand that economic and political institutions should be adapted to the poor man's will to eat and drink his fill out of the product of the labor he shares, are revolted by Ibsen's acceptance of the impulse towards greater freedom as sufficient ground for the repudiation of any customary duty, however sacred, that conflicts with it. Society, were it even as free as Lassalle's Social-Democratic republic, *must*, it seems to them, go to pieces when conduct is no longer regulated by inviolable covenants.

For what, during all these overthrowings of things sacred and things infallible, has been happening to that pre-eminently sanctified thing, Duty? Evidently it cannot have come off scatheless. First there was man's duty to God, with the priest as assessor. That was repudiated; and then came Man's duty to his neighbor, with Society as the assessor. Will this too be repudiated, and be succeeded by Man's duty to himself, assessed by himself? And if so, what will be the effect on the conception of Duty in the abstract? Let us see.

I have just called Lassalle a self-worshipper. In doing so I cast no reproach on him; for this is the last step in the evolution of the conception of duty. Duty arises at first, a gloomy tyranny, out of man's helplessness, his self-mistrust, in a word, his abstract fear. He personifies all that he abstractly fears as God, and straightway becomes the slave of his duty to God. He imposes that slavery fiercely on his children, threatening them with hell, and punishing them for their attempts to be happy. When, becoming bolder, he ceases to fear everything, and dares to love something, this duty of his to what he fears evolves into a sense of duty to what he loves. Sometimes he again personifies what he loves as God; and the God of Wrath becomes the God of Love: sometimes he at once becomes a humanitarian, an altruist, acknowledging only his duty to his neighbor. This stage is correlative to the rationalist stage in the evolution of philosophy and the capitalist phase in the evolution of industry. But in it the emancipated slave of God falls under the dominion of Society, which, having just reached a phase in which all the love is ground out of it by the competitive struggle for money, remorselessly crushes him until, in due course of the further growth of his courage, a sense at last arises in him of his duty to himself. And when this sense is fully grown the tyranny of duty perishes; for now the man's God is his own humanity; and he, self-satisfied at last, ceases to be selfish. The evangelist of this last step must therefore preach the repudiation of duty. This, to the unprepared of his generation, is indeed the wanton masterpiece of paradox. What! after all that has been said by men of noble life as to the secret of all right conduct being only Duty, Duty, Duty, is he to be told now that duty is the primal curse from which we must redeem ourselves before we can advance another step on the road along which, as we imagine (having forgotten the repudiations made by our fathers) duty and duty alone has brought us thus far? But why not? God Almighty was once the most sacred of our conceptions; and he had to be denied. Then Reason became the Infallible Pope, only to be deposed in turn. Is Duty more sacred than God or Reason?

Having now arrived at the prospect of the repudiation of duty by Man, I shall make a digression on the subject of ideals and idealists, as treated by Ibsen. I shall go round in a loop, and come back to the same point by way of the repudiation of duty by Woman; and then at last I shall be in a position to describe Ibsen's plays without risk of misunderstanding.

IDEALS AND IDEALISTS

WE have seen that as Man grows through the ages, he finds himself bolder by the growth of his courage: that is, of his spirit (for so the common people name it), and dares more and more to love and trust instead of to fear and fight. But his courage has other effects; he also raises himself from mere consciousness to knowledge by daring more and more to face facts and tell himself the truth. For in his infancy of helplessness and terror he could not face the inexorable; and facts being of all things the most inexorable, he masked all the threatening ones as fast as he discovered them; so that now every mask requires a hero to tear it off. The king of terrors, Death, was the Arch-Inexorable: Man could not bear the dread of that. He must persuade himself that Death can be propitiated, circumvented, abolished. How he fixed the mask of personal immortality on the face of Death for this purpose we all know. And he did the like with all disagreeables as long as they remained inevitable. Otherwise he must have gone mad with terror of the grim shapes around him, headed by the skeleton with the scythe and hourglass. The masks were his ideals, as he called them; and what, he would ask, would life be without ideals? Thus he became an idealist, and remained so until he dared to begin pulling the masks off and looking the spectres in the face – dared, that is, to be more and more a realist. But all men are not equally brave; and the greatest terror prevailed whenever some realist bolder than the rest laid hands on a mask which they did not yet dare to do without.

We have plenty of these masks around us still: some of them more fantastic than any of the Sandwich islanders' masks in the British Museum. In our novels and romances especially we see the most beautiful of all the masks: those

47

devised to disguise the brutalities of the sexual instinct in the earlier stages of its development, and to soften the rigorous aspect of the iron laws by which Society regulates its gratification. When the social organism becomes bent on civilization, it has to force marriage and family life on the individual, because it can perpetuate itself in no other way whilst love is still known only by fitful glimpses, the basis of sexual relationship being in the main mere physical appetite. Under these circumstances men try to graft pleasure on necessity by desperately pretending that the institution forced upon them is a congenial one, making it a point of public decency to assume always that men spontaneously love their kindred better than their chance acquaintances, and that the woman once desired is always desired: also that the family is woman's proper sphere, and that no really womanly woman ever forms an attachment, or even knows what it means, until she is requested to do so by a man. Now if anyone's childhood has been embittered by the dislike of his mother and the ill-temper of his father; if his wife has ceased to care for him and he is heartily tired of his wife; if his brother is going to law with him over the division of the family property, and his son acting in studied defiance of his plans and wishes, it is hard for him to persuade himself that passion is eternal and that blood is thicker than water. Yet if he tells himself the truth, all his life seems a waste and a failure by the light of it. It comes then to this, that his neighbors must either agree with him that the whole system is a mistake, and discard it for a new one, which cannot possibly happen until social organization so far outgrows the institution that Society can perpetuate itself without it; or else they must keep him in countenance by resolutely making believe that all the illusions with which it has been masked are realities.

For the sake of precision, let us imagine a community of a thousand persons, organized for the perpetuation of the species on the basis of the British family as we know it at

48

present. Seven hundred of them, we will suppose, find the British family arrangement quite good enough for them. Two hundred and ninety-nine find it a failure, but must put up with it since they are in a minority. The remaining person occupies a position to be explained presently. The 299 failures will not have the courage to face the fact that they are irremediable failures, since they cannot prevent the 700 satisfied ones from coercing them into conformity with the marriage law. They will accordingly try to persuade themselves that, whatever their own particular domestic arrangements may be, the family is a beautiful and holy natural institution. For the fox not only declares that the grapes he cannot get are sour: he also insists that the sloes he *can* get are sweet. Now observe what has happened. The family as it really is is a conventional arrangement, legally enforced, which the majority, because it happens to suit them, think good enough for the minority, whom it happens not to suit at all. The family as a beautiful and holy natural institution is only a fancy picture of what every family would have to be if everybody was to be suited, invented by the minority as a mask for the reality, which in its nakedness is intolerable to them. We call this sort of fancy picture an Ideal; and the policy of forcing individuals to act on the assumption that all ideals are real, and to recognize and accept such action as standard moral conduct, absolutely valid under all circumstances, contrary conduct or any advocacy of it being discountenanced and punished as immoral, may therefore be described as the policy of Idealism. Our 299 domestic failures are therefore become idealists as to marriage; and in proclaiming the ideal in fiction, poetry, pulpit and platform oratory, and serious private conversation, they will far outdo the 700 who comfortably accept marriage as a matter of course, never dreaming of calling it an 'institution', much less a holy and beautiful one, and being pretty plainly of opinion that Idealism is a crackbrained fuss about nothing. The idealists, hurt by this, will retort by calling them Philistines. We then have our society classified as 700 Philistines and 299 idealists, leaving one man unclassified: the man strong enough to face the truth the idealists are shirking.

Such a man says of marriage, 'This thing is a failure for many of us. It is insufferable that two human beings, having entered into relations which only warm affection can render tolerable, should be forced to maintain them after such affections have ceased to exist, or in spite of the fact that they have never arisen. The alleged natural attractions and repulsions upon which the family ideal is based do not exist; and it is historically false that the family was founded for the purpose of satisfying them. Let us provide otherwise for the social ends which the family subserves, and then abolish its compulsory character altogether.' What will be the attitude of the rest to this outspoken man? The Philistines will simply think him mad. But the idealists will be terrified beyond measure at the proclamation of their hidden thought – at the presence of the traitor among the conspirators of silence – at the rending of the beautiful veil they and their poets have woven to hide the unbearable face of the truth. They will crucify him, burn him, violate their own ideals of family affection by taking his children away from him, ostracize him, brand him as immoral, profligate, filthy, and appeal against him to the despised Philistines, specially idealized for the occasion as Society. How far they will proceed against him depends on how far his courage exceeds theirs. At his worst, they call him cynic and paradoxer; at his best, they do their utmost to ruin him if not to take his life. Thus, purblindly courageous moralists like Mandeville and Larochefoucauld, who merely state unpleasant facts without denying the validity of current ideals, and who indeed depend on those ideals to make their statements piquant, get off with nothing worse than this name of cynic, the free use of which is a familiar mark of the zealous idealist. But take the case of the man who has already served us as an example: Shelley. The idealists did not call Shelley a cynic; they called him a fiend until they invented a new illusion to enable them to enjoy the beauty of his lyrics, this illusion being nothing less than the pretence that since he was at bottom an idealist himself, his ideals must be identical with those of Tennyson and Longfellow, neither of whom ever wrote a line in which some highly respectable ideal was not implicit.[1]

Here the admission that Shelley, the realist, was an idealist too, seems to spoil the whole argument. And it certainly spoils its verbal consistency. For we unfortunately use this word ideal indifferently to denote both the institution which the ideal masks and the mask itself, thereby producing desperate confusion of thought, since the institution may be an effete and poisonous one, whilst the mask may be, and indeed generally is, an image of what we would fain have in its place. If the existing facts, with their masks on, are to be called ideals, and the future possibilities which the masks depict are also to be called ideals – if, again, the man who is defending existing institutions by maintaining their identity with their masks is to be confounded under one name with the man who is striving to realize the future possibilities by tearing the mask and the thing masked asunder, then the position cannot be intelligibly described by mortal pen: you and I, reader, will be at cross purposes at every sentence unless you allow me to distinguish pioneers like Shelley and Ibsen as realists from the idealists of my imaginary community of one thousand. If you ask why I have not allotted the terms the other way, and called Shelley and Ibsen idealists and the conventionalists realists, I reply that Ibsen himself, though he has not formally made the distinction, has so repeatedly harped on conventions and conventionalists as ideals and idealists that if I were now perversely to call them realities and realists, I should confuse readers of The Wild Duck and Rosmersholm more than I should help them. Doubtless I shall be reproached for puzzling people by thus limiting the meaning of the term ideal. But what, I ask, is that inevitable passing perplexity compared to the inextricable tangle I must produce if I follow the custom, and use the word indiscriminately in its two violently incompatible senses? If the term realist is objected to on account of some of its modern associations, I can only recommend you, if you must associate it with something else than my own description of its meaning (I do not deal in definitions), to associate it, not with Zola and Maupassant, but with Plato.

Now let us return to our community of 700 Philistines, 299 idealists, and 1 realist. The mere verbal ambiguity against which I have just provided is as nothing beside that which comes of any attempt to express the relations of these three sections, simple as they are, in terms of the ordinary systems of reason and duty. The idealist, higher in the ascent of evolution than the Philistine, yet hates the highest and strikes at him with a dread and rancor of which the easy-going Philistine is guiltless. The man who has risen above the danger and the fear that his acquisitiveness will lead him to theft, his temper to murder, and his affections to debauchery; this is he who is denounced as an arch-scoundrel and libertine, and thus confounded with the lowest because he is the highest. And it is not the ignorant and stupid who maintain this error, but the literate and the cultured. When the true prophet speaks, he is proved to be both rascal and idiot, not by those who have never read of how foolishly such learned demonstrations have come off in the past, but by those who have themselves written volumes on the crucifixions, the burnings, the stonings, the headings and hangings, the Siberia transportations, the calumny and ostracism which have been the lot of the pioneer as well as of the camp follower. It is from men of established literary reputation that we learn that William Blake was mad, that Shelley was spoiled by living in a low set, that Robert Owen was a man who did not know the world, that Ruskin was incapable of comprehending political economy, that Zola was a mere blackguard, and that Ibsen was 'a Zola with a wooden leg'. The great musician, accepted by the unskilled listener, is vilified by his fellow-musicians: it was the musical culture of Europe that pronounced Wagner the inferior of Mendelssohn and Meyerbeer. The great artist finds his foes among the painters, and not among the men in the street: it was the Royal Academy which placed forgotten nobodies above Burne Jones. It is not rational that it should be so; but it is so, for all that.

The realist at last loses patience with ideals altogether, and sees in them only something to blind us, something to numb us, something to murder self in us, something whereby, instead of resisting death, we can disarm it by committing suicide. The idealist, who has taken refuge with the ideals because he hates himself and is ashamed of himself, thinks that all this is so much the better. The realist, who has come to have a deep respect for himself and faith in the validity of his own will, thinks it so much the worse. To the one, human nature, naturally corrupt, is held back from ruinous excesses only by self-denying conformity to the ideals. To the other these ideals are only swaddling clothes which man has outgrown, and which insufferably impede his movements. No wonder the two cannot agree. The idealist says, 'Realism means egotism; and egotism means depravity.' The realist declares that when a man abnegates the will to live and be free in a world of the living and free, seeking only to conform to ideals for the sake of being, not himself, but 'a good man', then he is morally dead and rotten, and must be left unheeded to abide his resurrection, if that by good luck arrive before his bodily death.[2] Unfortunately, this is the sort of speech that nobody but a realist understands. It will be more amusing as well as more convincing to take an actual example of an idealist criticizing a realist.

THE WOMANLY WOMAN

In 1890 the literary sensation of the day was the Diary of Marie Bashkirtseff. An outline of it, with a running commentary, was given in The Review of Reviews (June 1890) by the editor, the late William Stead, who, having gained an immense following by a public service in rendering which he had to simulate a felony and suffer imprisonment for it in order to prove that it was possible, was engaged in a campaign with the object of establishing the ideal of sexual 'purity' as a condition of public life. He had certain Ibsenist qualities: faith in himself, wilfulness, conscientious unscrupulousness, and could always make himself heard. Prominent among his ideals was an ideal of womanliness. In support of that ideal he would, like all idealists, make and believe any statement, however obviously and grotesquely unreal. When he found Marie Bashkirtseff's account of herself utterly incompatible with the picture of a woman's mind presented to him by his ideal, he was confronted with the dilemma that either Marie was not a woman or else his ideal was false to nature. He actually accepted the former alternative. 'Of the distinctively womanly,' he says, 'there is in her but little trace. She was the very antithesis of a true woman.' William's next difficulty was, that self-control, being a leading quality in his ideal, could not have been possessed by Marie; otherwise she would have been more like his ideal. Nevertheless he had to record that she, without any compulsion from circumstances, made herself a highly skilled artist by working ten hours a day for six years. Let anyone who thinks that this is no evidence of self-control just try it for six months. William's verdict nevertheless was 'No self-control'. However, his fundamental quarrel with Marie came out in the following lines. 'Marie,' he said, 'was artist, musician, wit, philosopher, student, anything you like but a natural woman with a heart to love, and a soul to find its supreme satisfaction in sacrifice for lover or for child.' Now of all the idealist abominations that make society pestiferous, I doubt if there be any so mean as that of forcing self-sacrifice on a woman under pretence that she likes it; and, if she ventures to contradict the pretence, declaring her no true woman. In India they carried this piece of idealism to the length of declaring that a wife could not bear to survive her husband, but would be prompted by her own faithful, loving, beautiful nature to offer up her life on the pyre which consumed his dead body. The astonishing thing is that women, sooner than be branded as unsexed wretches, allowed themselves to be stupefied with drink, and in that unwomanly condition burnt alive. British Philistinism put down widow idealizing with the strong hand; and suttee is abolished in India. The English form of it still flourishes; and Stead, the rescuer of the children,[1] was one of its high priests. Imagine his feelings on coming across this entry in a woman's diary: 'I love myself.' Or this, 'I swear solemnly – by the Gospels, by the passion of Christ, by MYSELF – that in four years I will be famous.' The young woman was positively proposing to exercise for her own sake all the powers that were given to her, in Stead's opinion, solely that she might sacrifice them for her lover or child! No wonder he was driven to exclaim again, 'She was very clever, no doubt; but woman she was not.'

Now observe this notable result. Marie Bashkirtseff, instead of being a less agreeable person than the ordinary female conformer to the ideal of womanliness, was most conspicuously the reverse. Stead himself wrote as one infatuated with her mere diary, and pleased himself by representing her as a person who fascinated everybody, and was a source of delight to all about her by the mere exhilaration and hope-giving atmosphere of her wilfulness. The truth is, that in real life a self-sacrificing woman, or, as Stead would have put it, a womanly woman, is not only taken advantage of, but disliked as well for her pains. No man pretends that his soul finds its supreme satisfaction in self-sacrifice: such an affectation would stamp him as coward and weakling: the manly man is he who takes the Bashkirtseff view of himself. But men are not the less loved on this account. No one ever feels helpless by the side of the self-helper; whilst the self-sacrificer is always a drag, a responsibility, a reproach, an everlasting and unnatural trouble with whom no really strong soul can live. Only those who have helped themselves know how to help others, and to respect their right to help themselves.[2]

Although romantic idealists generally insist on self-surrender as an indispensable element in true womanly love, its repulsive effect is well known and feared in practice by both sexes. The extreme instance is the reckless self-abandonment seen in the infatuation of passionate sexual desire. Everyone who becomes the object of that infatuation shrinks from it instinctively. Love loses its charm when it is not free; and whether the compulsion is that of custom and law, or of infatuation, the effect is the same; it becomes valueless and even abhorrent, like the caresses of a maniac. The desire to give inspires no affection unless there is also the power to withhold; and the successful wooer, in both sexes alike, is the one who can stand out for honorable conditions, and, failing them, go without. Such conditions are evidently not offered to either sex by the legal marriage of today; for it is the intense repugnance inspired by the compulsory character of the legalized conjugal relation that leads, first to the idealization of marriage whilst it remains indispensable as a means of perpetuating society; then to its modification by divorce and by the abolition of penalties for refusal to comply with judicial orders for restitution of conjugal rights; and finally to 'ts disuse and disappearance as the responsibility for the maintenance and education of the rising generation is shifted from the parent to the community.[3]

Although the growing repugnance to face the Church of England marriage service has led many celebrants to omit those passages which frankly explain the object of the institution, we are not likely to dispense with legal ties and obligations, and trust wholly to the permanence of love, until the continuity of society no longer depends on the private nursery. Love, as a practical factor in society, is still a mere appetite. That higher development of it which Ibsen shews us occurring in the case of Rebecca West in Rosmersholm is only known to most of us by the descriptions of great poets, who themselves, as their biographies prove, have known it, not by sustained experience, but only by brief glimpses. Dante loved Beatrice with the higher love; but neither during her life nor after her death was he 'faithful' to her or to the woman he actually married. And he would be a bold bourgeois who would pretend to a higher mind than Dante. Tannhäuser may die in the conviction that one moment of the emotion he felt with St Elizabeth was fuller and happier than all the hours of passion he spent with Venus; but that does not alter the fact that love began for him with Venus, and that its earlier tentatives towards the final goal were attended with relapses. Now Tannhäuser's passion for Venus is a development of the humdrum fondness of the bourgeois Jack for his Jill, a development at once higher and more dangerous, just as idealism is at once higher and more dangerous than Philistinism. The fondness is the germ of the passion: the passion is the germ of the more perfect love. When Blake told men that through excess they would learn moderation, he knew that the way for the present lay through the Venusberg, and that the race would assuredly not perish there as some individuals have, and as the Puritan fears we all shall unless we find a way round. Also he no doubt foresaw the time when our children would be born on the other side of it, and so be spared that fiery purgation.

But the very facts that Blake is still commonly regarded as a crazy visionary, and that the current criticism of Rosmersholm entirely fails even to notice the evolution of Rebecca's passion for Rosmer into her love for him, much more to credit the moral transfiguration which accompanies it, shew how absurd it would be to pretend, for the sake of edification, that the ordinary marriage of today is a union between a William Blake and a Rebecca West, or that it would be possible, even if it were enlightened policy, to deny the satisfaction of the sexual appetite to persons who have not reached that stage. An overwhelming majority of such marriages as are not purely *de convenance* are entered into for the gratification of that appetite either in its crudest form or veiled only by those idealistic illusions which the youthful imagination weaves so wonderfully under the stimulus of desire, and which older people indulgently laugh at.

This being so, it is not surprising that our society, being directly dominated by men, comes to regard Woman, not as an end in herself like Man, but solely as a means of ministering to his appetite. The ideal wife is one who does everything that the ideal husband likes and nothing else. Now to treat a person as a means instead of an end is to deny that person's right to live. And to be treated as a means to such an end as sexual intercourse with those who deny one's right to live is insufferable to any human being. Woman, if she dares face the fact that she is being so treated, must either loathe herself or else rebel. As a rule, when circumstances enable her to rebel successfully – for instance, when the accident of genius enables her to 'lose her character' without losing her employment or cutting herself off from the society she values – she does rebel; but circumstances seldom do. Does she then loathe herself? By no means: she deceives herself in the idealist fashion by denying that the love which her suitor offers her is tainted with sexual appetite at all. It is, she declares, a beautiful, disinterested, pure, sublime devotion to another by which a man's life is exalted and purified, and a woman's rendered blest. And of all the cynics, the filthiest to her mind is the one who sees, in the man making honorable proposals to his future wife, nothing but the human male seeking his female. The man himself keeps her confirmed in her illusion;

for the truth is unbearable to him too: he wants to form an affectionate tie, and not to drive a degrading bargain. After all, the germ of the highest love is in them both; though as yet it is no more than the appetite they are disguising so carefully from themselves. Consequently every stockbroker who has just brought his business up to marrying point woos in terms of the romantic illusion; and it is agreed between the two that their marriage shall realize the romantic ideal. Then comes the breakdown of the plan. The young wife finds that her husband is neglecting her for his business; that his interests, his activities, his whole life except that one part of it to which only a cynic ever referred before her marriage, lies away from home; and that her business is to sit there and mope until she is wanted. Then what can she do? If she complains, he, the self-helper, can do without her; whilst she is dependent on him for her position, her livelihood, her place in society, her home, her name, her very bread.[4] All this is brought home to her by the first burst of displeasure her complaints provoke. Fortunately, things do not remain for ever at this point; perhaps the most wretched in a woman's life. The self-respect she has lost as a wife she regains as a mother, in which capacity her use and importance to the community compare favorably with those of most men of business. She is wanted in the house, wanted in the market, wanted by the children; and now, instead of weeping because her husband is away in the city, thinking of stocks and shares instead of his ideal woman, she would regard his presence in the house all day as an intolerable nuisance. And so, though she is completely disillusioned on the subject of ideal love, yet, since it has not turned out so badly after all, she countenances the illusion still from the point of view that it is a useful and harmless means of getting boys and girls to marry and settle down. And this conviction is the stronger in her because she feels that if she had known as much about marriage the day before her wedding as she did six months after, it would have been extremely hard to induce her to get married at all.

This prosaic solution is satisfactory only within certain limits. It depends altogether upon the accident of the woman having some natural vocation for domestic management and the care of children, as well as on the husband being fairly good-natured and livable-with. Hence arises the idealist illusion that a vocation for domestic management and the care of children is natural to women, and that women who lack them are not women at all, but members of the third, or Bashkirtseff sex. Even if this were true, it is obvious that if the Bashkirtseffs are to be allowed to live, they have a right to suitable institutions just as much as men and women. But it is not true. The domestic career is no more natural to all women than the military career is natural to all men; and although in a population emergency it might become necessary for every able-bodied woman to risk her life in childbed just as it might become necessary in a military emergency for every man to risk his life in the battlefield, yet even then it would by no means follow that the child-bearing would endow the mother with domestic aptitudes and capacities as it would endow her with milk. It is of course quite true that the majority of women are kind to children and prefer their own to other people's. But exactly the same thing is true of the majority of men, who nevertheless do not consider that their proper sphere is the nursery. The case may be illustrated more grotesquely by the fact that the majority of women who have dogs are kind to them, and prefer their own dogs to other people's; yet it is not proposed that women should restrict their activities to the rearing of puppies. If we have come to think that the nursery and the kitchen are the natural sphere of a woman, we have done so exactly as English children come to think that a cage is the natural sphere of a parrot; because they have never seen one anywhere else. No doubt there are Philistine parrots who agree with their owners that it is better to be in a cage than out, so long as there is plenty of hempseed and Indian corn there. There may even be idealist parrots who persuade themselves that the mission of a parrot is to minister to the happiness of a private family by whistling and saying 'Pretty Polly', and that it is in the sacrifice of its liberty to this altruistic pursuit that a true parrot finds the supreme satisfaction of its soul. I will not go so far as to affirm that there are theological parrots who are convinced that imprisonment is the will of God because it is unpleasant; but I am confident that there are rationalist parrots who can demonstrate that it would be a cruel kindness to let a parrot out to fall a prey to cats, or at least to forget its accomplishments and coarsen its naturally delicate fibres in an unprotected struggle for existence. Still, the only parrot a free-souled person can sympathize with is the one that insists on being let out as the first condition of making itself agreeable. A selfish bird, you may say; one that puts its own gratification before that of the family which is so fond of it – before even the greatest happiness of the greatest number: one that, in aping the independent spirit of a man, has unparroted itself and become a creature that has neither the home-loving nature of a bird nor the strength and enterprise of a mastiff. All the same, you respect that parrot in spite of your conclusive reasoning; and if it persists, you will have either to let it out or kill it.

The sum of the matter is that unless Woman repudiates her womanliness, her duty to her husband, to her children, to society, to the law and to everyone but herself, she cannot emancipate herself. But her duty to herself is no duty at all, since a debt is cancelled when the debtor and creditor are the same person. Its payment is simply a fulfilment of the individual will, upon which all duty is a restriction, founded on the conception of the will as naturally malign and devilish. Therefore Woman has to repudiate duty altogether. In that repudiation lies her freedom; for it is false to say that Woman is now directly the slave of Man: she is the immediate slave of duty; and as man's path to freedom is strewn with the wreckage of the duties and ideals he has trampled on, so must hers be. She may indeed mask her iconoclasm by proving in rationalist fashion, as Man has often done for the sake of a quiet life, that all these discarded idealist conceptions will be fortified instead of shattered by her emancipation. To a person with a turn for logic, such proofs are as easy as playing the piano is to Paderewski. But it will not be true. A whole basketful of ideals of the most sacred quality will be smashed by the achievement of equality for women and men. Those who shrink from such a clatter and breakage may comfort themselves with the reflection that the replacement of the broken goods will be prompt and certain. It is always a case of 'The ideal is dead: long live the ideal!' And the advantage of the work of destruction is that every new ideal is less of an illusion than the one it has supplanted; so that the destroyer of ideals, though denounced as an enemy of society, is in fact sweeping the world clear of lies.

My digression is now over. Having traversed my loop as I promised, and come back to Man's repudiation of duty by way of Woman's, I may at last proceed to give some more particular account of Ibsen's work without further preoccupation with Clement Scott's protest, or the many others of which it is the type. For we now see that the pioneer must necessarily provoke such outcry as he repudiates duties, tramples on ideals, profanes what was sacred, sanctifies what was infamous, always driving his plough through gardens of pretty weeds in spite of the laws made against trespassers for the protection of the worms which feed on the roots, always letting in light and air to hasten the putrefaction of decaying matter, and everywhere proclaiming that 'the old beauty is no longer beautiful, the new truth no longer true'. He can do no less; and what more and what else he does it is not given to all of his generation to understand. And if any man does not understand, and cannot foresee the harvest, what can he do but cry out in all sincerity against such destruction, until at last we come to know the cry of the blind like any other street cry, and to bear with it as an honest cry, albeit a false alarm?

THE PLAYS

BRAND, 1866

WE are now prepared to learn without misgiving that a typical Ibsen play is one in which the leading lady is an unwomanly woman, and the villain an idealist. It follows that the leading lady is not a heroine of the Drury Lane type; nor does the villain forge or assassinate, since he is a villain by virtue of his determination to do nothing wrong. Therefore readers of Ibsen – not playgoers – have sometimes so far misconceived him as to suppose that his villains are examples rather than warnings, and that the mischief and ruin which attend their actions are but the tribulations from which the soul comes out purified as gold from the furnace. In fact, the beginning of Ibsen's European reputation was the edification with which the pious received his great dramatic poem Brand. Brand is not his first play: indeed it is his seventh; and of its six forerunners all are notable and some splendid; but it is in Brand that he definitely, if not yet quite consciously, takes the field against idealism and, like another Luther, nails his thesis to the door of the Temple of Morality. With Brand therefore we must begin, lest we should be swept into an eddy of mere literary criticism, a matter altogether beside the purpose of this book, which is to distil the quintessence of Ibsen's message to his age.

Brand the priest is an idealist of heroic earnestness, strength and courage. Conventional, comfortable, sentimental churchgoing withers into selfish snobbery and cowardly weakness before his terrible word. 'Your God,' he cries, 'is an old man; mine is young'; and all Europe, hearing him, suddenly realizes that it has so far forgotten God as to worship an image of an elderly gentleman with a well-trimmed beard, an imposing forehead, and the expression of a headmaster. Brand, turning from such idolatrous follies with fierce scorn, declares himself the champion, not of things as they are, nor of things as they can be made, but of things as they ought to be. Things as they ought to be mean for him things as ordered by men conformed to his ideal of the perfect Adam, who, again, is not man as he is or can be, but man conformed to all the ideals; man as it is his duty to be. In insisting on this conformity, Brand spares neither himself nor anyone else. Life is nothing: self is nothing: the perfect Adam is everything. The imperfect Adam does not fall in with these views. A peasant whom he urges to cross a glacier in a fog because it is his duty to visit his dying daughter, not only flatly declines, but endeavors forcibly to prevent Brand from risking his own life. Brand knocks him down, and sermonizes him with fierce earnestness and scorn. Presently Brand has to cross a fiord in a storm to reach a dying man who, having committed a series of murders, wants 'consolation' from a priest. Brand cannot go alone: someone must hold the rudder of his boat whilst he manages the sail. The fisher folk, in whom the old Adam is strong, do not adopt his estimate of the gravity of the situation, and refuse to go. A woman, fascinated by his heroism and idealism, goes. That ends in their marriage and in the birth of a child to which they become deeply attached. Then Brand, aspiring from height to height of devotion to his ideal, plunges from depth to depth of murderous cruelty. First the child must die from the severity of the climate because Brand must not flinch from the post of duty and leave his congregation exposed to the peril of getting an inferior preacher in his place. Then he forces his wife to give the clothes of the dead child to a gipsy whose baby needs them. The bereaved mother does not grudge the gift; but she wants to hold back only one little garment as a relic of her darling. But Brand sees in this reservation the imperfection of the imperfect Eve. He forces her to regard the situation as a choice between the relic and his ideal. She sacrifices the relic to the ideal, and then dies, broken-hearted. Having killed her, and thereby placed himself beyond ever daring to doubt the idealism upon whose altar he has immolated her; having also refused to go to his mother's death-bed because she compromises with his principles in disposing of her property, he is hailed by the people as a saint, and finds his newly built church too small for his congregation. So he calls upon them to follow him to worship God in His own temple, the mountains. After a brief practical experience of this arrangement, they change their minds, and stone him. The very mountains themselves stone him, indeed; for he is killed by an avalanche.

PEER GYNT, 1867

Brand dies a saint, having caused more intense suffering by his saintliness than the most talented sinner could possibly have done with twice his opportunities. Ibsen does not leave this to be inferred. In another dramatic poem he gives us a rapscallion named Peer Gynt, an idealist who avoids Brand's errors by setting up as his ideal the realization of himself through the utter satisfaction of his own will. In this he would seem to be on the path to which Ibsen himself points; and indeed all who know the two plays will agree that whether or no it was better to be Peer Gynt than Brand, it was beyond all question better to be the mother or the sweetheart of Peer, scapegrace and liar as he was, than mother or wife to the saintly Brand. Brand would force his ideal on all men and women; Peer Gynt keeps his ideal for himself alone: it is indeed implicit in the ideal itself that it should be unique – that he alone should have the force to realize it. For Peer's first boyish notion of the self-realized man is not the saint, but the demi-god whose indomitable will is stronger than destiny, the fighter, the master, the man whom no woman can resist, the mighty hunter, the knight of a thousand adventures, the model, in short, of the lover in a lady's novel, or the hero in a boy's romance. Now, no such person exists, or ever did exist, or ever can exist. The man who cultivates an indomitable will and refuses to make way for anything or anybody, soon finds that he cannot hold a street crossing against a tram car, much less a world against the whole human race. Only by plunging into illusions to which every fact gives the lie can he persuade himself that his will is a force that can overcome all other forces, or that it is less conditioned by circumstances than a wheelbarrow is. However, Peer Gynt, being imaginative enough to conceive his ideal, is also imaginative enough to find illusions to hide its unreality, and to persuade himself that Peer Gynt, the shabby countryside loafer, is Peer Gynt, Emperor of Himself, as he writes over the door of his hut in the mountains. His hunting feats are invented; his military genius has no solider foundation than a street fight with a smith; and his reputation as an adventurous daredevil he has to gain by the bravado of carrying off the bride from a wedding at which the guests snub him. Only in the mountains can he enjoy his illusions undisturbed by ridicule; yet even in the mountains he finds obstacles he cannot force his way through, obstacles which withstand him as spirits with voices, telling him that he must go round. But he will not; he will go forward, he will cut his path sword in hand, in spite of fate. All the same, he has to go round; for the world-will is outside Peer Gynt as well as inside him.

Then he tries the supernatural, only to find that it means nothing more than the transmogrifying of squalid realities by lies and pretences. Still, like our amateurs of thaumaturgy, he is willing to enter into a conspiracy of make-believe up to a certain point. When the Trold king's daughter appears as a repulsive ragged creature riding on a pig, he is ready to accept her as a beautiful princess on a noble steed, on condition that she accepts his mother's tumble-down farmhouse, with the broken window panes stopped up with old clouts, as a splendid castle. He will go with her among the Trolds, and pretend that the gruesome ravine in which they hold their orgies is a glorious palace; he will partake of their filthy food and declare it nectar and ambrosia; he will applaud their obscene antics as exquisite dancing, and their discordant din as divine music; but when they finally propose to slit his eyes so that he may see and hear these things, not as they are, but as he has been pretending to see and hear them, he draws back, resolved to be himself even in self-deception. He leaves the mountains and becomes a prosperous man of business in America, highly respectable and ready for any profitable speculation; slave trade, Bible trade, whisky trade, missionary trade, anything! His commercial success in this phase persuades him that he is under the special care of God; but he is shaken in his opinion by an adventure in which he is marooned on the African coast, and does not recover his faith until the treacherous friends who marooned him are destroyed before his eyes by the blowing-up of the steam yacht they have just stolen from him, when he utters his celebrated exclamation, 'Ah, God is a Father to me after all; but economical he certainly is not.' He finds a white horse in the desert, and is accepted on its account as the Messiah by an Arab tribe, a success which moves him to declare that now at last he is really worshipped for himself, whereas in America people only respected his breast-pin, the symbol of his money. In commerce, too, he reflects, his eminence was a mere matter of chance, whilst as a prophet he is eminent by pure natural fitness for the post. This is ended by his falling in love with a dancing-girl, who, after leading him into every sort of undignified and ludicrous extravagance, ranging from his hailing her as the Eternal-Feminine of Goethe to the more practical folly of giving her his white horse and all his prophetic finery, runs away with the spoil, and leaves him once more helpless and alone in the desert. He wanders until he comes to the Great Sphinx, beside which he finds a German gentleman in great perplexity as to who the Sphinx is. Peer Gynt, seeing in that impassive, immovable, majestic figure, a symbol of his own ideal, is able to tell the German gentleman at once that the Sphinx is itself. This explanation dazzles the German, who, after some further discussion of the philosophy of self-realization, invites Peer Gynt to accompany him to a club of learned men in Cairo, who are ripe for enlightenment on this very question. Peer, delighted, accompanies the German to the club, which turns out to be a madhouse in which the lunatics have broken loose and locked up their keepers. It is in this madhouse, and by these madmen, that Peer Gynt is at last crowned Emperor of Himself. He receives their homage as he lies in the dust fainting with terror.

As an old man, Peer Gynt, returning to the scenes of his early adventures, is troubled with the prospect of meeting a certain button moulder who threatens to make short work of his realized self by melting it down in his crucible with a heap of other button-material. Immediately the old exaltation of the self realizer is changed into an unspeakable dread of the button moulder Death, to avoid whom Peer Gynt has already pushed a drowning man from the spar he is clinging to in a shipwreck lest it should not suffice to support two. At last he finds a deserted sweetheart of his youth still waiting for him and still believing in him. In the imagination of this old woman he finds the ideal Peer Gynt; whilst in himself, the loafer, the braggart, the confederate of sham magicians, the Charleston speculator, the false prophet, the dancing-girl's dupe, the bedlam emperor, the thruster of the drowning man into the waves, there is nothing heroic: nothing but commonplace self-seeking and shirking, cowardice and sensuality, veiled only by the romantic fancies of the born liar. With this crowningly unreal realization he is left to face the button moulder as best he can.[1]

Peer Gynt has puzzled a good many people by Ibsen's fantastic and subtle treatment of its metaphysical thesis. It is so far a difficult play, that the ideal of unconditional self-realization, however familiar its suggestions may be to the ambitious reader, is not understood by him. When it is stated to him by some one who does understand it, he unhesitatingly dismisses it as idiotic; and because he is perfectly right in doing so – because it is idiotic in the most accurate sense of the term – he does not easily recognize it as the common ideal of his own prototype, the pushing, competitive, success-craving man who is the hero of the modern world.

There is nothing novel in Ibsen's dramatic method of reducing these ideals to absurdity. Exactly as Cervantes took the old ideal of chivalry, and shewed what came of a man attempting to act as if it were real, so Ibsen takes the ideals of Brand and Peer Gynt, and subjects them to the same test. Don Quixote acts as if he were a perfect knight in a world of giants and distressed damsels instead of a country gentleman in a land of innkeepers and farm wenches; Brand acts as if he were the perfect Adam in a world where, by resolute rejection of all compromise with imperfection, it was immediately possible to change the rainbow 'bridge between flesh and spirit' into as enduring a structure as the tower of Babel was intended to be, thereby restoring man to the condition in which he walked with God in the garden; and Peer Gynt tries to act as if he had in him a special force that could be concentrated so as to prevail over all other forces. They ignore the real – ignore what they are and where they are, not only, like Nelson, shutting their eyes to the signals a brave man may disregard, but insanely steering straight on rocks no man's resolution can move or resist. Observe that neither Cervantes nor Ibsen is incredulous, in the Philistine way, as to the power of ideals over men. Don Quixote, Brand and Peer Gynt are, all three, men of action seeking to realize their ideals in deeds. However ridiculous Don Quixote makes himself, you cannot dislike or despise him, much less think that it would have been better for him to have been a Philistine like Sancho; and Peer Gynt, selfish rascal as he is, is not unlovable. Brand, made terrible by the consequences of his idealism to others, is heroic. Their castles in the air are more beautiful than castles of brick and mortar; but one cannot live in them; and they seduce man into pretending

70

that every hovel is such a castle, just as Peer Gynt pretended that the Trold king's den was a palace.

EMPEROR AND GALILEAN, 1873

When Ibsen, by merely giving the rein to the creative impulse of his poetic nature, had produced Brand and Peer Gynt, he was nearly forty. His will, in setting his imagination to work, had produced a tough puzzle for his intellect. In no case does the difference between the will and the intellect come out more clearly than in that of the poet, save only that of the lover. Had Ibsen died in 1867, he, like many another great poet, would have gone to his grave without having ever rationally understood his own meaning. Nay, if in that year an intellectual expert – a commentator, as we call him – having read Brand, had put forward the explanation which Ibsen himself must have arrived at before he constructed Ghosts and The Wild Duck, he would perhaps have repudiated it with as much disgust as a maiden would feel if anyone were prosaic enough to give her the physiological explanation of her dreams of meeting a fairy prince. Only simpletons go to the creative artist presuming that he must be able to answer their 'What does this obscure passage mean?' That is the very question the poet's own intellect, which had no part in the conception of the poem, may be asking him. And this curiosity of the intellect, this restless life in it which differentiates it from dead machinery, and troubles our lesser artists but little, is one of the marks of the greater sort. Shakespear, in Hamlet, made a drama of the self-questioning that came upon him when his intellect rose up in alarm, as well it might, against the vulgar optimism of his Henry V, and yet could mend it to no better purpose than by the equally vulgar pessimism of Troilus and Cressida. Dante took pains to understand himself; so did Goethe. Richard Wagner, one of the greatest poets of our own day, has left us as many volumes of criticism of art and life as he has left musical scores; and he has expressly described how the keen intellectual activity he brought to the analysis of his music dramas was in abeyance during their creation. Just so do we find Ibsen, after composing his two great dramatic poems, entering on a struggle to become intellectually conscious of what he had done.

We have seen that with Shakespear such an effort became itself creative and produced a drama of questioning. With Ibsen the same thing occurred: he harked back to an abandoned project of his, and wrote two huge dramas on the subject of the apostasy of the Emperor Julian. In this work we find him at first preoccupied with a piece of old-fashioned freethinking; the dilemma that moral responsibility presupposes free-will, and that free-will sets man above God. Cain, who slew because he willed, willed because he must, and must have willed to slay because he was himself, comes upon the stage to claim that murder is fertile, and death the ground of life, though, not having read Weismann on death as a method of evolution, he cannot say what is the ground of death. Judas asks whether, when the Master chose him, he chose foreknowingly. This part of the drama has no very deep significance. It is easy to invent conundrums which dogmatic evangelicalism cannot answer; and no doubt, whilst it was still a nine days' wonder that evangelicalism could not solve all enigmas, such invention seemed something much deeper than the mere intellectual chess-play which it is seen to be now that the nine days are past. In his occasional weakness for such conundrums, and later on in his harping on the hereditary transmission of disease, we see Ibsen's active intellect busy, not only with the problems peculiar to his own plays, but with the fatalism and pessimism of the middle of the nineteenth century, when the typical advanced culture was attainable by reading Strauss's Leben Jesu, the popularizations of Helmholtz and Darwin by Tyndall and Huxley, and George Eliot's novels, vainly protested against by Ruskin as peopled with 'the sweepings of a Pentonville omnibus'.

The traces of this period in Ibsen's writings shew how well he knew the crushing weight with which the sordid cares of the ordinary struggle for money and respectability fell on the world when the romance of the creeds was discredited, and progress seemed for the moment to mean, not the growth of the spirit of man, but an effect of the survival of the fittest brought about by the destruction of the unfit, all the most frightful examples of this systematic destruction being thrust into the utmost prominence by those who were fighting the Church with Mill's favorite dialectical weapon, the incompatibility of divine omnipotence with divine benevolence. His plays are full of an overwhelming sense of the necessity for rousing ourselves into self-assertion against this numbing fatalism; and yet he certainly had not at this time freed his intellect from an acceptance of its scientific validity as our Samuel Butler did, though Butler was more like Ibsen than any man in Europe, having the same grim hoaxing humor, the same grip of spiritual realities behind material facts, the same toughness of character holding him unshaken against the world.

Butler revelled in Darwinism for six weeks, and then, grasping the whole scope and the whole terror of it, warned us (we did not listen until we had revelled for half a century) that Darwin had 'banished mind from the universe', meaning from Evolution. Ibsen, belonging to an earlier generation, and intellectually nursed on northern romance and mysticism rather than on the merely industrious and prosaic science of the interval between the discovery of Evolution at the end of the eighteenth century and the discovery and overrating of Natural Selection as a method of evolution in the middle of the nineteenth, was, when Darwin arrived, past the age at which Natural Selection could have swept him away as it swept Butler and his contemporaries. But, like them, he seems to have welcomed it for the mortal blow it dealt to the current travesties of Christianity, which were really only reductions of the relations between man and God to the basis of the prevalent Commercialism, shewing how God may be cheated, and how salvation can be got for nothing through the blood of Christ by sweaters, adulterators, quacks, sharks and hypocrites; also how God, though the most dangerously capricious and short-tempered of Anarchists, is also the most sentimental of dupes. It is against this conception of God as a sentimental dupe that Brand rages. Ibsen evidently regarded the brimstone conception, 'the Almighty Fiend' of Shelley, as not worth his powder and shot, partly, no doubt, because he knew that the Almighty Fiend's votaries would never read or understand his works, and partly because the class he addressed, the cultured class, had thrown off that superstition, and were busy with the sentimental religion of love in which we are still wallowing, and which only substitutes twaddle for terror.

At first sight this may seem an improvement; but it is no defence against that fear of man which is so much more mischievous than the fear of God. The cruelty of Natural Selection was a powerful antidote to such sentimentalism; and Ibsen, who was perhaps no expert in recent theories of evolution, was quite ready to rub it in uncritically for the sake of its value as a tonic. Indeed, as a fearless observer of the cruelty of Nature, he was quite independent of Darwin: what we find in his works is an unmistakable Darwinian atmosphere, but not the actual Darwinian discoveries and technical theory. If Natural Selection, the gloomiest and most formidable of the castles of Giant Despair, had stopped him, he would no doubt, like Butler, have set himself deliberately to play Greatheart and reduce it; but his genius pushed him past it and left it to be demolished philosophically by Butler, and practically by the mere march of the working class, which, by its freedom from the economic bias of the middle classes, has escaped their characteristic illusions, and solved many of the enigmas they found insoluble because they did not wish to have them solved. For instance, according to the theory of Natural Selection, progress can take place only through an increase in the severity of the material conditions of existence; and as the working classes were quite determined that progress should consist of just the opposite, they had no difficulty in seeing that it generally does occur in that way, whereas the middle class wished, on the contrary, to be convinced that the poverty of the working classes and all the hideous evils attending it were inevitable conditions of progress, and that every penny in the pound on the rates spent in social amelioration, and every attempt on the part of the workers to raise their wages by Trade Unionism or otherwise, were vain defiances of biologic and economic science.

How far Ibsen was definitely conscious of all this is doubtful; but one of his most famous utterances pointed to the working class and the women as the great emancipators. His prophetic belief in the spontaneous growth of the will made him a meliorist without reference to the operation of Natural Selection; but his impression of the light thrown by physical and biological science on the facts of life seems to have been the gloomy one of the middle of the nineteenth century. External nature often plays her most ruthless and destructive part in his works, which have an extraordinary fascination for the pessimists of that period, in spite of the incompatibility of his individualism with that mechanical utilitarian ethic of theirs which treats Man as the sport of every circumstance, and ignores his will altogether.

Another inessential but very prominent feature in Ibsen's dramas will be understood easily by anyone who has observed how a change of religious faith intensifies our concern about our own salvation. An ideal, pious or secular, is practically used as a standard of conduct; and whilst it remains unquestioned, the simple rule of right is to conform to it. In the theological stage, when the Bible is accepted as the revelation of God's will, the pious man, when in doubt as to whether he is acting rightly or wrongly, quiets his misgivings by searching the Scripture until he finds a text which endorses his action.[2] The rationalist, for whom the Bible has no authority, brings his conduct to such tests as asking himself, after Kant, how it would be if everyone did as he proposes to do; or by calculating the effect of his action on the greatest happiness of the greatest number; or by judging whether the liberty of action he is claiming infringes the equal liberty of others, etc., etc. Most men are ingenious enough to pass examinations of this kind successfully in respect to everything they really want to do. But in periods of transition, as, for instance, when faith in the infallibility of the Bible is shattered, and faith in that of reason not yet perfected, men's uncertainty as to the rightness and wrongness of their actions keeps them in a continual perplexity, amid which casuistry seems the most important branch of intellectual activity. Life, as depicted by Ibsen, is very full of it. We find the great double drama of Emperor and Galilean occupied at first with Julian's case regarded as a case of conscience. It is compared, in the manner already described, with the cases of Cain and Judas, the three men being introduced as 'corner stones under the wrath of necessity', 'great freedmen under necessity', and so forth. The qualms of Julian are theatrically effective in producing the most exciting suspense as to whether he will dare to choose between Christ and the imperial purple; but the mere exhibition of a man struggling between his ambition and his creed belongs to a phase of intellectual interest which Ibsen had passed even before the production of Brand, when he wrote his Kongs Emnerne (The Pretenders). Emperor and Galilean might have been appropriately, if prosaically, named 'The Mistake of Maximus the Mystic'. It is Maximus who forces the choice on Julian, not as between ambition and principle; between Paganism and Christianity; between 'the old beauty that is no longer beautiful and the new truth that is no longer true', but between Christ and Julian himself. Maximus knows that there is no going back to 'the first empire' of pagan sensualism. 'The second empire', Christian or self-abnegatory idealism, is already rotten at heart. 'The third empire' is what he looks for; the empire of Man asserting the eternal validity of his own will. He who can see that not on Olympus, not nailed to the cross, but in himself is God, he is the man to build Brand's bridge between the flesh and the spirit, establishing this third empire in which the spirit shall not be unknown, nor the flesh starved, nor the will tortured and baffled. Thus throughout the first part of the double drama we have Julian prompted step by step to the stupendous conviction that he no less than the Galilean is God. His final resolution to seize the throne is expressed in his interruption of the Lord's prayer, which he hears intoned by worshippers in church as he wrestles in the gloom of the catacombs with his own fears and the entreaties and threats of his soldiers urging him to take the final decisive step. At the cue 'Lead us not into temptation; but deliver us from evil' he rushes to the church with his soldiers, exclaiming 'For mine is the kingdom'. Yet he halts on the threshold, dazzled by the light, as his follower Sallust points the declaration by adding, 'and the power, and the glory'.

Once on the throne Julian becomes a mere pedant-tyrant, trying to revive Paganism mechanically by cruel enforcement of external conformity to its rites. In his moments of exaltation he half grasps the meaning of Maximus, only to relapse presently and pervert it into a grotesque mixture of superstition and monstrous vanity. We have him making such speeches as this, worthy of Peer Gynt at his most ludicrous: 'Has not Plato long ago enunciated the truth that only a god can rule over men? What did he mean by that saying? Answer me: what did he mean? Far be it from me to assert that Plato, incomparable sage though he was, had any individual, even the greatest, in his prophetic eye,' etc. In this frame of mind Christ appears to him, not as the prototype of himself, as Maximus would have him feel, but as a rival god over whom he must prevail at all costs. It galls him to think that the Galilean still reigns in the hearts of men whilst the emperor can only extort lip honor from them by brute force; for in his wildest excesses of egotism he never so loses his saving sense of the realities of things as to mistake the trophies of persecution for the fruits of faith. 'Tell me who shall conquer,' he demands of Maximus, 'the emperor or the Galilean?'

'Both the emperor and the Galilean shall succumb,' says Maximus. 'Whether in our time or in hundreds of years I know not; but so it shall be when the right man comes.'

'Who is the right man?' says Julian.

'He who shall swallow up both emperor and Galilean,'[3] replies the seer. 'Both shall succumb; but you shall not therefore perish. Does not the child succumb in the youth and the youth in the man: yet neither child nor youth perishes. You know I have never approved of your policy as emperor. You have tried to make the youth a child again. The empire of the flesh is fallen a prey to the empire of the spirit. But the empire of the spirit is not final, any more than the youth is. You have tried to hinder the youth from growing: from becoming a man. Oh fool, who have drawn your sword against that which is to be: against the third empire, in which the twin-natured shall reign. For him the Jews have a name. They call him Messiah, and are waiting for him.'

Still Julian stumbles on the threshold of the idea without entering into it. He is galled out of all comprehension by the rivalry of the Galilean, and asks despairingly who shall break his power. Then Maximus drives the lesson home.

MAXIMUS. Is it not written, 'Thou shalt have none other gods but me?'

JULIAN. Yes – yes – yes.

MAXIMUS. The seer of Nazareth did not preach this god or that: he said 'God is I: I am God.'

JULIAN. And that is what makes the emperor powerless? The third empire? The Messiah? Not the Jews' Messiah, but the Messiah of the two empires, the spirit and the world?

MAXIMUS. The God-Emperor.

JULIAN. The Emperor-God.

MAXIMUS. Logos in Pan, Pan in Logos.

JULIAN. How is he begotten?

78

MAXIMUS. He is self-begotten in the man who wills.

But it is of no use. Maximus's idea is a synthesis of relations in which not only is Christ God in exactly the same sense as that in which Julian is God, but Julian is Christ as well. The persistence of Julian's jealousy of the Galilean shews that he has not comprehended the synthesis at all, but only seized on that part of it which flatters his own egotism. And since this part is only valid as a constituent of the synthesis, and has no reality when isolated from it, it cannot by itself convince Julian. In vain does Maximus repeat his lesson in every sort of parable, and in such pregnant questions as 'How do you know, Julian, that you were not in him whom you now persecute?' He can only wreak him to utter commands to the winds, and to exclaim, in the excitement of burning his fleet on the borders of Persia, 'The third empire is here, Maximus. I feel that the Messiah of the earth lives within me. The spirit has become flesh and the flesh spirit. All creation lies within my will and power. More than the fleet is burning. In that glowing, swirling pyre the crucified Galilean is burning to ashes; and the earthly emperor is burning with the Galilean. But from the ashes shall arise, phoenix-like, the God of earth and the Emperor of the spirit in one, in one, in one.' At which point he is informed that a Persian refugee, whose information has emboldened him to burn his ships, has fled from the camp and is a manifest spy. From that moment he is a broken man. In his next and last emergency, when the Persians fall upon his camp, his first desperate exclamation is a vow to sacrifice to the gods. 'To what gods, oh fool?' cries Maximus. 'Where are they; and what are they?' 'I will sacrifice to this god and that god: I will sacrifice to many,' he answers desperately. 'One or other must surely hear me. *I must call on something without me and above me.*' A flash of lightning seems to him a response from above; and with this encouragement he throws himself into the fight, clinging, like Macbeth, to an ambiguous oracle which leads him to suppose that only in the Phrygian regions need he fear defeat. He imagines he sees the Nazarene in the ranks of the enemy; and in fighting madly to

79

reach him he is struck down, in the name of Christ, by one of his own soldiers. Then his one Christian General, Jovian, calls on his 'believing brethren' to give Caesar what is Caesar's. Declaring that the heavens are open and the angels coming to the rescue with their swords of fire, he rallies the Galileans of whom Julian has made slave-soldiers. The pagan free legions, crying out that the god of the Galileans is on the Roman side, and that he is the strongest, follow Jovian as he charges the enemy, who fly in all directions whilst Julian, sinking back from a vain effort to rise, exclaims, 'Thou hast conquered, O Galilean.'

Julian dies quietly in his tent, averring, in reply to a Christian friend's inquiry, that he has nothing to repent of. 'The power which circumstances placed in my hands,' he says, 'and which is an emanation of divinity, I am conscious of having used to the best of my skill. I have never wittingly wronged anyone. If some should think that I have not fulfilled all expectations, they should in justice reflect that there is a mysterious power outside us, which in a great measure governs the issue of human undertakings.' He still does not see eye to eye with Maximus, though there is a flash of insight in his remark to him, when he learns that the village where he fell is called the Phrygian region, that 'the world-will has laid an ambush for him'. It was something for Julian to have seen that the power which he found stronger than his individual will was itself will; but inasmuch as he conceived it, not as the whole of which his will was but a part, but as a rival will, he was not the man to found the third empire. He had felt the godhead in himself, but not in others. Being only able to say, with half conviction, 'The kingdom of heaven is within ME,' he had been utterly vanquished by the Galilean who had been able to say, 'The kingdom of heaven is within YOU.' But he was on the way to that full truth. A man cannot believe in others until he believes in himself; for his conviction of the equal worth of his fellows must be filled by the overflow of his conviction of his own worth. Against the spurious Christianity of asceticism, starving that indispensable prior conviction, Julian rightly rebelled, and Maximus rightly incited him to rebel. But Maximus could not fill the prior conviction even to fulness, much less to overflowing; for the third empire was not yet, and is not yet.

However, the tyrant dies with a peaceful conscience; and Maximus is able to tell the priest at the bedside that the world-will will answer for Julian's soul. What troubles the mystic is his having misled Julian by encouraging him to bring upon himself the fate of Cain and Judas. As water can be boiled by fire, man can be prompted and stimulated from without to assert his individuality; but just as no boiling can fill a half-empty well, no external stimulus can enlarge the spirit of man to the point at which he can self-beget the Emperor-God in himself by willing. At that point 'to will is to have to will'; and it is with these words on his lips that Maximus leaves the stage, still sure that the third empire is to come.

It is not necessary to translate the scheme of Emperor and Galilean into terms of the antithesis between idealism and realism. Julian, in this respect, is a reincarnation of Peer Gynt. All the difference is that the subject which was instinctively projected in the earlier poem, is intellectually constructed in the later history, Julian plus Maximus the Mystic being Peer plus one who understands him better than Ibsen did when he created him.

The interest for us of Ibsen's interpretation of original Christianity is obvious. The deepest sayings recorded in the gospels are now nothing but eccentric paradoxes to most of those who reject the supernatural view of Christ's divinity. Those who accept that view often consider that such acceptance absolves them from attaching any sensible meaning to his words at all, and so might as well pin their faith to a stock or stone. Of these attitudes the first is superficial, and the second stupid. Ibsen's interpretation, whatever may be its validity, will certainly hold the field long after the current 'Crosstianity', as it has been aptly called, becomes unthinkable.

THE OBJECTIVE ANTI-IDEALIST PLAYS

IBSEN had now written three immense dramas, all dealing with the effect of idealism on individual egotists of exceptional imaginative excitability. This he was able to do whilst his intellectual consciousness of his theme was yet incomplete, by simply portraying sides of himself. He has put himself into the skin of Brand and Peer Gynt. He has divided himself between Maximus and Julian. These figures have accordingly a certain direct vitality which we shall find in none of his later male figures until it reappears under the shadow of death, less as vitality than as mortality putting on immortality, in the four great plays with which he closed and crowned his life's work. There are flashes of it in Relling, in Lövborg, in Ellida's stranger from the sea; but they are only flashes: henceforth for many years, indeed until his warfare against vulgar idealism is accomplished and a new phase entered upon in The Master Builder, all his really vivid and solar figures are women. For, having at last completed his intellectual analysis of idealism, he could now construct methodical illustrations of its social working, instead of, as before, blindly projecting imaginary personal experiences which he himself had not yet succeeded in interpreting. Further, now that he understood the matter, he could see plainly the effect of idealism as a social force on people quite unlike himself: that is to say, on everyday people in everyday life: on shipbuilders, bank managers, parsons and doctors, as well as on saints, romantic adventurers and emperors.

With his eyes thus opened, instances of the mischief of idealism crowded upon him so rapidly that he began deliberately to inculcate their lesson by writing realistic prose plays of modern life, abandoning all production of art for art's sake. His skill as a playwright and his genius as an artist were thenceforth used only to secure attention and effectiveness for his detailed attack on idealism. No more verse, no more tragedy for the sake of tears or comedy for the sake of laughter, no more seeking to produce specimens of art forms in order that literary critics might fill the public belly with the east wind. The critics, it is true, soon declared that he had ceased to be an artist; but he, having something else to do with his talent than to fulfil critics' definitions, took no notice of them, not thinking their ideal sufficiently important to write a play about.

THE LEAGUE OF YOUTH, 1869

The first of the series of realistic prose plays is called Pillars of Society; but before describing this, a word must be said about a previous work which seems to have determined the form the later series took. Between Peer Gynt and Emperor and Galilean, Ibsen had let fall an amusing comedy called The League of Youth (*De Unges Forbund*) in which the imaginative egotist reappears farcically as an ambitious young lawyer-politician who, smarting under a snub from a local landowner and county magnate, relieves his feelings with such a passionate explosion of Radical eloquence that he is cheered to the echo by the progressive party. Intoxicated with this success, he imagines himself a great leader of the people and a wielder of the mighty engine of democracy. He narrates to a friend a dream in which he saw kings swept helplessly over the surface of the earth by a mighty wind. He has hardly achieved this impromptu when he receives an invitation to dine with the local magnate, whose friends, to spare his feelings, have misled him as to the person aimed at in the new demagogue's speech. The invitation sets the egotist's imagination on the opposite tack: he is presently pouring forth his soul in the magnate's drawing-room to the very friend to whom he related the great dream.

'My goal is this: in the course of time I shall get into

Parliament, perhaps into the Ministry, and marry happily into a rich and honorable family. I intend to reach it by my own exertions. I must and shall reach it without help from anyone. Meanwhile I shall enjoy life here, drinking in beauty and sunshine. Here there are fine manners: life moves gracefully here: the very floors seem laid to be trodden only by lacquered shoes: the arm-chairs are deep; and the ladies sink exquisitely into them. Here the conversation goes lightly and elegantly, like a game at battledore; and no blunders come plumping in to make an awkward silence. Here I feel for the first time what distinction means. Yes: we have indeed an aristocracy of culture; and to it I will belong. Don't you yourself feel the refining influence of the place,' etc., etc.

For the rest, the play is an ingenious comedy of intrigue, clever enough in its mechanical construction to entitle the French to claim that Ibsen owes something to his technical education as a playwright in the school of Scribe. One or two episodes are germs of later plays; and the suitability of the realistic prose comedy form to these episodes no doubt confirmed Ibsen in his choice of it.

PILLARS OF SOCIETY, 1877

Pillars of Society is the history of one Karsten Bernick, a 'pillar of society' who, in pursuance of the duty of maintaining the respectability of his father's firm of shipbuilders, has averted a disgraceful exposure by allowing another man to bear the discredit not only of a love affair in which he himself had been the sinner, but of a theft which was never committed at all, having been merely alleged as an excuse for the firm being out of funds at a critical period. Bernick is an abject slave to the idealizings of one Rörlund, a schoolmaster, about respectability, duty to society, good example, social influence, health of the community, and so on. When Bernick falls in love with a married actress, he feels that no man has a right to shock the feelings of Rörlund and the community for his own selfish gratification. However, a clandestine intrigue will shock nobody, since nobody need know of it. He accordingly adopts this method of satisfying himself and preserving the moral tone of the community at the same time. Unluckily, the intrigue is all but discovered; and Bernick has either to see the moral security of the community shaken to its foundation by the terrible scandal of his exposure, or else to deny what he did and put it on another man. As the other man happens to be going to America, where he can easily conceal his imputed shame, Bernick's conscience tells him that it would be little short of a crime against society to neglect such an opportunity; and he accordingly lies his way back into the good opinion of Rörlund and Company at the emigrant's expense.

There are three women in the play for whom the schoolmaster's ideals have no attractions. First, there is the actress's daughter, who wants to get to America because she hears that people there are not good; for she is heartily tired of good people, since it is part of their goodness to look down on her because of her mother's disgrace. The schoolmaster, to whom she is engaged, condescends to her for the same reason. The second has already sacrificed her happiness and wasted her life in conforming to the Rörlund ideal of womanliness; and she earnestly advises the younger woman not to commit that folly, but to break her engagement with the schoolmaster, and elope promptly with the man she loves. The third is a naturally free woman who has snapped her fingers at the current ideals all her life; and it is her presence that at last encourages the liar to break with the ideals by publicly telling the truth about himself.

The comic personage of the piece is a useless hypochondriac whose function in life, as described by himself, is 'to hold up the banner of the ideal'. This he does by sneering at everything and everybody for not resembling the heroic incidents and characters he reads about in novels and tales of adventure. But his obvious peevishness and folly make him much less dangerous than the pious idealist, the earnest and respectable Rörlund. The play concludes with Bernick's admission that the spirits of Truth and Freedom are the true pillars of society, a phrase which sounds so like an idealistic commonplace that it is necessary to add that Truth in this passage does not mean the nursery convention of truth-telling satirized by Ibsen himself in a later play, as well as by Labiche and other comic dramatists. It means the unflinching recognition of facts, and the abandonment of the conspiracy to ignore such of them as do not bolster up the ideals. The idealist rule as to truth dictates the recognition only of those facts or idealistic masks of facts which have a respectable air, and the mentioning of these on all occasions and at all hazards. Ibsen urges the recognition of all facts; but as to mentioning them, he wrote a whole play, as we shall see presently, to shew that you must do that at your own peril, and that a truth-teller who cannot hold his tongue on occasion may do as much mischief as a whole universityful of trained liars. The word Freedom means freedom from the tyranny of the Rörlund ideals.

A DOLL'S HOUSE, 1879

Unfortunately, Pillars of Society, as a propagandist play, is disabled by the circumstance that the hero, being a fraudulent hypocrite in the ordinary police-court sense of the phrase, would hardly be accepted as a typical pillar of society by the class he represents. Accordingly, Ibsen took care next time to make his idealist irreproachable from the standpoint of the ordinary idealist morality. In the famous Doll's House, the pillar of society who owns the doll is a model husband, father, and citizen. In his little household, with the three darling children and the affectionate little wife, all on the most loving terms with one another, we have the sweet home, the womanly woman, the happy family life of the idealist's dream. Mrs Nora Helmer is happy in the belief that she has attained a valid realization of all these illusions; that she is an ideal wife and mother; and that Helmer is an ideal husband who would, if the necessity arose, give his life to save her reputation. A few simply contrived incidents disabuse her effectually on all these points. One of her earliest acts of devotion to her husband has been the secret raising of a sum of money to enable him to make a tour which was necessary to restore his health. As he would have broken down sooner than go into debt, she has had to persuade him that the money was a gift from her father. It was really obtained from a moneylender, who refused to make her the loan unless she induced her father to endorse the promissory note. This being impossible, as her father was dying at the time, she took the shortest way out of the difficulty by writing the name herself, to the entire satisfaction of the moneylender, who, though not at all duped, knew that forged bills are often the surest to be paid. Since then she has slaved in secret at scrivener's work until she has nearly paid off the debt.

At this point Helmer is made manager of the bank in which he is employed; and the moneylender, wishing to obtain a post there, uses the forged bill to force Nora to exert her influence with Helmer on his behalf. But she, having a hearty contempt for the man, cannot be persuaded by him that there was any harm in putting her father's name on the bill, and ridicules the suggestion that the law would not recognize that she was right under the circumstances. It is her husband's own contemptuous denunciation of a forgery formerly committed by the moneylender himself that destroys her self-satisfaction and opens her eyes to her ignorance of the serious business of the world to which her husband belongs: the world outside the home he shares with her. When he goes on to tell her that commercial dishonesty is generally to be traced to the influence of bad mothers, she begins to perceive that the happy way in which she plays with the children, and the care she takes to dress them nicely, are not sufficient to constitute her a fit person to train them. To redeem the forged bill, she resolves to borrow the balance due upon it from an intimate friend of the family. She has learnt to coax her husband into giving her what she asks by appealing to his affection for her: that is, by playing all sorts of pretty tricks until he is wheedled into an amorous humor. This plan she has adopted without thinking about it, instinctively taking the line of least resistance with him. And now she naturally takes the same line with her husband's friend. An unexpected declaration of love from him is the result; and it at once explains to her the real nature of the domestic influence she has been so proud of.

All her illusions about herself are now shattered. She sees herself as an ignorant and silly woman, a dangerous mother, and a wife kept for her husband's pleasure merely; but she clings all the harder to her illusion about him: he is still the ideal husband who would make any sacrifice to rescue her from ruin. She resolves to kill herself rather than allow him to destroy his own career by taking the forgery on himself to save her reputation. The final disillusion comes when he, instead of at once proposing to pursue this ideal line of conduct when he hears of the forgery, naturally enough flies into a vulgar rage and heaps invective on her for disgracing him. Then she sees that their whole family life has been a fiction: their home a mere doll's house in which they have been playing at ideal husband and father, wife and mother. So she leaves him then and there and goes out into the real world to find out its reality for herself, and to gain some position not fundamentally false, refusing to see her children again until she is fit to be in charge of them, or to live with him until she and he become capable of a more honorable relation to one another. He at first cannot understand what has happened, and flourishes the shattered ideals over her as if they were as potent as ever. He presents the course most agreeable to him – that of her staying at home and avoiding a scandal – as her duty to her husband, to her children, and to her religion; but the magic of these disguises is gone; and at last even he understands what has really happened, and sits down alone to wonder whether that more honorable relation can ever come to pass between them.

GHOSTS, 1881

In his next play, Ibsen returned to the charge with such an uncompromising and outspoken attack on marriage as a useless sacrifice of human beings to an ideal, that his meaning was obscured by its very obviousness. Ghosts, as it is called, is the story of a woman who has faithfully acted as a model wife and mother, sacrificing herself at every point with selfless thoroughness. Her husband is a man with a huge capacity and appetite for sensuous enjoyment. Society, prescribing ideal duties and not enjoyment for him, drives him to enjoy himself in underhand and illicit ways. When he marries his model wife, her devotion to duty only makes life harder for him; and he at last takes refuge in the caresses of an undutiful but pleasure-loving housemaid, and leaves his wife to satisfy her conscience by managing his business affairs while he satisfies his cravings as best he can by reading novels, drinking, and flirting, as aforesaid, with the servants. At this point even those who are most indignant with Nora Helmer for walking out of the doll's house must admit that Mrs Alving would be justified in walking out of *her* house. But Ibsen is determined to shew you what comes of the scrupulous line of conduct you were so angry with Nora for not pursuing. Mrs Alving feels that her place is by her husband for better for worse, and by her child. Now the ideal of wifely and womanly duty which demands this from her also demands that she shall regard herself as an outraged wife, and her husband as a scoundrel. And the family ideal calls upon her to suffer in silence lest she shatter her innocent son's faith in the purity of home life by letting him know the disreputable truth about his father. It is her duty to conceal that truth from the world and from him. In this she falters for one moment only. Her marriage has not been a love match: she has, in pursuance of her duty as a daughter, contracted it for the sake of her family, although her heart inclined to a highly respectable clergyman, a professor of her own idealism, named Manders. In the humiliation of her first discovery of her husband's infidelity, she leaves the house and takes refuge with Manders; but he at once leads her back to the path of duty, from which she does not again swerve. With the utmost devotion she now carries out an elaborate scheme of lying and imposture. She so manages her husband's affairs and so shields his good name that everybody believes him to be a public-spirited citizen of the strictest conformity to current ideals of respectability and family life. She sits up of nights listening to his lewd and silly conversation, and even drinking with him, to keep him from going into the streets and being detected by the neighbors in what she considers his vices. She provides for the servant he has seduced, and brings up his illegitimate daughter as a maid in her own household. And, as a crowning sacrifice, she sends her son away to Paris to be educated there, knowing that if he stays at home the shattering of his ideals must come sooner or later.

Her work is crowned with success. She gains the esteem of her old love the clergyman, who is never tired of holding up her household as a beautiful realization of the Christian ideal of marriage. Her own martyrdom is brought to an end at last by the death of her husband in the odor of a most sanctified reputation, leaving her free to recall her son from Paris and enjoy his society, and his love and gratitude, in the flower of his early manhood.

But when her son comes home, the facts refuse as obstinately as ever to correspond to her ideals. Oswald has inherited his father's love of enjoyment; and when, in dull rainy weather, he returns from Paris to the solemn strictly ordered house where virtue and duty have had their temple for so many years, his mother sees him shew the unmistakable signs of boredom with which she is so miserably familiar from of old; then sit after dinner killing time over the bottle; and finally – the climax of anguish – begin to flirt with the maid who, as his mother alone knows, is his own father's daughter. But there is this worldwide difference in her insight to the cases of the father and the son. She did not love the father: she loves the son with the intensity of a heart-starved woman who has nothing else left to love. Instead of recoiling from him with pious disgust and Pharisaical conscience of moral superiority, she sees at once that he has a right to be happy in his own way, and that she has no right to force him to be dutiful and wretched in hers. She sees, too, her injustice to the unfortunate father, and the cowardice of the monstrous fabric of lies and false appearances she has wasted her life in manufacturing. She resolves that the son's life shall not be sacrificed to ideals which are to him joyless and unnatural. But she finds that the work of the ideals is not to be undone quite so easily. In driving the father to steal his pleasures in secrecy and squalor, they had brought upon him the diseases bred by such conditions; and her son now tells her that those diseases have left their mark on him, and that he carries poison in his pocket against the time, foretold to him by a Parisian surgeon, when general paralysis of the insane may destroy his faculties. In desperation she undertakes to rescue him from this horrible apprehension by making his life happy. The house shall be made as bright as Paris for him: he shall have as much champagne as he wishes until he is no longer driven to that dangerous resource by the dulness of his life with her: if he loves the girl he shall marry her if she were fifty times his half-sister. But the half-sister, on learning the state of his health, leaves the house; for she, too, is her father's daughter, and is not going to sacrifice her life in devotion to an invalid. When the mother and son are left alone in their dreary home, with the rain still falling outside, all she can do for him is to promise that if his doom overtakes him before he can poison himself, she will make a final sacrifice of her natural feelings by performing that dreadful duty, the first of all her duties that has any real basis. Then the weather clears up at last; and the sun, which the young man has so longed to see, appears. He asks her to give it to him to play with; and a glance at him shews her that the ideals have claimed their victim, and that the time has come for her to save him from a real horror by sending him from her out of the world, just as she saved him from an imaginary one years before by sending him out of Norway.

This last scene of Ghosts is so appallingly tragic that the emotions it excites prevent the meaning of the play from being seized and discussed like that of A Doll's House. In England nobody, as far as I know, seems to have perceived that Ghosts is to A Doll's House what the late Sir Walter Besant intended his own sequel[1] to that play to be. Besant attempted to shew what might come of Nora's repudiation of that idealism of which he was one of the most popular professors. But the effect made on Besant by A Doll's House was very faint compared to that produced on the English critics by the first performance of Ghosts in this country. In the earlier part of this essay I have shewn that since Mrs Alving's early conceptions of duty are as valid to ordinary critics as to Pastor Manders, who must appear to them as an admirable man, endowed with Helmer's good sense without Helmer's selfishness, a pretty general disapproval of the moral of the play was inevitable. Fortunately, the newspaper press went to such bedlamite lengths on this occasion that Mr William Archer, the well-known dramatic critic and translator of Ibsen, was able to put the whole body of hostile criticism out of court by simply quoting its excesses in an article entitled 'Ghosts and Gibberings', which appeared in The Pall Mall Gazette of the 8th of April 1891. Mr Archer's extracts, which he offers as a nucleus for a 'Dictionary of Abuse' modelled upon the Wagner *Schimpf-Lexicon*, are worth reprinting here as samples of contemporary idealist criticism of the drama.

DESCRIPTIONS OF THE PLAY

'Ibsen's positively abominable play entitled *Ghosts* ... This disgusting representation ... Reprobation due to such as aim at infecting the modern theatre with poison after desperately inoculating themselves and others ... An open drain; a loathsome sore unbandaged; a dirty act done publicly; a lazar-house with all its doors and windows open ... Candid foulness ... Kotzebue turned bestial and cynical. Offensive cynicism ... Ibsen's melancholy and malodorous world ... Absolutely loathsome and fetid ... Gross, almost putrid indecorum ... Literary carrion ... Crapulous stuff ... Novel and perilous nuisance' (*Daily Telegraph* leading article). 'This mass of vulgarity, egotism, coarseness, and absurdity' (*Daily Telegraph* criticism). 'Unutterably offensive ... Prosecution under Lord Campbell's Act ... Abominable piece ... Scandalous' (*Standard*). 'Naked loathsomeness ... Most dismal and repulsive production' (*Daily News*). 'Revoltingly suggestive and blasphemous ... Characters either contradictory in themselves, uninteresting or abhorrent' (*Daily Chronicle*). 'A repulsive and degrading work' (*Queen*). 'Morbid, unhealthy, unwholesome and disgusting story ... A piece to bring the stage into disrepute and dishonour with every right-thinking man and woman' (*Lloyd's*). 'Merely dull dirt long drawn out.' (*Hawk*). 'Morbid horrors of the hideous tale ... Ponderous dullness of the didactic talk ... If any repetition of this outrage be attempted, the authorities will doubtless wake from their lethargy' (*Sporting and Dramatic News*). 'Just a wicked nightmare' (*The Gentlewoman*). 'Lugubrious diagnosis of sordid impropriety ... Characters are prigs, pedants and profligates ... Morbid caricatures ... Maunderings of nookshotten Norwegians ... It is no more of a play than an average Gaiety burlesque' (*Black and White*). 'Most loathsome of all Ibsen's plays ... Garbage and offal' (*Truth*). 'Ibsen's putrid play called *Ghosts* ... So loathsome an enterprise' (*Academy*). 'As foul and filthy a concoction as has ever been allowed to disgrace the boards of an English theatre . . . Dull and disgusting . . . Nastiness and malodorousness laid on thickly as with a trowel' (*Era*). 'Noisome corruption' (*Stage*).

DESCRIPTIONS OF IBSEN

'An egotist and a bungler' (*Daily Telegraph*). 'A crazy fanatic . . . A crazy, cranky being . . . Not only consistently dirty but deplorably dull' (*Truth*). 'The Norwegian pessimist *in petto*' [*sic*] (*Black and White*). 'Ugly, nasty, discordant, and downright dull . . . A gloomy sort of ghoul, bent on groping for horrors by night, and blinking like a stupid old owl when the warm sunlight of the best of life dances into his wrinkled eyes' (*Gentlewoman*). 'A teacher of the aestheticism of the Lock Hospital' (*Saturday Review*).

DESCRIPTIONS OF IBSEN'S ADMIRERS

'Lovers of prurience and dabblers in impropriety who are eager to gratify their illicit tastes under the pretence of art' (*Evening Standard*). 'Ninety-seven per cent of the people who go to see *Ghosts* are nasty-minded people who find the discussion of nasty subjects to their taste in exact proportion to their nastiness' (*Sporting and Dramatic News*). 'The sexless . . . The unwomanly woman, the unsexed females, the whole army of unprepossessing cranks in petticoats . . . Educated and muck-ferreting dogs . . . Effeminate men and male women . . . They all of them – men and women alike – know that they are doing not only a nasty but an illegal thing . . . The Lord Chamberlain left them alone to wallow in *Ghosts* . . . Outside a silly clique, there is not the slightest interest in the Scandinavian humbug or all his works . . . A wave of human folly' (*Truth*).[2]

AN ENEMY OF THE PEOPLE, 1882

After this, the reader will understand the temper in which Ibsen set about his next play, An Enemy of the People, in which, having done sufficient execution among the ordinary middle-class domestic and social ideals, he puts his finger for a moment on commercial political ideals. The play deals with a local majority of middle-class people who are pecuniarily interested in concealing the fact that the famous baths which attract visitors to their town and customers to their shops and hotels are contaminated by sewage. When an honest doctor insists on exposing this danger, the townspeople immediately disguise themselves ideally. Feeling the disadvantage of appearing in their true character as a conspiracy of interested rogues against an honest man, they pose as Society, as The People, as Democracy, as the solid Liberal Majority, and other imposing abstractions, the doctor, in attacking them, of course being thereby made an enemy of The People, a danger to Society, a traitor to Democracy, an apostate from the great Liberal party, and so on. Only those who take an active part in politics can appreciate the grim fun of the situation, which, though it has an intensely local Norwegian air, will be at once recognized as typical in England, not, perhaps, by the professional literary critics, who are for the most part *fainéants* as far as political life is concerned, but certainly by everyone who has got as far as a seat on the committee of the most obscure Ratepayers' Association.

As An Enemy of the People contains one or two references to Democracy which are anything but respectful, it is necessary to examine Ibsen's criticism of it with precision. Democracy is really only an arrangement by which the governed are allowed to choose (as far as any choice is possible, which in capitalistic society is not saying much) the members of the representative bodies which control the executive. It has never been proved that this is the best arrangement; and it has been made effective only to the very limited extent short of which the dissatisfaction which it appeases might take the form of actual violence. Now

95

when men had to submit to kings, they consoled themselves by making it an article of faith that the king was always right, idealizing him as a Pope, in fact. In the same way we who have to submit to majorities set up Voltaire's pope, *Monsieur Tout-le-monde*, and make it blasphemy against Democracy to deny that the majority is always right, although that, as Ibsen says, is a lie. It is a scientific fact that the majority, however eager it may be for the reform of old abuses, is always wrong in its opinion of new developments, or rather is always unfit for them (for it can hardly be said to be wrong in opposing developments for which it is not yet fit). The pioneer is a tiny minority of the force he heads; and so, though it is easy to be in a minority and yet be wrong, it is absolutely impossible to be in the majority and yet be right as to the newest social prospects. We should never progress at all if it were possible for each of us to stand still on democratic principles until we saw whither all the rest were moving, as our statesmen declare themselves bound to do when they are called upon to lead. Whatever clatter we may make for a time with our filing through feudal serf collars and kicking off old mercantilist fetters, we shall never march a step forward except at the heels of 'the strongest man, he who is able to stand alone' and to turn his back on 'the damned compact Liberal majority'. All of which is no disparagement of parliaments and adult suffrage, but simply a wholesome reduction of them to their real place in the social economy as pure machinery; machinery which has absolutely no principles except the principles of mechanics, and no motive power in itself whatsoever. The idealization of public organizations is as dangerous as that of kings or priests. We need to be reminded that though there is in the world a vast number of buildings in which a certain ritual is conducted before crowds called congregations by a functionary called a priest, who is subject to a central council controlling all such functionaries on a few points, there is not therefore any such thing in the concrete as the ideal Catholic Church, nor ever was, nor ever will be. There may, too, be a highly elaborate organization of public affairs;

but there is no such thing as the ideal State. There may be a combination of persons living by the practice of medicine, surgery, or physical or biological research; or by drawing up wills and leases, and preparing, pleading, or judging cases at law; or by painting pictures, writing books, and acting plays; or by serving in regiments and battle ships; or by manual labor or industrial service. But when any of these combinations, through its organizers or leaders, claims to deliver the Verdict of Science, or to act with the Authority of the Law, or to be as sacred as the Mission of Art, or to revenge criticism of themselves as outrages on the Honor of His Majesty's Services, or to utter the Voice of Labor, there is urgent need for the guillotine, or whatever may be the mode in vogue of putting presumptuous persons in their proper place. All abstractions invested with collective consciousness or collective authority, set above the individual, and exacting duty from him on pretence of acting or thinking with greater validity than he, are man-eating idols red with human sacrifices.

This position must not be confounded with Anarchism, or the idealization of the repudiation of Governments. Ibsen did not refuse to pay the tax collector, but may be supposed to have regarded him, not as the vicar of an abstraction called THE STATE, but simply as the man sent round by a committee of citizens (mostly fools as far as Maximus the Mystic's Third Empire is concerned) to collect the money for the police or the paving and lighting of the streets.

THE WILD DUCK, 1884

After An Enemy of the People, Ibsen, as I have said, left the vulgar ideals for dead, and set about the exposure of those of the choicer spirits, beginning with the incorrigible idealists who had idealized his very self, and were becoming known as Ibsenites. His first move in this direction was such a tragicomic slaughtering of sham Ibsenism that his astonished victims plaintively declared that The Wild Duck, as the new play was called, was a satire on his former works; whilst the pious, whom he had disappointed so severely by his interpretation of Brand, began to hope that he was coming back repentant to the fold. The household to which we are introduced in The Wild Duck is not, like Mrs Alving's, a handsome one made miserable by superstitious illusions, but a shabby one made happy by romantic illusions. The only member of it who sees it as it really is is the wife, a good-natured Philistine who desires nothing better. The husband, a vain, petted, spoilt dawdler, believes that he is a delicate and high-souled man, devoting his life to redeeming his old father's name from the disgrace brought on it by imprisonment for breach of the forest laws. This redemption he proposes to effect by making himself famous as a great inventor some day when he has the necessary inspiration. Their daughter, a girl in her teens, believes intensely in her father and in the promised invention. The disgraced grandfather cheers himself by drink whenever he can get it; but his chief resource is a wonderful garret full of rabbits and pigeons. The old man has procured a number of second-hand Christmas trees; and with these he has turned the garret into a sort of toy forest, in which he can play at bear hunting, which was one of the sports of his youth and prosperity. The weapons employed in the hunting expeditions are a gun which will not go off, and a pistol which occasionally brings down a rabbit or a pigeon. A crowning touch is given to the illusion by a wild duck, which, however, must not be shot, as it is the special property of the girl, who reads and dreams whilst her mother cooks, washes, sweeps, and carries on the photographic work which is supposed to be the business of her husband. Mrs Ekdal does not appreciate Hjalmar's highly strung sensitiveness of character, which is constantly suffering agonizing jars from her vulgarity; but then she does not appreciate that other fact that he is a lazy and idle impostor. Downstairs there is a disgraceful clergyman named Molvik, a hopeless drunkard; but even he respects himself and is tolerated because of a special illusion invented for him by another lodger, Dr Relling, upon whom the lesson of the household above has not been thrown away. Molvik, says the doctor, must break out into drinking fits because he is daimonic, an imposing explanation which completely relieves the reverend gentleman from the imputation of vulgar tippling.

Into this domestic circle there comes a new lodger, an idealist of the most advanced type. He greedily swallows the daimonic theory of the clergyman's drunkenness, and enthusiastically accepts the photographer as the high-souled hero he supposes himself to be; but he is troubled because the relations of the man and his wife do not constitute an ideal marriage. He happens to know that the woman, before her marriage, was the cast-off mistress of his own father; and because she has not told her husband this, he conceives her life as founded on a lie, like that of Bernick in Pillars of Society. He accordingly sets himself to work out the woman's salvation for her, and establish ideally frank relations between the pair, by simply blurting out the truth, and then asking them, with fatuous self-satisfaction, whether they do not feel much the better for it. This wanton piece of mischief has more serious results than a mere domestic scene. The husband is too weak to act on his bluster about outraged honor and the impossibility of his ever living with his wife again; and the woman is merely annoyed with the idealist for telling on her; but the girl takes the matter to heart and shoots herself. The doubt cast on her parentage, with her father's theatrical repudiation of her, destroy her ideal place in the home, and make her a source of discord there; so she sacrifices herself, thereby carrying out the teaching of the idealist mischief-maker, who has talked a good deal to her about the duty and beauty of self-sacrifice, without foreseeing that he might be taken in mortal earnest. The busybody thus finds that people cannot be freed from their failings from without. They must free themselves. When Nora is strong enough to live out of the doll's house, she will go out of it of her own accord if the door stands open; but if before that period you take her by the scruff of the neck and thrust her out, she will only take refuge in the next establishment of the kind that offers to receive her. Woman has thus two enemies to deal with; the old-fashioned one who wants to keep the door locked, and the new-fashioned one who wants to thrust her into the street before she is ready to go. In the cognate case of a hypocrite and liar like Bernick, exposing him is a mere police measure; he is none the less a liar and hypocrite when you have exposed him. If you want to make a sincere and truthful man of him, all you can wisely do is to remove what you can of the external obstacles to his exposing himself, and then wait for the operation of his internal impulse to confess. If he has no such impulse, then you must put up with him as he is. It is useless to make claims on him which he is not yet prepared to meet. Whether, like Brand, we make such claims because to refrain would be to compromise with evil, or, like Gregers Werle, because we think their moral beauty must recommend them at sight to every one, we shall alike incur Relling's impatient assurance that 'life would be quite tolerable if we could only get rid of the confounded duns that keep on pestering us in our poverty with the claims of the ideal.'

ROSMERSHOLM, 1886

Ibsen did not in The Wild Duck exhaust the subject of the danger of forming ideals for other people, and interfering in their lives with a view to enabling them to realize those ideals. Cases far more typical than that of the meddlesome lodger are those of the priest who regards the ennobling of mankind as a sort of trade process of which his cloth gives him a monopoly, and the clever woman who pictures a noble career for the man she loves, and devotes herself to helping him to achieve it. In Rosmersholm, the play with which Ibsen followed up The Wild Duck, there is an unpractical country parson, a gentleman of ancient stock, whose family has been for many years a centre of social influence. The tradition of that influence reinforces his priestly tendency to regard the ennoblement of the world as an external operation to be performed by himself; and the need of such ennoblement is very evident to him; for his nature is a fine one: he looks at the world with some dim prevision of 'the third empire'. He is married to a woman of passionately affectionate nature, who is very fond of him, but does not regard him as a regenerator of the human race. Indeed she does not share any of his dreams, and only acts as an extinguisher on the sacred fire of his idealism. He, she, her brother Kroll the headmaster, Kroll's wife, and their set, form a select circle of the best people in the place, comfortably orbited in our social system, and quite planetary in ascertained position and unimpeachable respectability. Into the orbit comes presently a wandering star, one Rebecca Gamvik, an unpropertied orphan, who has been allowed to read advanced books, and is a Freethinker and a Radical: things that disqualify a poor woman for admission to the Rosmer world. However, one must live somewhere; and as the Rosmer world is the only one in which an ambitious and cultivated woman can find powerful allies and educated companions, Rebecca, being both ambitious and cultivated, makes herself agreeable to the Rosmer circle with such success that the affectionate and impulsive but unintelligent Mrs Rosmer becomes wildly fond of her, and is not content until she has persuaded her to come and live with them. Rebecca, then a mere adventuress fighting for a foothold in polite society (which has hitherto shewn itself highly indignant at her thrusting herself in where nobody has thought of providing room for her), accepts the offer all the more readily because she has taken the measure of Parson Rosmer, and formed the idea of playing upon his aspirations, and making herself a leader in politics and society by using him as a figurehead.

But now two difficulties arise. First, there is Mrs Rosmer's extinguishing effect on her husband; an effect which convinces Rebecca that nothing can be done with him whilst his wife is in the way. Second – a contingency quite unallowed for in her provident calculations – she finds herself passionately enamored of him. The poor parson, too, falls in love with her; but he does not know it. He turns to the woman who understands him like a sunflower to the sun, and makes her his real friend and companion. The wife feels this soon enough; and he, quite unconscious of it, begins to think that her mind must be affected, since she has become so intensely miserable and hysterical about nothing – nothing that he can see. The truth is that she has come under the curse of Rebecca's ideal; she sees herself standing, a useless obstacle, between her husband and the woman he really loves, the woman who can help him to a glorious career. She cannot even be the mother in the household; for she is childless. Then comes Rebecca, fortified with a finely reasoned theory that Rosmer's future is staked against his wife's life, and says that it is better for all their sakes that she should quit Rosmersholm. She even hints that she must go at once if a grave scandal is to be avoided. Mrs Rosmer, regarding a scandal in Rosmersholm as the most terrible thing that can happen, and seeing that it could be averted by the marriage of Rebecca and Rosmer if she were out of the way, writes a letter secretly to Rosmer's bitterest enemy, the editor of the local Radical paper, a man who has forfeited his moral reputation by an intrigue which Rosmer has pitilessly denounced. In this letter she implores him not to believe or publish any stories that he may hear about Rosmer, to the effect that he is in any way to blame for anything that may happen to her. Then she sets Rosmer free to marry Rebecca, and to realize his ideals, by going out into the garden, and throwing herself into the mill-stream that runs there.

Now follows a period of quiet mourning at Rosmersholm. Everybody except Rosmer suspects that Mrs Rosmer was not mad, and guesses why she committed suicide. Only it would not do to compromise the aristocratic party by treating Rosmer as the Radical editor was treated. So the neighbors shut their eyes and condole with the bereaved clergyman; and the Radical editor holds his tongue because Radicalism is growing respectable, and he hopes, with Rebecca's help, to get Rosmer over to his side presently. Meanwhile the unexpected has again happened to Rebecca. Her passion is worn out; but in the long days

of mourning she has found the higher love; and it is now for
Rosmer's own sake that she urges him to become a man of
action, and brood no more over the dead. When his friends
start a Conservative paper and ask him to become editor, she
induces him to reply by declaring himself a Radical and Freethinker. To his utter amazement, the result is, not an animated
discussion of his views, but just such an attack on his home life
and private conduct as he had formerly made on those of the
Radical editor. His friends tell him plainly that the compact of
silence is broken by his defection, and that there will be no
mercy for the traitor to the party. Even the Radical editor not
only refuses to publish the fact that his new ally is a Freethinker
(which would destroy all his social weight as a Radical recruit),
but brings up the dead woman's letter as a proof that the attack
is sufficiently well-founded to make it unwise to go too far.
Rosmer, who at first had been simply shocked that men whom
he had always honored as gentlemen should descend to such
hideous calumny, now sees that he really did love Rebecca, and
is indeed guilty of his wife's death. His first impulse is to shake
off the spectre of the dead woman by marrying Rebecca; but
she, knowing that the guilt is hers, puts that temptation behind
her and refuses. Then, as he thinks it all over, his dream of
ennobling the world slips away from him: such work can only
be done by a man conscious of his own innocence. To save him
from despair, Rebecca makes a great sacrifice. She 'gives him
back his innocence' by confessing how she drove his wife to
kill herself; and, as the confession is made in the presence of
Kroll, she ascribes the whole plot to her ambition, and says not
a word of her passion. Rosmer, confounded as he realizes what
helpless puppets they have all been in the hands of this clever
woman, for the moment misses the point that unscrupulous
ambition, though it explains her crime, does not account for
her confession. He turns his back on her and leaves the house
with Kroll. She quietly packs up her trunk, and is about to
vanish from Rosmersholm without another word when he
comes back alone to ask why she confessed. She tells him why,

offering him her self-sacrifice as a proof that his power of ennobling others was no vain dream, since it is his companionship that has changed her from the selfish adventuress she was to the devoted woman she has just proved herself to be. But he has lost faith in himself, and cannot believe her. The proof seems to him subtle, artful: he cannot forget that she duped him by flattering this very weakness of his before. Besides, he knows now that it is not true: people are not ennobled from without. She has no more to say; for she can think of no further proof. But he has thought of an unanswerable one. Dare she make all doubt impossible by sacrificing her share in his future in the only absolutely final way: that is, by doing for his sake what his wife did? She asks what would happen if she had the heart and the will to do it. 'Then,' he replies, 'I should have to believe in you. I should recover my faith in my mission. Faith in my power to ennoble human souls. Faith in the human soul's power to attain nobility.' 'You shall have your faith again,' she answers. At this pass the inner truth of the situation comes out; and the thin veil of a demand for proof, with its monstrous sequel of asking the woman to kill herself in order to restore the man's good opinion of himself, falls away. What is really driving Rosmer is the superstition of expiation by sacrifice. He sees that when Rebecca goes into the millstream he must go too. And he speaks his real mind in the words, 'There is no judge over us: therefore we must do justice upon ourselves.' But the woman's soul is free of this to the end; for when she says, 'I am under the power of the Rosmersholm view of life *now*. What I have sinned it is fit I should expiate,' we feel in that speech a protest against the Rosmersholm view of life: the view that denied her right to live and be happy from the first, and now at the end, even in denying its God, exacts her life as a vain blood-offering for its own blindness. The woman has the higher light: she goes to her death out of fellowship with the man who is driven thither by the superstition which has destroyed his will. The story ends with his taking her solemnly as his wife, and casting himself with her into the millstream.

It is unnecessary to repeat here what is said on page 47 as to the vital part played in this drama by the evolution of the lower into the higher love. Peer Gynt, during the prophetic episode in his career, shocks the dancing girl Anitra into a remonstrance by comparing himself to a cat. He replies, with his wisest air, that from the standpoint of love there is perhaps not so much difference between a tomcat and a prophet as she may imagine. The number of critics who have entirely missed the point of Rebecca's transfiguration seems to indicate that the majority of men, even among critics of dramatic poetry, have not got beyond Peer Gynt's opinion in this matter. No doubt they would not endorse it as a definitely stated proposition, aware, as they are, that there is a poetic convention to the contrary. But if they fail to recognize the only possible alternative proposition when it is not only stated in so many words by Rebecca West, but when without it her conduct dramatically contradicts her character – when they even complain of the contradiction as a blemish on the play, I am afraid there can be no further doubt that the extreme perplexity into which the first performance of Rosmersholm in England plunged the Press was due entirely to the prevalence of Peer Gynt's view of love among the dramatic critics.

THE LADY FROM THE SEA, 1888

Ibsen's next play, though it deals with the old theme, does not insist on the power of ideals to kill, as the two previous plays do. It rather deals with the origin of ideals in unhappiness, in dissatisfaction with the real. The subject of The Lady from the Sea is the most poetic fancy imaginable. A young woman, brought up on the sea-coast, marries a respectable doctor, a widower, who idolizes her and places her in his household with nothing to do but dream and be made much of by everybody. Even the housekeeping is done by her stepdaughter: she has no responsibility, no care, and no trouble. In other words, she is an idle, helpless, utterly dependent article of luxury. A man turns red at the thought of being such a thing; but he thoughtlessly accepts a pretty and fragile-looking woman in the same position as a charming natural picture. The lady from the sea feels an indefinite want in her life. She reads her want into all other lives, and comes to the conclusion that man once had to choose whether he would be a land animal or a creature of the sea; and that having chosen the land, he has carried about with him ever since a secret sorrow for the element he has forsaken. The dissatisfaction that gnaws her is, as she interprets it, this desperate longing for the sea. When her only child dies and leaves her without the work of a mother to give her a valid place in the world, she yields wholly to her longing, and no longer cares for her husband, who, like Rosmer, begins to fear that she is going mad.

At last a seaman appears and claims her as his wife on the ground that they went years before through a rite which consisted of their marrying the sea by throwing their rings into it. This man, who had to fly from her in the old time because he killed his captain, and who fills her with a sense of dread and mystery, seems to her to embody the mystic attraction the sea has for her. She tells her husband that she must go away with the seaman. Naturally the doctor expostulates – declares that he cannot for her own sake let her do so mad a thing. She replies that he can only prevent her by locking her up, and asks him what satisfaction it will be to him to have her body under lock and key whilst her heart is with the other man. In vain he urges that he will only keep her under restraint until the seaman goes – that he must not, dare not, allow her to ruin herself. Her argument remains unanswerable. The seaman openly declares that she will come; so that the distracted husband asks him does he suppose he can force her from her home. To this the seaman replies that, on the contrary, unless she comes of her own free will there is no satisfaction to him in her coming at all: the unanswerable argument again. She echoes it by demanding her freedom to choose. Her husband must cry off his law-made and Church-made bargain; renounce his claim to the fulfilment of her vows; and leave her free to go back to the sea with her old lover. Then the doctor, with a heavy heart, drops his prate about his heavy responsibility for her actions, and throws the responsibility on her by crying off as she demands. The moment she feels herself a free and responsible woman, all her childish fancies vanish: the seaman becomes simply an old acquaintance whom she no longer cares for; and the doctor's affection produces its natural effect. In short, she says 'No' to the seaman, and takes over the housekeeping keys from her stepdaughter without any further maunderings over that secret sorrow for the abandoned sea.

It should be noted here that Ellida [call her Eleeda], the Lady from the Sea, seems more fantastic to English readers than to Norwegian ones. The same thing is true of many other characters drawn by Ibsen, notably Peer Gynt, who, if born in England, would certainly not have been a poet and metaphysician as well as a blackguard and a speculator. The extreme type of Norwegian, as depicted by Ibsen, imagines himself doing wonderful things, but does nothing. He dreams as no Englishman dreams, and drinks to make himself dream the more, until his effective will is destroyed, and he becomes a broken-down, disreputable sot, carrying about the tradition that he is a hero, and discussing himself on that assumption. Although the number of persons who dawdle their life away over fiction in England must be frightful, and is probably increasing, yet their talk is not the talk of Ulric Brendel, Rosmer, Ellida, or Peer Gynt; and it is for this reason that Rosmersholm and the Lady from the Sea strike English audiences as more fantastic and less literal than A Doll's House and the plays in which the leading figures are men and women of action, though to a Norwegian there is probably no difference in this respect.

HEDDA GABLER, 1890

Hedda Gabler has no ethical ideals at all, only romantic ones. She is a typical nineteenth-century figure, falling into the abyss between the ideals which do not impose on her and the realities she has not yet discovered. The result is that though she has imagination, and an intense appetite for beauty, she has no conscience, no conviction: with plenty of cleverness, energy, and personal fascination she remains mean, envious, insolent, cruel in protest against others' happiness, fiendish in her dislike of inartistic people and things, a bully in reaction from her own cowardice. Hedda's father, a general, is a widower. She has the traditions of the military caste about her; and these narrow her activities to the customary hunt for a socially and pecuniarily eligible husband. She makes the acquaintance of a young man of genius who, prohibited by an idea-ridden society from taking his pleasures except where there is nothing to restrain him from excess, is going to the bad in search of his good, with the usual consequences. Hedda is intensely curious about the side of life which is forbidden to her, and in which powerful instincts, absolutely ignored and condemned in her circle, steal their satisfaction. An odd intimacy springs up between the inquisitive girl and the rake. Whilst the general reads the paper in the afternoon, Lövborg and Hedda have long conversations in which he describes to her all his disreputable adventures. Although she is the questioner, she never dares to trust him: all the questions are indirect; and the responsibility for his interpretations rests on him alone. Hedda has no conviction whatever that these conversations are disgraceful; but she will not risk a fight with society on the point; it is easier to practise hypocrisy, the homage that truth pays to falsehood, than to endure ostracism. When he proceeds to make advances to her, Hedda has again no conviction that it would be wrong for her to gratify his instinct and her own; so that she is confronted with the alternative of sinning against herself and him, or sinning against social ideals in which she has no faith.

Making the coward's choice, she carries it out with the utmost bravado, threatening Lövborg with one of her father's pistols, and driving him out of the house with all that ostentation of outraged purity which is the instinctive defence of women to whom chastity is not natural, much as libel actions are mostly brought by persons concerning whom libels are virtually, if not technically, justifiable.

Hedda, deprived of her lover, now finds that a life of conformity without faith involves something more terrible than the utmost ostracism: to wit, boredom. This scourge, unknown among revolutionists, is the curse which makes the security of respectability as dust in the balance against the unflagging interest of rebellion, and which forces society to eke out its harmless resources for killing time by licensing gambling, gluttony, hunting, shooting, coursing and other vicious distractions for which even idealism has no disguise. These licenses, being expensive, are available only for people who have more than enough money to keep up appearances; and as Hedda's father, being in the army instead of in commerce, is too poor to leave her much more than the pistols, her boredom is only mitigated by dancing, at which she gains much admiration, but no substantial offers of marriage.

At last she has to find somebody to support her. A good-natured mediocrity of a professor is the best that is to be had; and though she regards him as a member of an inferior class, and despises almost to loathing his family circle of two affectionate old aunts and the inevitable general servant who has helped to bring him up, she marries him *faute de mieux*, and immediately proceeds to wreck this prudent provision for her livelihood by accommodating his income to her expenditure instead of accommodating her expenditure to his income. Her nature so rebels against the whole sordid transaction that the prospect of bearing a child to her husband drives her almost frantic, since it will not only expose her to the intimate solicitude of his aunts in the course of a derangement of her health in which she can see nothing that is not repulsive and humiliating, but will make her one of his family in earnest.

To amuse herself in these galling circumstances, she forms an underhand alliance with a visitor who belongs to her old set, an elderly gallant who quite understands how little she cares for her husband, and proposes a *ménage à trois* to her. She consents to his coming there and talking to her as he pleases behind her husband's back; but she keeps her pistols in reserve in case he becomes seriously importunate. He, on the other hand, tries to get some hold over her by placing her husband under pecuniary obligations, as far as he can do it without being out of pocket.

Meanwhile Lövborg is drifting to disgrace by the nearest way: drink. In due time he descends from lecturing at the university on the history of civilization to taking a job in an out-of-the-way place as tutor to the little children of Sheriff Elvsted. This functionary, on being left a widower with a number of children, marries their governess, finding that she will cost him less and be bound to do more for him as his wife. As for her, she is too poor to dream of refusing such a settlement in life. When Lövborg comes, his society is heaven to her. He does not dare tell her about his dissipations; but he tells her about his unwritten books, which he never discussed with Hedda. She does not dare to remonstrate with him for drinking; but he gives it up as soon as he sees that it shocks her. Just as Mr Fearing, in Bunyan's story, was in a way the bravest of the pilgrims, so this timid and unfortunate Mrs Elvsted trembles her way to a point at which Lövborg, quite reformed, publishes one book which makes him celebrated for the moment, and completes another, fair-copied in her handwriting, to which he looks for a solid position as an original thinker. But he cannot now stay tutoring Elvsted's children; so off he goes to town with his pockets full of the money the published book has brought him. Left once more in her old lonely plight, knowing that without her Lövborg will probably relapse into dissipation, and that without him her life will not be worth living, Mrs

Elvsted must either sin against herself and him or against the institution of marriage under which Elvsted purchased his housekeeper. It never occurs to her that she has any choice. She knows that her action will count as 'a dreadful thing'; but she sees that she must go; and accordingly Elvsted finds himself without a wife and his children without a governess, and so disappears unpitied from the story.

Now it happens that Hedda's husband, Jörgen Tesman, is an old friend and competitor (for academic honors) of Lövborg, and also that Hedda was a schoolfellow of Mrs Elvsted, or Thea, as she had better now be called. Thea's first business is to find out where Lövborg is; for hers is no preconcerted elopement: she has hurried to town to keep Lövborg away from the bottle, a design she dare not hint at to himself. Accordingly, the first thing she does in town is to call on the Tesmans, who have just returned from their honeymoon, to beg them to invite Lövborg to their house so as to keep him in good company. They consent, with the result that the two pairs are brought together under the same roof, and the tragedy begins to work itself out.

Hedda's attitude now demands a careful analysis. Lövborg's experience with Thea has enlightened his judgment of Hedda; and as he is, in his gifted way, an arrant *poseur* and male coquet, he immediately tries to get on romantic terms with her (for have they not 'a past'?) by impressing her with the penetrating criticism that she is and always was a coward. She admits that the virtuous heroics with the pistol were pure cowardice; but she is still so void of any other standard of conduct than conformity to the conventional ideals, that she thinks her cowardice consisted in not daring to be wicked. That is, she thinks that what she actually did was the right thing; and since she despises herself for doing it, and feels that he also rightly despises her for doing it, she gets a passionate feeling that what is wanted is the courage to do wrong. This unlooked-for reaction of idealism, this monstrous but very common setting-up of wrong-doing as an ideal, and of the wrongdoer as hero or heroine *qua* wrongdoer, leads Hedda to conceive that when

111

Lövborg tried to seduce her he was a hero, and that in allowing Thea to reform him he has played the recreant. In acting on this misconception she is restrained by no consideration for any of the rest. Like all people whose lives are valueless, she has no more sense of the value of Lövborg's or Tesman's or Thea's lives than a railway shareholder has of the value of a shunter's. She gratifies her intense jealousy of Thea by deliberately taunting Lövborg into breaking loose from her influence by joining a carouse at which he not only loses his manuscript, but finally gets into the hands of the police through behaving outrageously in the house of a disreputable woman whom he accuses of stealing it, not knowing that it has been picked up by Tesman and handed to Hedda for safe keeping. Now Hedda's jealousy of Thea is not jealousy of her bodily fascination: at that Hedda can beat her. It is jealousy of her power of making a man of Lövborg, of her part in his life as a man of genius. The manuscript which Tesman gives to Hedda to lock up safely is in Thea's handwriting. It is the fruit of Lövborg's union with Thea: he himself speaks of it as 'their child'. So when he turns his despair to romantic account by coming to the two women and making a tragic scene, telling Thea that he has cast the manuscript, torn into a thousand pieces, out upon the fiord; and then, when she is gone, telling Hedda that he has brought 'the child' to a house of ill-fame and lost it there, she, deceived by his posing, and thirsting to gain faith in the beauty of her own influence over him from a heroic deed of some sort, makes him a present of one of her pistols, only begging him to 'do it beautifully', by which she means that he is to kill himself in some manner that will make his suicide a romantic memory and an imaginative luxury to her for ever. He takes it unblushingly, and leaves her with the air of a man who is looking his last on earth. But the moment he is out of sight of his audience, he goes back to the house where he still supposes the manuscript to lie stolen, and there renews the wrangle of the night before, using the pistol to threaten the woman, with the result that he gets shot in the abdomen, leaving the weapon to fall into the hands of the police. Meanwhile Hedda deliberately burns 'the child'. Then comes her elderly gallant to disgust her with the unromantically ugly details of the deed which Lövborg promised her to do so beautifully, and to make her understand that he himself has now got her into his power by his ability to identify the pistol. She must either be the slave of this man, or else face the scandal of the connection of her name at the inquest with a squalid debauch ending in a murder. Thea, too, is not crushed by Lövborg's death. Ten minutes after she has received the news with a cry of heartfelt loss, she sits down with Tesman to reconstruct 'the child' from the old notes she had piously preserved. Over the congenial task of collecting and arranging another man's ideas Tesman is perfectly happy, and forgets his beautiful Hedda for the first time. Thea the trembler is still mistress of the situation, holding the dead Lövborg, gaining Tesman, and leaving Hedda to her elderly admirer, who smoothly remarks that he will answer for Mrs Tesman not being bored whilst her husband is occupied with Thea in putting the pieces of the book together. However, he has again reckoned without General Gabler's second pistol. She shoots herself then and there; and so the story ends.

THE LAST FOUR PLAYS

DOWN AMONG THE DEAD MEN

IBSEN now lays down the completed task of warning the world against its idols and anti-idols, and passes into the shadow of death, or rather into the splendor of his sunset glory; for his magic is extraordinarily potent in these four plays, and his purpose more powerful. And yet the shadow of death is here; for all four, except Little Eyolf, are tragedies of the dead, deserted and mocked by the young who are still full of life. The Master Builder is a dead man before the curtain rises: the breaking of his body to pieces in the last act by its fall from the tower is rather the impatient destruction of a ghost of whose delirious whisperings Nature is tired than of one who still counts among the living. Borkman and the two women, his wife and her sister, are not merely dead: they are buried; and the creatures we hear and see are only their spirits in torment. 'Never dream of life again,' says Mrs Borkman to her husband, 'lie quiet where you are.' And the last play of all is frankly called When We Dead Awaken. Here the quintessence of Ibsenism reaches its final distillation; morality and reformation give place to mortality and resurrection; and the next event is the death of Ibsen himself: he, too, creeping ghost-like through the blackening mental darkness until he reaches his actual grave, and can no longer make Europe cry with pity by sitting at a copybook, like a child, trying to learn again how to write, only to find that divine power gone for ever from his dead hand. He, the crustiest, grimmest hero since Beethoven, could not die like him, shaking his fist at the thunder and alive to the last: he must follow the path he had traced for Solness and Borkman, and survive himself. But as these two were dreamers to the last, and never so luminous in their dreams as when they could no longer put the least of them into action; so we may believe

114

that when Ibsen could no longer remember the alphabet, or use a dictionary, his soul may have been fuller than ever before of the unspeakable. Do not snivel, reader, over the contrast he himself drew between the man who was once the greatest writer in the world, and the child of seventy-six trying to begin again at pothooks and hangers. Depend on it, whilst there was anything left of him at all there was enough of his iron humor to grin as widely as the skeleton with the hour-glass who was touching him on the shoulder.

THE MASTER BUILDER, 1892

Halvard Solness is a dead man who has been a brilliantly successful builder, and, like the greatest builders, his own architect. He is sometimes in the sublime delirium that precedes bodily death, and sometimes in the horror that varies the splendors of delirium. He is mortally afraid of young rivals; of the younger generation knocking at the door. He has built churches with high towers (much as Ibsen built great historical dramas in verse). He has come to the end of that and built 'homes for human beings' (much as Ibsen took to writing prose plays of modern life). He has come to the end of that too, as men do at the end of their lives; and now he must take to dead men's architecture, the building of castles in the air. Castles in the air are the residences not only of those who have finished their lives, but of those who have not yet begun them. Another peculiarity of castles in the air is that they are so beautiful and so wonderful that human beings are not good enough to live in them: therefore when you look round you for somebody to live with you in your castle in the air, you find nobody glorious enough for that sanctuary. So you resort to the most dangerous of all the varieties of idolization: the idolization of the person you are most in love with; and you take him or her to live with you in your castle. And as imaginative young people, because they are young, have no illusions about youth, whilst old people, because they are old, have no illusions about age, elderly gentlemen very often idolize adolescent girls, and adolescent girls idolize elderly gentlemen. When the idolization is not reciprocal, the idolizer runs terrible risks if the idol is selfish and unscrupulous. Cases of girls enslaved by elderly gentlemen whose scrupulous respect for their maiden purity is nothing but an excuse for getting a quantity of secretarial or domestic service out of them that is limited only by their physical endurance, without giving them anything in return, are not at all so rare as they would be if the theft of a woman's youth and devotion were as severely condemned by public opinion as the comparatively amiable and negligible theft of a few silver spoons and forks. On the other hand doting old gentlemen are duped and ruined by designing young women who care no more for them than a Cornish fisherman cares for a conger eel. But sometimes, when the two natures are poetic, we have scenes of Bettina and Goethe, which are perhaps wholesome as well as pleasant for both parties when they are good enough and sensible enough to face the inexorable on the side of age and to recognize the impossible on the side of youth. On these conditions, old gentlemen are indulged in fancies for poetic little girls; and the poetic little girls have their emotions and imaginations satisfied harmlessly until they find a suitable mate.

But the master builder, though he gets into just such a situation, does not get out of it so cheaply, because he is not outwardly an old, or even a very elderly gentleman. 'He is a man no longer young, but healthy and vigorous, with closely cut curly hair, dark moustache, and dark thick eyebrows.' Also he is daimonic, not sham daimonic like Molvik in The Wild Duck, but really daimonic, with luck, a star, and mystic 'helpers and servers', who find the way through the maze of life for him. In short, a very fascinating man, whom nobody, himself least of all, could suspect of having shot his bolt and being already dead. Therefore a man for whom a girl's castle in the air is a very dangerous place, as she may easily thrust

116

upon him adventures that would tax the prime of an unexhausted man, and are mere delirious madness for a spent one.

Grasp this situation and you will be able to follow a performance of The Master Builder without being puzzled; though to the unprepared theatregoer it is a bewildering business. You see Solness in his office, ruthlessly exploiting the devotion of the girl secretary Kaia, who idolizes him, and giving her nothing in return but a mesmerizing word occasionally. You see him with equal ruthlessness apparently, but really with the secret terror of 'the priest who slew the slayer and shall himself be slain', trying to suppress a young rival who is as yet only a draughtsman in his employment. To keep the door shut against the younger generation already knocking at it: that is all he can do now, except build castles in the air; for, as I have said, the effective part of the man is dead. Then there is his wife, who, knowing that he is failing in body and mind, can do nothing but look on in helpless terror. She cannot make a happy home for Solness, because her own happiness has been sacrificed to his genius. Or rather, her own genius, which is for 'building up the souls of little children', has been sacrificed to his. For they began their family life in an old house that was part of her property: the sort of house that may be hallowed by old family associations and memories of childhood, but that it pays the speculative builder to pull down and replace by rows of villas. Now the ambitious Solness knows this but dares not propose such a thing to his wife, who cherishes all the hallowing associations, and even keeps her dolls: nine lovely dolls, feeling them 'under her heart, like little unborn children'. Everything in the house is precious to her: the old silk dresses, the lace, the portraits. Solness knows that to touch these would be tearing her heart up by the roots. So he says nothing; does nothing; only notes a crack in the old chimney which should be repaired if the house is to be safe against fire, and does not repair it. Instead, he pictures to himself a fire, with his wife out in the sledge with his two children, and nothing but charred ruins facing her when she returns; but what matter, since the children have escaped and are still with her? He even calls upon his helpers and servers to consider whether this vision might not become a reality. And it does. The house is burnt; the villas rise on its site and cover the park; and Halvard Solness becomes rich and successful.

But the helpers and servers have not stuck to the program for all that. The fire did not come from the crack in the chimney when all the domestic fires were blazing. It came at night when the fires were low, and began in a cupboard quite away from the chimney. It came when Mrs Solness and the children were in bed. It shattered the mother's health; it killed the children she was nursing; it devoured the portraits and the silk dresses and the old lace; it burnt the nine lovely dolls; and it broke the heart under which the dolls had lain like little unborn children. That was the price of the master builder's success. He is married to a dead woman; and he is trying to atone by building her a new villa: a new tomb to replace the old home; for he is gnawed with remorse.

But the fire was not only a good building speculation: it also led to his obtaining commissions to build churches. And one triumphant day, when he was celebrating the completion of the giant tower he had added to the old church at Lysanger, it suddenly flashed on him that his house had been burnt, his wife's life laid waste, and his own happiness destroyed, so that he might become a builder of churches. Now it happens that one of his difficulties as a builder is that he has a bad head for heights, and cannot venture even on a second floor balcony. Yet in the fury of that thought he mounts to the pinnacle of his tower, and there, face to face with God, who has, he feels, wasted the wife's gift of building up the souls of little children to make the husband a builder of steeples, he declares that he will never set hand to church-building again, and will henceforth build nothing but homes for happier men than he. Which vow he keeps, only to find that the home, too, is a devouring idol, and that men and women have no longer any use for it.

In spite of his excitement, he very nearly breaks his neck after all; for among the crowd below there is a little devil of a girl who waves a white scarf and makes his head swim. This tiny animal is no other than the younger stepdaughter of Ellida, The Lady from the Sea, Hilda Wangel, of whose taste for 'thrilling' sensations we had a glimpse in that play. On the same evening Solness is entertained at a club banquet, in consequence of which he is not in the most responsible condition when he returns to sup at the house of Dr Wangel, who is putting him up for the night. He meets the imp there; thinks her like a little princess in her white dress; kisses her; and promises her to come back in ten years and carry her off to the kingdom of Orangia. Perhaps it is only just to mention that he stoutly denies these indiscretions afterwards; though he admits that when he wishes something to happen between himself and somebody else, the somebody else always imagines it actually has happened.

The play begins ten years after the climbing of the tower. The younger generation knocks at the door with a vengeance. Hilda, now a vigorous young woman, and a great builder of castles in the air, bursts in on him and demands her kingdom; and very soon she sends him up a tower again (the tower of the new house) and waves her scarf to him as madly as ever. This time he really does break his neck; and so the story ends.

LITTLE EYOLF, 1894

Though the most mischievous ideals are social ideals which have become institutions, laws and creeds, yet their evil must come to a personal point before they can strike down the individual. Jones is not struck down by an ideal in the abstract, but by Smith making monstrous claims or inflicting monstrous injuries on him in the name of an ideal. And it is fair to add that the ideals are sometimes beneficent, and their repudiation sometimes cruel. For ideals are in practice not so much matters of conscience as excuses for doing what we like; and thus it happens that of two people worshipping the same ideals, one will be a detestable tyrant and the other a kindly and helpful friend of mankind. What makes the bad side of idealism so dangerous is that wicked people are allowed to commit crimes in the name of the ideal that would not be tolerated for a moment as open devilment. Perhaps the worst, because the commonest and most intimate cases, are to be found in family life. Even during the Reign of Terror, the chances of any particular Frenchman or Frenchwoman being guillotined were so small as to be negligible. Under Nero, a Christian was far safer from being smeared with pitch and set on fire than he was from domestic trouble. If the private lives that have been wasted by idealistic persecution could be recorded and set against the public martyrdoms and slaughterings and torturings and imprisonments, our millions of private Neros and Torquemadas and Calvins, Bloody Maries and Cleopatras and Semiramises, would eclipse the few who have come to the surface of history by the accident of political or ecclesiastical conspicuousness.

Thus Ibsen, at the beginning of his greatness, shewed us Brand sacrificing his wife; and this was only the first of a series of similar exhibitions, ending, so far, in Solness sacrificing his wife and being himself sacrificed to a girl's enthusiasm. And he brings Solness to the point of rebelling furiously against the tyranny of his wife's ideal of home, and declaring that 'building homes for happy human beings is not worth a rap: men are not happy in these homes: I should not have been happy in such a home if I had had one.' It is not surprising to find that Little Eyolf is about such a home.

This home clearly cannot be a working-class home. And here let it be said that the comparative indifference of the working class to Ibsen's plays is neither Ibsen's fault nor that of the working class. To the man who works for his living in modern society, home is not the place where he lives, nor his wife the woman he lives with. Home is the roof under which he sleeps and eats; and his wife is the woman who makes his bed, cooks his meals, and looks after their children when they are neither in school nor in the streets, or who at least sees that the servants do these things. The man's work keeps him from home from eight to twelve hours a day. He is unconscious through sleep for another eight hours. Then there is the public house and the club. There is eating, washing, dressing, playing with the children or the dog, entertaining or visiting friends, reading, and pursuing hobbies such as gardening and the like. Obviously the home ideal cannot be tested fully under these conditions, which enable a married pair to see less and know less of one another than they do of those who work side by side with them. It is in the propertied class only that two people can really live together and devote themselves to one another if they want to. There are certain businesses which men and women can conduct jointly, and certain professions which men can pursue at home; and in these the strain of idealism on marriage is more severe than when the two work separately. But the full strain comes on with the modern unearned income from investments, which does not involve even the management of an estate. And it is under this full strain that Ibsen tests it in Little Eyolf.

Shakespear, in a flash of insight which has puzzled many commentators, and even set them proposing alterations of a passage which they found unthinkable, has described one of his characters as 'a fellow almost damned in a fair wife'. There is no difficulty or obscurity about this phrase at all: you have only to look round at the men who have ventured to marry very fascinating women to see that most of them are not merely 'almost damned' but wholly damned. Allmers, in Little Eyolf, is a fellow almost damned in a fair wife. She, Rita Allmers, has brought him 'gold and green forests' (a reminiscence from an early play called The Feast at Solhoug), and not only troubles and uncentres him as only a woman can trouble and uncentre a man who is susceptible to her bodily attraction, but is herself furiously and jealously in love with him. In short, they form the ideal home of romance; and it would be hard to find a compacter or more effective formula for a small private hell. The 'almost damned' are commonly saved by the fact that the devotion is usually on one side only, and that the lovely lady (or gentleman; for a woman almost damned in a fair husband is also a common object in domestic civilization), if she has only one husband, relieves the boredom of his devotion by having fifty courtiers. But Rita will neither share Allmers with anyone else nor be shared. He must be wholly and exclusively hers; and she must be wholly and exclusively his. By her gold and green forests she snatches him from his work as a schoolmaster and imprisons him in their house, where the poor wretch pretends to occupy himself by writing a book on Human Responsibility, and forming the character of their son, little Eyolf. For your male sultana takes himself very seriously indeed, as do most sultanas and others who are so closely shut up with their own vanities and appetites that they think the world a little thing to be moulded and arranged at their silly pleasure like a lump of plasticine. Rita is jealous of the book, and hates it not only because Allmers occupies himself with it instead of with her, but talks about it to his half-sister Asta, of whom she is of course also jealous. She is jealous of little Eyolf, and hates him too, because he comes between her and her prey.

One day, when the baby child is lying on the table, they have an amorous fit and forget all about him. He falls off the table and is crippled for life. He and his crutch become thenceforth a standing reproach to them. They hate themselves; they hate each other; they hate him; their atmosphere of ideal conjugal love breeds hate at every turn: hatred masquerading as a loving bond that has been drawn closer and sanctified by their common misfortune. After ten years of this hideous slavery the man breaks loose: actually insists on going for a short trip into the mountains by himself. It is true that he reassures Rita by coming back before his time;

but her conclusion that this was because he could not abstain from her society is rudely shattered by his conduct on his return. She dresses herself beautifully to receive him, and makes the seraglio as delightful as possible for their reunion; but he purposely arrives tired out, and takes refuge in the sleep of exhaustion, without a caress. As she says, quoting a popular poem when reproaching him for this afterwards, 'There stood your champagne and you tasted it not.' It soon appears that he has come to loathe his champagne, and that the escape into the mountains has helped him to loathe his situation to some extent, even to discovering the absurdity of his book on Human Responsibility, and the cruelty of his educational experiments on Eyolf. In future he is going to make Eyolf 'an open-air little boy', which of course involves being a good deal in the open air with him, and out of the seraglio. Then the woman's hatred of the child unveils itself; and she openly declares what she really feels as to this little creature, with its 'evil eyes', that has come between them.

At this point, very opportunely, comes the Rat Wife, who, like the Pied Piper, clears away rats for a consideration. Has Rita any little gnawing things she wants to get rid of? Here, it seems, is a helper and server for Rita. The Rat Wife's method is to bewitch the rats so that when she rows out to sea they follow her and are drowned. She describes this with a heart-breaking poetry that frightens Rita, who makes Allmers send her away. But a helper and server is not so easily exorcized. Rita's little gnawing thing, Eyolf, has come under the spell; and when the Rat Wife rows out to sea, he follows her and is drowned.

The family takes the event in a very proper spirit. Horror, lamentation, shrieks and tears, and all the customary homages to death and attestations of bereavement are duly and even sincerely gone through; for the shock of such an accident makes us all human for a moment. But next morning Allmers finds some difficulty in keeping it up, miserable as he is. He finds himself forgetting about Eyolf for several minutes, and thinking about other things, even about his breakfast; and in his idealistic self-devotion to artificial attitudes he reproaches himself and tries to force himself to keep thinking of Eyolf and being overwhelmed with grief about him. Besides, it is an excuse for avoiding his wife. The revulsion against his slavery to her has made her presence unbearable to him. He can bear nobody but his half-sister Asta, whose relation to him is a most blessed comfort and relief because their blood kinship excludes from it all the torment and slavery of his relation to Rita. But this consolation is presently withdrawn; for Asta has just discovered, in some old correspondence, convincing proofs that she is not related to him at all; and the effect of the discovery has been to remove the inhibition which has hitherto limited her strong affection for him; so that she now perceives that she must leave him. Hitherto, she has refused, for his sake, the offers of Borgheim, an engineer who wants to marry her, but who, like Rita, wants to take her away and make her exclusively his own; for he, too, cannot share with anyone. And though both Allmers and Rita implore her to stay, dreading now nothing so much as being left alone with one another, she knows that she cannot stay innocently, and accepts the engineer and vanishes lest a worse thing should befall.

And now Rita has her man all to herself. Eyolf dead, Asta gone, the Book on Human Responsibility thrown into the waste paper basket: there are no more rivals now, no more distractions: the field is clear for the ideal union of 'two souls with but a single thought, two hearts that beat as one'. The result may be imagined.

The situation is insufferable from the beginning. Allmers' attempts to avoid seeing or speaking to Rita are of course impracticable. Equally impracticable are their efforts to behave kindly to one another. They are presently at it hammer and tongs, each tearing the mask from the other's grief for the child, and leaving it exposed as their remorse: hers for having jealously hated Eyolf; his for having sacrificed him to his passion for Rita, and to the schoolmasterly vanity and folly which sees in the child nothing more than the vivisector sees in a guinea-pig: something to experiment on with a view to rearranging the world to suit his own little ideas. If ever two cultivated souls of the propertied middle class were stripped naked and left bankrupt, these two are. They cannot bear to live; and yet they are forced to confess that they dare not kill themselves.

The solution of their problem, as far as it is solved, is, as coming from Ibsen, very remarkable. It is not, as might have been expected after his long propaganda of Individualism, that they should break up the seraglio and go out into the world until they have learnt to stand alone, and through that accept companionship on honorable conditions only. Ibsen here explicitly insists for the first time that 'we are members one of another', and that though the strongest man is he who stands alone, the man who is standing alone for his own sake solely is literally an idiot. It is indeed a staring fact in history and contemporary life that nothing is so gregarious as selfishness, and nothing so solitary as the selflessness that loathes the word Altruism because to it there are no 'others'; it sees and feels in every man's case the image of its own. 'Inasmuch as ye have done it unto one of the least of these my brethren ye have done it unto me' is not Altruism or Othersism. It is an explicit repudiation of the patronizing notion that 'the least of these' is *another* to whom you are invited to be very nice and kind: in short, it accepts entire identification of 'me' with 'the least of these'. The fashionably sentimental version, which runs, in effect, 'If you subscribe eighteen-pence to give this little dear a day in the country I shall regard it as a loan of one-and-sixpence to myself' is really more conceitedly remote from the spirit of the famous Christian saying than even the sham political economy that took in Mr Gradgrind. Accordingly, if you would see industrial sweating at its vilest, you must go, not to the sempstresses who work for commercial firms, but to the victims of pious Altruistic Ladies' Work Guilds and the like, in which ladies with gold and green forests offer to 'others' their blouses to be stitched at prices that the most sordid East End slave-driver would recoil from offering.

Thus we see that in Ibsen's mind, as in the actual history of the nineteenth century, the way to Communism lies through the most resolute and uncompromising Individualism. James Mill, with an inhuman conceit and pedantry which leaves the fable of Allmers and Eyolf far behind, educated John Stuart Mill to be the arch Individualist of his time, with the result that John Stuart Mill became a Socialist quarter of a century before the rest of his set moved in that direction. Herbert Spencer lived to write despairing pamphlets against the Socialism of his ablest pupils. There is no hope in Individualism for egotism. When a man is at last brought face to face with himself by a brave Individualism, he finds himself face to face, not with an individual, but with a species, and knows that to save himself, he must save the race. He can have no life except a share in the life of the community; and if that life is unhappy and squalid, nothing that he can do to paint and paper and upholster and shut off his little corner of it can really rescue him from it.

It happens so to that bold Individualist Mrs Rita Allmers. The Allmers are, of course, snobs, and have always been very determined that the common little children down at the pier should be taught their place as Eyolf's inferiors. They even go the length of discussing whether these dirty little wretches should not be punished for their cowardice in not rescuing Eyolf. Thereby they raise the terrible question whether they themselves, who are afraid to commit suicide in their misery, would have been any braver. There is nobody to comfort them; for the income from the gold and green forests, by enabling them to cut themselves off from all industry of the place, has led them into something like total isolation. They hate their neighbors as themselves. They are alone together with nothing to do but wear each other out and drive each other mad to an extent impossible under any other conditions. And Rita's plight is the more desperate of the two, because as she has been the more unscrupulous, the more exacting, she has left him something to look forward to: freedom from her. He is bent on that, at least: he will not live with her on any terms, not stay anywhere within reach of her: the one thing he craves is that he may never see her or speak to her again. That is the end of the 'two souls with but a single thought', etc. But to her his release is only a supreme privation, the end of everything that gave life any meaning for her. She has not even egotism to fall back on.

At this pass, an annoyance of which she has often complained occurs again. The children down at the pier make a noise, playing and yelling as if Eyolf had never existed. It suddenly occurs to her that these are children too, just like Eyolf, and that they are suffering a good deal from neglect. After all, they too are little Eyolfs. Inasmuch as she can do it unto one of the least of these his brethren she can do it unto him. She determines to take the dirty little wretches in hand and look after them. It is at all events a more respectable plan than that of the day before, which was to throw herself away on the first man she met if Allmers dared to think of anybody but her. And it has the domestic advantage that Allmers has nothing to fear from a woman who has something else to do than torment him with passions that devour and jealousies that enslave him. The world and the home suddenly take on their natural aspect. Allmers offers to stay and help her. And so they are delivered from their evil dream, and, let us hope, live happily every after.

JOHN GABRIEL BORKMAN, 1896

In Little Eyolf the shadow of death lifted for a moment; but now we enter it again. Here the persons of the drama are not only dead but buried. Borkman is a Napoleon of finance. He has the root of finance in him in a born love of money in its final reality: a love, that is, of precious metals. He does not dream of beautiful ladies calling to him for knightly rescue from dragons and tyrants, but of metals imprisoned in undiscovered mines, calling to him to release them and send them out into all lands fertilizing, encouraging, creating. Music to him means the ring of the miner's pick and hammer: the eternal night underground is as magical to him as the moonlit starlit night of the upper air to the romantic poet. This love of metal is common enough: no man feels towards a cheque for £20 as he does towards twenty gold sovereigns: he will part from the paper with less of a pang than from the coins. There are misers whose fingers tremble when they touch gold, but close steadily on banknotes. True love of money is, in fact, a passion based on a physical appetite for precious metals. It is not greed: you cannot call a man who starves himself sooner than part with one sovereign from his sack of sovereigns, greedy. If he did the same for the love of God, you would call him a saint, if for the love of a woman, a perfect gentle knight. Men grow rich according to the strength of their obsession by this passion: its great libertines become Napoleons of finance: its narrow debauchees become misers, petty moneylenders, and the like. It must not be looked for in all our millionaires, because most of these are rich by pure accident (our abandonment of industry to the haphazard scrambles of private adventurers necessarily produces occasional windfalls which enrich the man who happens to be on the spot), as may be seen when the lucky ones are invited to display their supposed Napoleonic powers in spending their windfalls, when they reveal themselves as quite ordinary mortals, if not indeed sometimes as exceptionally resourceless ones. Besides, finance is one business, and industrial organization another: the man with a passion for altering the map by digging isthmuses never thinks of money save as a means to his end. But those who as financiers have passionately 'made' money instead of merely holding their hats under an accidental shower of it will be found to have a genuine disinterested love of it. It is not easy to say how common this passion is. Poverty is general, which would seem to indicate a general lack of it; but poverty is mainly the result of organized robbery and oppression (politely called Capitalism) starving the passion for gold as it starves all the passions. The evidence is further confused by the decorative instinct: some men will load their fingers and shirt-fronts with rings and studs, whilst others of equal means are ringless and fasten their shirts with sixpennorth of mother-of-pearl. But it is significant that Plato, and, following him, Sir Thomas More, saw with Ibsen, and made complete indifference to the precious metals, minted or not, a necessary qualification for aristocracy. This indifference is, as a matter of fact, so characteristic of our greatest non-industrial men that when they do not happen to inherit property they are generally poor and in difficulties. Therefore we who have never cared for money enough to do more than keep our heads above water, and are therefore tempted to regard ourselves as others regard us (that is, as failures, or, at best, as persons of no account) may console ourselves with the reflection that money-hunger is no more respectable than gluttony, and that unless its absence or feebleness is only a symptom of a general want of power to care for anything at all, it usually means that the soul has risen above it to higher concerns.

All this is necessary to the appreciation of Ibsen's present-ment of the Napoleon of finance. Ibsen does not take him superficially: he goes to the poetic basis of the type: the love of gold – actual metallic gold – and the idealization of gold through that love.

Borkman meets the Misses Rentheim: two sisters: the elder richer than the younger. He falls in love with the younger; and she falls in love with him; but the love of gold is the master passion: he marries the elder. Yet he respects his secondary passion in the younger. When he speculates with other people's securities he spares hers. On the point of bringing off a great stroke of finance, the other securities are missed; and he is imprisoned for embezzlement. That is the end of him. He comes out of prison a ruined man and a dead man, and would not have even a tomb to sleep in but for the charity of Ella Rentheim, whose securities he spared when he broke her heart. She maintains his old home for him.

He now enters the grimmest lying in state ever exposed to public view by mortal dramatist. His wife, a proud woman, must live in the same house with the convicted thief who has disgraced her, because she has nowhere else to lay her head; but she will not see him nor speak to him. She sits downstairs in the drawing-room eating the bitter bread of her sister's charity, and listening with loathing to her husband's steps as he paces to and fro in the long gallery upstairs 'like a sick wolf'. She listens not for days but for years. And her one hope is that her son Erhart will rehabilitate the family name; repay the embezzled money; and lead her from her tomb up again into honor and prosperity. To this task she has devoted *his* life.

Borkman has quite another plan. He is still Napoleon, and will return from his Elba to scatter his enemies and complete the stroke that ill-luck and the meddlesomeness of the law frustrated. But he is proud: prouder than Napoleon. He will not come back to the financial world until it finds out that it cannot do without him and comes to ask him to resume his place at the head of the board. He keeps himself in readiness for that deputation. He is always dressed for it; and when he hears steps on the threshold he stands up by the table; puts one hand into the breast of his coat; and assumes the attitude of a conqueror receiving suppliants. And this also goes on not for days but for years, long after the world has forgotten him, and there is nobody likely to come for him except Peer Gynt's button moulder.

Borkman, like all madmen, cannot nourish his delusion without some response from without. One of the victims of his downfall is a clerk who once wrote a tragedy, and has lived ever since in his own imagination as a poet. His family ridicules his tragedy and his pretensions; and as he is a poor ineffectual little creature who has never lived enough to feel dignified among the dead, like Borkman, he too finds it hard to keep his illusion alive without help. Fortunately he has admired Borkman, the great financier; and Borkman, when he has ruined him and ruined himself, is quite willing to be admired by this humble victim, and even to reward him by a pretence of believing in his poetic genius. Thus the two form one of those Mutual Admiration Societies on which the world so largely subsists, and make the years in the long gallery tolerable by flattering each other. There are even moments when Borkman is nerved to the point of starting for his second advent as a great financial redeemer. On such occasions the woman downstairs hears the footsteps of the sick wolf on the stairs approaching the hatstand where his hat and stick have waited unused all the years of his entombment; but they never reach that first stage of the journey. They always turn back into the gallery again.

This melancholy household of the dead crumbles to dust at the knock of the younger generation at the door. Erhart, dedicated by his mother to the task of paying his father's debts and retrieving his ruin, and by his aunt to the task of sweetening her last days with his grateful love, has dedicated himself to his own affairs – for the moment mostly love affairs – and has not the faintest intention of concerning himself with the bygone career of the crazy ex-felon upstairs or the sentimentalities of the old maid downstairs. He detests the house and the atmosphere, and associates his aunt's broken heart with nothing more important than the scent of stale lavender, which he dislikes. He spends his time happily in the house of a pretty lady in the neighborhood, who has been married and divorced, and knows how to form an adolescent youth. And as to the unpardonable enemy of the family, one Hinkel, who betrayed Borkman to the police and rose on his ruins, Erhart cares so little for that old story that he goes to Hinkel's parties and enjoys himself there very much. And when at last the pretty lady raises his standard of happiness to a point at which the old house and the old people become impossible, unthinkable, unbearable, he goes off with her to Italy and leaves the dead to bury their dead.

The details of this catastrophe make the play. The fresh air and the light of day break into the tomb; and its inhabitants crumble into dust. Foldal, the poet clerk, lets slip the fact that he has not the slightest belief in Borkman's triumphant return to the world; and Borkman retorts by telling him he is no poet. After this comedy comes the tragedy of the son's defection; and amid the recriminations of the broken heart, the baffled pride, and the shattered dreams, the castles in the air vanish and reveal the open grave they have hidden. Poor Foldal, limping home after being run over by a sledge in which his daughter is running away to act as 'second string' and chaperone for Erhart and the pretty lady, is the only one who is wanted in the world, since he must still work for his derisive family. But Borkman returns to his dream, and ventures out of doors at last, not this time to resume his place as governor of the bank, but to release the imprisoned metal that rings and sings to him from the earth. In other words, to die in the open, mad but happy, whilst the two sisters, 'we two shadows', end their strife over his body.

WHEN WE DEAD AWAKEN, 1900

This play, the last work of Ibsen, and at first the least esteemed, has had its prophecy so startlingly fulfilled in England that nobody will now question the intensity of its inspiration. With us the dead have awakened in the very manner prefigured in the play. The simplicity and brevity of the story is so obvious, and the enormous scope of the conception so difficult to comprehend, that many of Ibsen's most devoted admirers failed to do it justice. They knew that he was a man of seventy, and were prepossessed with the belief that at such an age his powers must be falling off. It certainly was easier at that time to give the play up as a bad job than to explain it. Now that the great awakening of women which we call the Militant Suffrage Movement is upon us, and you may hear our women publicly and passionately paraphrasing Ibsen's heroine without having read a word of the play, the matter is simpler. There is no falling-off here in Ibsen. It may be said that this is physically impossible; but those who say so forget that the natural decay of a writer's powers may shew itself in two ways. The inferiority of the work produced is only one way. The other is the production of equally good or even better work with much greater effort than it would have cost its author ten years earlier. Ibsen produced this play with great difficulty in twice as long a period as had before sufficed; and even at that the struggle left his mind a wreck; for he not only never wrote another play, but, like an overstrained athlete, lost even the normal mental capacity of an ordinary man. Yet it would be hard to say that the play was not worth the sacrifice. It shews no decay of Ibsen's highest qualities: his magic is nowhere more potent. It is shorter than usual: that is all. The extraordinarily elaborate private history, family and individual, of the personages, which lies behind the action of the other plays, is replaced by a much simpler history of a few people in their general human relations without any family history at all. And the characteristically conscientious fitting of the play to the mechanical conditions of old-fashioned stages has given way to demands that even the best equipped and largest modern stages cannot easily comply with; for the second act takes place in a valley; and though it is easy to represent a valley by a painted scene when the action is confined to one spot in the foreground, it is a different matter when the whole valley has to be practicable, and the movements of the figures cover distances which do not exist on the stage, and cannot, as far as my experience goes, be satisfactorily simulated by the stage carpenter, though they are easy enough for the painter. I should attach no importance at all to this in a writer less mindful of technical limitations and less ingenious in circumventing them than Ibsen, who was for some years a professional stage manager; but in his case it is clear that in calling on the theatre to expand to his requirements instead of, as his custom was, limiting his scene of action to the possibilities of a modest provincial theatre, he knew quite well what he was doing. Here then, we have three differences, from the earlier plays. None of them are inferiorities. They are proper to the difference of subject, and in fact increased the difficulty of the playwright's task by throwing him back on sheer dramatic power, unaided by the cheaper interest that can be gained on the stage by mere ingenuity of construction. Ibsen, who has always before played on the spectator by a most elaborate gradual development which would have satisfied Dumas, here throws all his cards on the table as rapidly as possible, and proceeds to deal intensively with a situation that never alters.

This situation is simple enough in its general statement, though it is so complex in its content that it raises the whole question of domestic civilization. Take a man and a woman at the highest pitch of natural ability and charm yet attained, and enjoying all the culture that modern art and literature can offer them; and what does it all come to? Contrast them with an essentially uncivilized pair, with a man who lives for hunting and eating and ravishing, and whose morals are those of the bully with the strong hand: in short, a man from the Stone Age as we conceive it (such men are still common enough in the classes that can afford the huntsman's life); and couple him with a woman who has no interest or ambition in life except to be captured by such a man (and of these we have certainly no lack). Then face this question. What is there to choose between these two pairs? Is the cultured gifted man less hardened, less selfish towards the woman, than the paleolithic man? Is the woman less sacrificed, less enslaved, less dead spiritually in the one case than

134

in the other? Modern culture, except when it has rotted into mere cynicism, shrieks that the question is an insult. The Stone Age, anticipating Ibsen's reply, guffaws heartily and says, 'Bravo, Ibsen!' Ibsen's reply is that the sacrifice of the woman of the Stone Age to fruitful passions which she herself shares is as nothing compared to the wasting of the modern woman's soul to gratify the imagination and stimulate the genius of the modern artist, poet, and philosopher. He shews us that no degradation ever devized or permitted is as disastrous as this degradation; that through it women die into luxuries for men, and yet can kill them; that men and women are becoming conscious of this; and that what remains to be seen as perhaps the most interesting of all imminent social developments is what will happen 'when we dead awaken'.

Ibsen's greatest contemporary outside his own art was Rodin the French sculptor. Whether Ibsen knew this, or whether he was inspired to make his hero a sculptor just as Dickens was inspired to make Pecksniff an architect, is not known. At all events, having to take a type of the highest and ablest masculine genius, he made him a sculptor, and called his name, not Rodin, but Rubeck: a curious assonance, if it was not intentional. Rubeck is as able an individual as our civilization can produce. The difficulty of presenting such an individual in fiction is that it can be done only by a writer who occupies that position himself; for a dramatist cannot conceive anything higher than himself. No doubt he can invest an imaginary figure with all sorts of imaginary gifts. A drunken author may make his hero sober; an ugly, weak, puny, timid one may make him a Hyperion or a Hercules; a deaf mute may write novels in which the lover is an orator and his mistress a prima donna; but whatever ornaments and accomplishments he may pile up on his personages, he cannot give them greater souls than his own. Defoe could invent wilder adventures for Robinson Crusoe than Shakespear for Hamlet; but he could not make that mean adventurer, with his dull eulogies of the virtues of 'the middle station of life', anything even remotely like Shakespear's prince.

For Ibsen this difficulty did not exist. He knew quite well that he was one of the greatest men living; so he simply said, 'Suppose ME to be a sculptor instead of a playwright', and the thing was done. Thus he came forward himself to plead to his own worst indictment of modern culture. One of the touches by which he identifies himself has all the irony of his earliest work. Rubeck has to make money out of human vanity, as all sculptors must nowadays, by portrait busts; but he revenges himself by studying and bringing out in his sitters 'the respectable pompous horse faces, and self-opinionated donkey-muzzles, and lop-eared low-browed dog-skulls, and fatted swine-snouts, and dull brutal bull fronts' that lurk in so many human faces. All artists who deal with humanity do this, more or less. Leonardo da Vinci ruled his notebook in columns headed fox, wolf, etc., and made notes of faces by ticking them off in these columns, finding this, apparently, as satisfactory a memorandum as a drawing. Domestic animals, terriers, pugs, poultry, parrots, and cockatoos, are specially valuable to the caricaturist, as giving the original types which explain many faces. Ibsen must have classified his acquaintances a good deal in this way, not without an occasional chuckle; and his attribution of the practice to Rubeck is a confession of it.

Rubeck makes his reputation, as sculptors often do, by a statue of a woman. Not, be it observed, of a dress and a pair of boots, with a head protruding from them, but of a woman from the hand of Nature. It is worth noting here that we have hardly any portraits, either painted or carved, of our famous men and women or even of our nearest and dearest friends. Charles Dickens is known to us as a guy with a human head and face on top. Shakespear is a laundry advertisement of a huge starched collar with his head sticking out of it. Dr Johnson is a face looking through a wig perched on a snuffy suit of old clothes. All the great women of history are fashion plates of their period. Bereaved parents, orphans, and widows weep fondly over photographs of uniforms, frock coats, gowns, and hats, for the sake of the little scrap of humanity that is allowed to peep through these trappings. Women with noble figures and plain or elderly faces are outdressed and outfaced by rivals who, if revealed as they really are, would be hardly human. Carlyle staggers humanity by inviting the House of Commons to sit unclothed, so that we, and they themselves, shall know them for what they really are.

Hence it is that the artist who adores mankind as his highest subject always comes back to the reality beneath the clothes. His claim to be allowed to do this is so irresistible that in every considerable city in England you will find, supported by the rates of prudish chapel goers, and even managed and inspected by committees of them, an art school where, in the 'life class' (significant term!) young women posed in ridiculous and painful attitudes by a drawing master, and mostly under the ugliest circumstances of light, color, and surroundings, earn a laborious wage by allowing a crowd of art students to draw their undraped figures. It is a joylessly grotesque spectacle: one wonders whether anything can really be learnt from it; for never have I seen one of these school models in an attitude which any human being would, unless the alternative were starvation, voluntarily sustain for thirty seconds, or assume on any natural occasion or provocation whatever. Male models are somewhat less slavish; and the stalwart laborer or olive-skinned young Italian who poses before a crowd of easels with ludicrously earnest young ladies in blue or vermilion gowns and embroidered pinafores drawing away at him for dear life is usually much more comfortably and possibly posed. But Life will not yield up her more intimate secrets for eighteenpence an hour; and these earnest young ladies and artsome young men, when they have filled portfolios with such sordid life studies, know less about living humanity than they did before, and very much less about even the mechanism of the body and the shape of its muscles than they could learn less inhumanly from a series of modern kinematographs of figures in motion.

Rubeck does not make his statues in a class at a municipal art school by looking at a weary girl in a tortured attitude with a background of match-boarding, under a roof of girders, and with the ghastly light of a foggy, smoky manufacturing town making the light side of her flesh dirty yellow and the shadowed side putrid purple. He knows better than that. He finds a beautiful woman, and tells her his vision of a statue of The Resurrection Day in the form of a woman 'filled with a sacred joy at finding herself unchanged in the higher, freer, happier region after the long dreamless sleep of death'. And the woman, immediately seizing his inspiration and sharing it, devotes herself to the work, not merely as his model, but as his friend, his helper, fellow worker, comrade, all things, save one, that may be humanly natural and necessary between them for an unreserved co-operation in the great work. The one exception is that they are not lovers; for the sculptor's ideal is a virgin, or, as he calls it, a pure woman.

And her reward is that when the work is finished and the statue achieved, he says 'Thank you for a priceless EPISODE,' at which significant word, revealing as it does that she has, after all, been nothing to him but a means to his end, she leaves him and drops out of his life. To earn her living she must then pose, not to him, but before crowds in Variety Theatres in living pictures, gaining much money by her beauty, winning rich husbands, and driving them all to madness or to death by 'a fine sharp dagger which she always has with her in bed', much as Rita Allmers nearly killed her husband. And she calls the statue her child and Rubeck's, as the book in Hedda Gabler was the child of Thea and Eilert Lövborg. But finally she too goes mad under the strain.

Rubeck presently meets a pretty Stone Age woman, and marries her. And as he is not a Stone Age man, and she is bored to distraction by his cultured interests, he disappoints her as thoroughly as she disgusts and wearies him: the symptoms being that though he builds her a splendid villa, full of works of art and so forth, neither he nor she can settle down quietly; and they take trips here, trips there, trips anywhere to escape being alone and at home together.

But the retribution for his egotism takes a much subtler form, and strikes at a much more vital place in him: namely, his artistic inspiration. Working with Irene, the lost model, he had achieved a perfect work of art; and, having achieved it, had supposed that he was done with her. But art is not so simple as that. The moment she forsakes him and leaves him to the Stone Age woman and to his egotism, he no longer sees the perfection of his work. He becomes dissatisfied with it. He sees that it can be improved: for instance, why should it consist of a figure of Irene alone? Why should he not be in it himself? Is he not a far more important factor in the conception? He changes the single figure design to a group. He adds a figure of himself. He finds that the woman's figure, with its wonderful expression of gladness, puts his own image out of countenance. He rearranges the group so as to give himself more prominence. Even so the gladness out-shines him; and at last he 'tones it down', striking the gladness out with his chisel, and making his own expression the main interest of the group. But he cannot stop there. Having destroyed the thing that was superior to him, he now wants to introduce things that are inferior. He carves clefts in the earth at the feet of his figure, and from these clefts he makes emerge the folk with the horse faces and the swine snouts that are nearer the beast than his own fine face. Then he is satisfied with his work; and it is in this form that it makes him famous and is finally placed in a public museum. In his days with Irene, they used to call these museums the prisons of works of art. Precisely what the Italian Futurist painters of today are calling them.

And now the play begins. Irene comes from her madhouse to a 'health resort'. Thither also comes Rubeck, wandering about with the Stone Age woman to avoid being left at home with her. Thither also comes the man of the Stone Age with his dogs and guns, and carries off the Stone Age woman, to her husband's great relief. Rubeck and Irene meet; and as they talk over old times, she learns, bit by bit, what has happened to the statue, and is about to kill him when she realizes, also bit by bit, that the history of its destruction is the history of his own, and that as he used her up and left her dead, so with her death the life went out of him. But, like Nora in A Doll's House, she sees the possibility of a miracle. The dead may awaken if only they can find an honest and natural relation in which they shall no longer sacrifice and slay one another. She asks him to climb to the top of a mountain with her and see that promised land. Half way up, they meet the Stone Age pair hunting. There is a storm coming. It is death to go up and danger to climb down. The Stone Age man faces the danger and carries his willing prey down. The others are beyond the fear of death, and go up. And that is the end of them and of the plays of Henrik Ibsen.

The end, too, let us hope, of the idols, domestic, moral, religious and political, in whose name we have been twaddled into misery and confusion and hypocrisy unspeakable. For Ibsen's dead hand still keeps the grip he laid on their masks when he first tore them off; and whilst that grip holds, all the King's horses and all the King's men will find it hard to set those Humpty-Dumpties up again.

THE LESSON OF THE PLAYS

In following this sketch of the plays written by Ibsen to illustrate his thesis that the real slavery of today is slavery to ideals of goodness, it may be that readers who have conned Ibsen through idealist spectacles have wondered that I could so pervert the utterances of a great poet. Indeed I know already that many of those who are most fascinated by the poetry of the plays will plead for any explanation of them rather than that given by Ibsen himself in the plainest terms through the mouths of Mrs Alving, Relling, and the rest. No great writer uses his skill to conceal his meaning. There is a tale by a famous Scotch story-teller which would have suited Ibsen exactly if he had hit on it first. Jeanie Deans sacrificing her sister's life on the scaffold to ideal truthfulness is far more horrible than the sacrifice in Rosmersholm; and the *deus ex machina* expedient by which Scott makes the end of his story agreeable is no solution of the ethical problem raised, but only a puerile evasion of it. He dared not, when it came to the point, allow Effie to be hanged for the sake of Jeanie's ideals.[1] Nevertheless, if I were to pretend that Scott wrote The Heart of Midlothian to shew that people are led to do as mischievous, as unnatural, as murderous things by their religious and moral ideals as by their envy and ambition, it would be easy to confute me from the pages of the book itself. And Ibsen, like Scott, has made his opinion plain. If any one attempts to maintain that Ghosts is a polemic in favor of indissoluble monogamic marriage, or that The Wild Duck was written to inculcate that truth should be told for its own sake, they must burn the text of the plays if their contention is to stand. The reason that Scott's story is tolerated by those who shrink from Ghosts is not that it is less terrible, but that Scott's views are familiar to all well-brought-up ladies and gentlemen, whereas Ibsen's are for the moment so strange to them as to be

141

unthinkable. He is so great a poet that the idealist finds himself in the dilemma of being unable to conceive that such a genius should have an ignoble meaning, and yet equally unable to conceive his real meaning otherwise than as ignoble. Consequently he misses the meaning altogether in spite of Ibsen's explicit and circumstantial insistence on it, and proceeds to substitute a meaning congenial to his own ideal of nobility.

Ibsen's deep sympathy with his idealist figures seems to countenance this confusion. Since it is on the weaknesses of the higher types of character that idealism seizes, his most tragic examples of vanity, selfishness, folly, and failure are not vulgar villains, but men who in an ordinary novel or melodrama would be heroes. Brand and Rosmer, who drive those they love to death, do so with all the fine airs of the Sophoclean or Shakespearean good man persecuted by Destiny. Hilda Wangel, who kills the Master Builder literally to amuse herself, is the most fascinating of sympathetic girl-heroines. The ordinary Philistine commits no such atrocities: he marries the woman he likes and lives with her more or less happily ever after; but that is not because he is greater than Brand or Rosmer, he is less. The idealist is a more dangerous animal than the Philistine just as a man is a more dangerous animal than a sheep. Though Brand virtually murdered his wife, I can understand many a woman, comfortably married to an amiable Philistine, reading the play and envying the victim her husband. For when Brand's wife, having made the sacrifice he has exacted, tells him that he was right; that she is happy now; that she sees God face to face; and then reminds him that 'whoso sees Jehovah dies', he instinctively clasps his hands over her eyes; and that action raises him at once far above the criticism that sneers at idealism from beneath, instead of surveying it from the clear ether above, which can only be reached through its mists.

If, in my account of the plays, I have myself suggested false judgments by describing the errors of the idealists in the terms of the life they have risen above rather than in those of the life they fall short of, I can only plead, with but moderate disrespect for the general reader, that if I had done otherwise I should have failed wholly to make my exposition intelligible. Indeed accurate terms for realist morality, though they are to be found in the Bible, are so out of fashion and forgotten that in this very distinction between idealism and realism, I am forced to insist on a sense of the words which, had not Ibsen forced my hand, I should perhaps have conveyed otherwise, to avoid the conflict of many of its applications with the vernacular use of the words.

This, however, was a trifle compared to the difficulty which arose from our inveterate habit of labelling men with the abstract names of their qualities without the slightest reference to the underlying will which sets these qualities in action. At an anniversary celebration of the Paris Commune of 1871, I was struck by the fact that no speaker could find a eulogy for the Federals which would not have been equally appropriate to the peasants of La Vendée who fought for their tyrants against the French revolutionists, or to the Irishmen and Highlanders who fought for the Stuarts at the Boyne or Culloden. The statements that the slain members of the Commune were heroes who died for a noble ideal would have left a stranger quite as much in the dark about them as the counter statements, once common enough in our newspapers, that they were incendiaries and assassins. Our obituary notices are examples of the same ambiguity. Of all the public men lately deceased when Ibsenism was first discussed in England, none was made more interesting by strongly marked personal characteristics than the famous atheist orator, Charles Bradlaugh. He was not in the least like any other notable member of the House of Commons. Yet when the obituary notices appeared, with the usual string of qualities: eloquence, determination, integrity, strong common-sense, and so on, it would have been possible, by merely expunging all names and other external details from these notices, to leave the reader entirely unable to say whether the subject of them was Gladstone, Lord Morley, William Stead, or any one else no

more like Bradlaugh than Garibaldi or the late Cardinal New-
man, whose obituary certificates of morality might nevertheless have been reprinted almost verbatim for the occasion
without any gross incongruity. Bradlaugh had been the subject
of many sorts of newspaper notices in his time. Thirty years
ago, when the middle classes supposed him to be a revolutionist, the string of qualities which the press hung upon him were
all evil ones, great stress being laid on the fact that as he was an
atheist it would be an insult to God to admit him to Parliament.
When it became apparent that he was an anti-socialist force in
politics, he, without any recantation of his atheism, at once had
the string of evil qualities exchanged for a rosary of good ones;
but it is hardly necessary to add that neither the old badge nor
the new could ever give any inquirer the least clue to the sort of
man he actually was: he might have been Oliver Cromwell or
Wat Tyler or Jack Cade, Penn or Wilberforce or Wellington, the
late Mr Hampden of flat-earth-theory notoriety or Proudhon or
the Archbishop of Canterbury, for all the distinction such labels
could give him one way or the other. The worthlessness of
these abstract descriptions is recognized in practice every day.
Tax a stranger before a crowd with being a thief, a coward, and
a liar; and the crowd will suspend its judgment until you
answer the question, 'What's he done?' Attempt to take up a
collection for him on the ground that he is an upright, fearless,
high-principled hero; and the same question must be
answered before a penny goes into the hat.

The reader must therefore discount those partialities which
I have permitted myself to express in telling the stories of the
plays. They are as much beside the mark as any other example
of the sort of criticism which seeks to create an impression
favorable or otherwise to Ibsen by simply pasting his characters all over with good or bad conduct marks. If any person cares
to describe Hedda Gabler as a modern Lucretia who preferred
death to dishonor, and Thea Elvsted as an abandoned, perjured strumpet who deserted the man she had sworn before her
God to love, honor and obey until her death, the play contains

conclusive evidence establishing both points. If the critic goes on to argue that as Ibsen manifestly means to recommend Thea's conduct above Hedda's by making the end happier for her, the moral of the play is a vicious one, that, again, cannot be gainsaid. If, on the other hand, Ghosts be defended, as the dramatic critic of Piccadilly did defend it, because it throws into divine relief the beautiful figure of the simple and pious Pastor Manders, the fatal compliment cannot be parried. When you have called Mrs Alving an emancipated woman or an unprincipled one, Alving a debauchee or a victim of society, Nora a fearless and noble-hearted woman or a shocking little liar and an unnatural mother, Helmer a selfish hound or a model husband and father, according to your bias, you have said something which is at once true and false, and in both cases perfectly idle.

The statement that Ibsen's plays have an immoral tendency, is, in the sense in which it is used, quite true. Immorality does not necessarily imply mischievous conduct: it implies conduct, mischievous or not, which does not conform to current ideals. All religions begin with a revolt against morality, and perish when morality conquers them and stamps out such words as grace and sin, substituting for them morality and immorality. Bunyan places the town of Morality, with its respectable leading citizens Mr Legality and Mr Civility, close to the City of Destruction. In the United States today he would be imprisoned for this. Born as I was in the seventeenth-century atmosphere of mid-nineteenth century Ireland, I can remember when men who talked about morality were suspected of reading Tom Paine, if not of being downright atheists. Ibsen's attack on morality is a symptom of the revival of religion, not of its extinction. He is on the side of the prophets in having devoted himself to shewing that the spirit or will of Man is constantly outgrowing the ideals, and that therefore thoughtless conformity to them is constantly producing results no less tragic than those which follow thoughtless violation of them. Thus the main effect of his plays is to keep before the public the importance of being always prepared to act immorally. He reminds men that they ought to be as careful how they yield to a temptation to tell the truth as to a temptation to hold their tongues, and he urges upon women who either cannot or will not marry that the inducements held out to them by society to preserve their virginity and refrain from motherhood may be called temptations as logically as the inducements to the contrary held out by individuals and by their own temperaments, the practical decision depending on circumstances just as much as a decision between walking and taking a cab, however less trivial both the action and the circumstances may be. He protests against the ordinary assumption that there are certain moral institutions which justify all means used to maintain them, and insists that the supreme end shall be the inspired, eternal, ever growing one, not the external unchanging, artificial one; not the letter but the spirit; not the contract but the object of the contract; not the abstract law but the living well. And because the will to change our habits and thus defy morality arises before the intellect can reason out any racially beneficent purpose in the change, there is always an interval during which the individual can say no more than that he wants to behave immorally because he likes, and because he will feel constrained and unhappy if he acts otherwise. For this reason it is enormously important that we should 'mind our own business' and let other people do as they like unless we can prove some damage beyond the shock to our feelings and prejudices. It is easy to put revolutionary cases in which it is so impossible to draw the line that they will always be decided in practice more or less by physical force; but for all ordinary purposes of government and social conduct the distinction is a commonsense one. The plain working truth is that it is not only good for people to be shocked occasionally, but absolutely necessary to the progress of society that they should be shocked pretty often. But it is not good for people to be garrotted occasionally, or at all. That is why it is a mistake to treat an atheist as you treat a garrotter, or to put 'bad taste' on the footing of theft and murder. The need for freedom of evolution is the sole basis of toleration, the sole valid argument against Inquisitions and Censorships, the sole reason for not burning heretics and sending every eccentric person to the madhouse.

In short, our ideals, like the gods of old, are constantly demanding human sacrifices. Let none of them, says Ibsen, be placed above the obligation to prove itself worth the sacrifices it demands; and let everyone religiously refuse to sacrifice himself and others from the moment he loses his faith in the validity of the ideal. Of course it will be said here by incorrigibly slipshod readers that this, far from being immoral, is the highest morality; but I really will not waste further definition on those who will neither mean one thing or another by a word nor allow me to do so. Suffice it that among those who are not ridden by current ideals no question as to the ethical soundness of Ibsen's plays will ever arise; and among those who are so ridden his plays will be denounced as immoral, and cannot be defended against the accusation.

There can be no question as to the effect likely to be produced on an individual by his conversion from the ordinary acceptance of current ideals as safe standards of conduct, to the vigilant openmindedness of Ibsen. It must at once greatly deepen the sense of moral responsibility. Before conversion the individual anticipates nothing worse in the way of examination at the judgment bar of his conscience than such questions as, 'Have you kept the commandments?' 'Have you obeyed the law?' 'Have you attended church regularly? paid your rates and taxes to Caesar? and contributed, in reason, to charitable institutions?' It may be hard to do all these things; but it is still harder not to do them, as our ninety-nine moral cowards in the hundred well know. And even a scoundrel can do them all and yet live a worse life than the smuggler or prostitute who must answer 'No' all through the catechism. Substitute for such a technical examination one in which the whole point to be settled is, 'Guilty or Not Guilty?', one in which there is no more and no less respect for virginity than for

147

incontinence, for subordination than for rebellion, for legality than for illegality, for piety than for blasphemy: in short, for the standard qualities than for the standard faults, and immediately, instead of lowering the ethical standard by relaxing the tests of worth, you raise it by increasing their stringency to a point at which no mere Pharisaism or moral cowardice can pass them.

Naturally this does not please the Pharisee. The respectable lady of the strictest Church principles, who has brought up her children with such relentless regard to their ideal morality that if they have any spirit left in them by the time they arrive at years of independence they use their liberty to rush deliriously to the devil; this unimpeachable woman has always felt it unjust that the respect she wins should be accompanied by deep-seated detestation, whilst the latest spiritual heiress of Nell Gwynne, whom no respectable person dare bow to in the street, is a popular idol. The reason is – though the idealist lady does not know it – that Nell Gwynne is a better woman than she; and the abolition of the idealist test which brings her out a worse one, and its replacement by the realist test which would shew the true relation between them, would be a most desirable step forward in public morals, especially as it would act impartially, and set the good side of the Pharisee above the bad side of the Bohemian as ruthlessly as it would set the good side of the Bohemian above the bad side of the Pharisee.[2] For as long as convention goes counter to reality in these matters, people will be led into Hedda Gabler's error of making an ideal of vice. If we maintain the convention that the distinction between Catherine of Russia and Queen Victoria, between Nell Gwynne and Mrs Proudie, is the distinction between a bad woman and a good woman, we need not be surprised when those who sympathize with Catherine and Nell conclude that it is better to be a loose woman than a strict one, and go on recklessly to conceive a prejudice against teetotalism and monogamy, and a prepossession in favour of alcoholic excitement and promiscuous amours. Ibsen himself is kinder to the man who has gone his own way as a rake and a drunkard than to the man who is respectable because he dare not be otherwise. We find that the franker and healthier a boy is, the more certain is he to prefer pirates and highwaymen, or Dumas musketeers, to 'pillars of society' as his favorite heroes of romance. We have already seen both Ibsenites and anti-Ibsenites who seem to think that the cases of Nora and Mrs Elvsted are meant to establish a golden rule for women who wish to be 'emancipated': the said golden rule being simply, 'Run away from your husband'. But in Ibsen's view of life, that would come under the same condemnation as the ecclesiastical rule, 'Cleave to your husband until death do you part'. Most people know of a case or two in which it would be wise for a wife to follow the example of Nora or even of Mrs Elvsted. But they must also know cases in which the results of such a course would be as tragi-comic as those of Gregers Werle's attempt in The Wild Duck to do for the Ekdal household what Lona Hessel did for the Bernick household. What Ibsen insists on is that there is no golden rule; that conduct must justify itself by its effect upon life and not by its conformity to any rule or ideal. And since life consists in the fulfilment of the will, which is constantly growing, and cannot be fulfilled today under the conditions which secured its fulfilment yesterday, he claims afresh the old Protestant right of private judgment in questions of conduct as against all institutions, the so-called Protestant Churches themselves included.

Here I must leave the matter, merely reminding those who may think that I have forgotten to reduce Ibsenism to a formula for them, that its quintessence is that there is no formula.

WHAT IS THE NEW ELEMENT IN THE NORWEGIAN SCHOOL?

I NOW come to the question: Why, since neither human nature nor the specific talent of the playwright has changed since the days of Charles Dickens and Dumas *père*, are the works of Ibsen, of Strindberg, of Tolstoy, of Gorki, of Tchekov, of Brieux, so different from those of the great fictionists of the first half of the nineteenth century? Tolstoy actually imitated Dickens. Ibsen was not Dickens's superior as an observer, nor is Strindberg, nor Gorki, nor Tchekov, nor Brieux. Tolstoy and Ibsen together, gifted as they were, were not otherwise gifted or more gifted than Shakespear and Molière. Yet a generation which could read all Shakespear and Molière, Dickens and Dumas, from end to end without the smallest intellectual or ethical perturbation, was unable to get through a play by Ibsen or a novel by Tolstoy without having its intellectual and moral complacency upset, its religious faith shattered, and its notions of right and wrong conduct thrown into confusion and sometimes even reversed. It is as if these modern men had a spiritual force that was lacking in even the greatest of their forerunners. And yet, what evidence is there in the lives of Wagner, Ibsen, Tolstoy, Strindberg, Gorki, Tchekov and Brieux, that they were or are better men in any sense than Shakespear, Molière, Dickens and Dumas?

I myself have been told by people that the reading of a single book of mine or the witnessing of a single play has changed their whole lives; and among these are some who tell me that they cannot read Dickens at all, whilst all of them have read books and seen plays by authors obviously quite as gifted as I am, without finding anything more in them than pastime.

The explanation is to be found in what I believe to be a general law of the evolution of ideas. 'Every jest is an earnest in the womb of time,' says Peter Keegan in John Bull's Other Island. 'There's many a true word spoken in jest,' says the first villager you engage in philosophic discussion. All very serious revolutionary propositions begin as huge jokes. Otherwise they would be stamped out by the lynching of their first exponents. Even these exponents themselves have their revelations broken to them mysteriously through their sense of humor. Two friends of mine, travelling in remote parts of Spain, were asked by the shepherd what their religion was. 'Our religion,' replied one of them, a very highly cultivated author and traveller, with a sardonic turn, 'is that there is no God.' This reckless remark, taken seriously, might have provided nineteenth-century scepticism with a martyr. As it was, the countryside rang with laughter for days afterwards as the stupendous joke was handed round. But it was just by tolerating the blasphemy as a joke that the shepherds began to build it into the fabric of their minds. Being now safely lodged there, it will in due time develop its earnestness; and at last travellers will come who will be taken quite seriously when they say that the imaginary hidalgo in the sky whom the shepherds call God does indeed not exist. And they will remain godless, and call their streets Avenue Paul Bert and so forth, until in due time another joker will arrive with sidesplitting intimations that Shakespear's 'There's a divinity that shapes our ends, rough hew them how we will' was a strictly scientific statement of fact, and that 'neo-Darwinism' consists for the most part of grossly unscientific statements of superstitious nonsense. Which jest will in its due time come to its own as very solid earnest.

The same phenomenon may be noticed in our attitude towards matters of fact so obvious that no dispute can arise as to their existence. And here the power of laughter is astonishing. It is not enough to say merely that men enable themselves to endure the unbearablest nuisances and the deadliest scourges by setting up a merry convention that they are amusing. We must go further and face the fact that they actually are amused by them – that they are not laughing with the wrong side of the mouth. If you doubt it, read the popular fiction of the pre-Dickensian age, from the novels of Smollett to Tom Cringle's Log. Poverty in rags is a joke, yellow fever is a joke, drunkenness is a joke, dysentery is a joke, kickings, floggings, falls, frights, humiliations and painful accidents of all sorts are jokes. Henpecked husbands and termagant mothers-in-law are prime jokes. The infirmities of age and the inexperience and shyness of youth are jokes; and it is first-rate fun to insult and torment those that suffer from them.

We take some of these jokes seriously enough now. Humphrey Clinker may not have become absolutely unreadable (I have not tried him for more than forty years); but there is certainly a good deal in the book that is now simply disgusting to the class of reader that in its own day found it uproariously amusing. Much of Tom Cringle has become mere savagery: its humors are those of a donkey race. Also, the fun is forced; one sees beneath the determination of the old sea dog to put a hearty smiling English face on pain and discomfort, that he has not merely looked on at it, and that he did not really like it. The mask of laughter wears slowly off the shames and the evils; but men finally see them as they really are.

Sometimes the change occurs, not between two generations, but actually in the course of a single work by one author. Don Quixote and Mr Pickwick are recognized examples of characters introduced in pure ridicule, and presently gaining the affection and finally the respect of their authors. To them may be added Shakespear's Falstaff. Falstaff is introduced as a subordinate stage figure with no other function than to be robbed by the Prince and Poins, who was originally meant to be the *raisonneur* of the piece, and the chief figure among the prince's dissolute associates. But Poins soon fades into nothing, like several characters in Dickens's early works; whilst Falstaff develops into an enormous joke and an exquisitely mimicked human type. Only in the end the joke withers. The question comes to Shakespear: *Is* this really a laughing matter? Of course there can be only one answer; and Shakespear gives it as best he can by the mouth of the prince become king, who might, one thinks, have the decency to wait until he has redeemed his own character before assuming the right to lecture his boon companion. Falstaff, rebuked and humiliated, dies miserably. His followers are hanged, except Pistol, whose exclamation, 'Old do I wax; and from my weary limbs honour is cudgelled', is a melancholy exordium to an old age of beggary and imposture.

But suppose Shakespear had begun where he left off! Suppose he had been born at a time when, as the result of a long propaganda of health and temperance, sack had come to be called alcohol, alcohol had come to be called poison, corpulence had come to be regarded as either a disease or a breach of good manners, and a conviction had spread throughout society that the practice of consuming 'a half-pennyworth of bread to an intolerable deal of sack' was the cause of so much misery, crime and racial degeneration that whole States prohibited the sale of potable spirits altogether, and even moderate drinking was more and more regarded as a regrettable weakness! Suppose (to drive the change well home) the women in the great theatrical centres had completely lost that amused indulgence for the drunken man which still exists in some out-of-the-way places, and felt nothing but disgust and anger at the conduct and habits of Falstaff and Sir Toby Belch! Instead of Henry IV and The Merry Wives of Windsor, we should have had something like Zola's L'Assommoir. Indeed, we actually have Cassio, the last of Shakespear's gentleman-drunkards, talking like a temperance reformer, a fact which suggests that Shakespear had been roundly lectured for the offensive vulgarity of Sir Toby by some woman of refinement who refused to see the smallest fun in giving a knight such a name as Belch, with characteristics to correspond to it. Suppose, again, that the first performance of The Taming of the Shrew had led to a modern Feminist demonstration in the theatre, and forced upon Shakespear's consideration a whole century of agitatresses, from Mary Wollstonecraft to Mrs Fawcett and Mrs Pankhurst, is it not likely that the jest of Katharine and Petruchio would have become the earnest of Nora and Torvald Helmer?

In this light the difference between Dickens and Strindberg becomes intelligible. Strindberg simply refuses to regard the cases of Mrs Raddle and Mrs Macstinger and Mrs Jo Gargery as laughing matters. He insists on taking them seriously as cases of a tyranny which effects more degradation and causes more misery than all the political and sectarian oppressions known to history. Yet it cannot be said that Strindberg, even at his fiercest, is harder on women than Dickens. No doubt his case against them is far more complete, because he does not shirk the specifically sexual factors in it. But this really softens it. If Dickens had allowed us, were it but for an instant, to see Jo Gargery and Mrs Jo as husband and wife, he would perhaps have been accused by fools of immodesty; but we should have at least some more human impression than the one left by an unredeemed shrew married to a grown-up terrified child. It was George Gissing, a modern realist, who first pointed out the power and truth to nature of Dickens's women, and the fact that, funny as they are, they are mostly detestable. Even the amiable ones are silly and sometimes disastrous. When the few good ones are agreeable they are not specifically feminine: they are the Dickensian good man in petticoats; yet they lack that strength which they would have had if Dickens had seen clearly that there is no such species in creation as 'Woman, lovely woman', the woman being simply the female of the human species, and that to have one conception of humanity for the woman and another for the man, or one law for the woman and another for the man, or one artistic convention for woman and another for man, or, for the matter of that, a skirt for the woman and a pair of breeches for the man, is as unnatural, and in the long run as unworkable, as one law for the mare and another for the horse. Roughly it may be said that all Dickens's studies from life of the differentiated creatures our artificial sex institutions have made of women are, for all their truth, either vile or ridiculous or both. Betsy Trotwood is a dear because she is an old bachelor in petticoats, a manly woman, like all good women; good men being equally all womanly men. Miss Havisham, an insanely womanly woman, is a horror, a monster, though a Chinese monster: that is, not a natural one, but one produced by deliberate perversion of her humanity. In comparison, Strindberg's women are positively amiable and attractive. The general impression that Strindberg's women are the revenge of a furious woman-hater for his domestic failures, whilst Dickens is a genial idealist (he had little better luck domestically, by the way), is produced solely by Dickens either making fun of the affair or believing that women are born so and must be admitted to the fellowship of the Holy Ghost on a feminine instead of a human basis; whilst Strindberg takes womanliness with deadly seriousness as an evil not to be submitted to for a moment without vehement protest and demand for quite practicable reform. The nurse in his play who wheedles her old nursling and then slips a strait waistcoat on him revolts us; but she is really ten times more lovable and sympathetic than Sairey Gamp, an abominable creature whose very soul is putrid, and who is yet true to life. It is very noteworthy that none of the modern writers who take life as seriously as Ibsen have ever been able to bring themselves to depict depraved people so pitilessly as Dickens and Thackeray and even the genial Dumas *père*. Ibsen was grim enough in all conscience: no man has said more terrible things both privately and publicly; and yet there is not one of Ibsen's characters who is not, in the old phrase, the temple of the Holy Ghost, and who does not move you at moments by the sense of that mystery. The Dickens-Thackeray spirit is, in comparison, that of a Punch and Judy showman, who is never restrained from whacking his little figures unmercifully by the sense that they, too, are images of God, and, 'but for the grace of God', very like himself. Dickens does deepen very markedly towards this as he grows older, though it is impossible to pretend that Mrs Wilfer is treated with less levity than Mrs Nickleby; but to Ibsen, from beginning to end, every human being is a sacrifice, whilst to Dickens he is a farce. And there you have the whole difference. No character drawn by Dickens is more ridiculous than Hjalmar Ekdal in The Wild Duck, or more eccentric than old Ekdal, whose toy game-preserve in the garret is more fantastic than the house of Miss Havisham; and yet these Ekdals wring the heart whilst Micawber and Chivery (who sits between the lines of clothes hung out to dry because 'it reminds him of groves' as Hjalmar's garret reminds old Ekdal of bear forests) only shake the sides.

It may be that if Dickens could read these lines he would say that the defect was not in him but in his readers; and that if we will return to his books now that Ibsen has opened our eyes we will have to admit that he also saw more in the soul of Micawber than mere laughing gas. And indeed one cannot forget the touches of kindliness and gallantry which ennoble his mirth. Still, between the man who occasionally remembered and the man who never forgot, between Dick Swiveller and Ulrik Brendel, there is a mighty difference. The most that can be said to minimize it is that some of the difference is certainly due to the difference in the attitude of the reader. When an author's works produce violent controversy, and are new, people are apt to read them with that sort of seriousness which is very appropriately called deadly; that is, with a sort of solemn paralysis of every sense except a quite abstract and baseless momentousness which has no more to do with the contents of the author's works than the horrors of a man in delirium tremens have to do with real rats and snakes. The Bible is a sealed literature to most of us because we cannot read it naturally and unsophisticatedly: we are like the old lady who was edified by the word Mesopotamia, or Samuel Butler's Chowbok, who was converted to Christianity by the effect on his imagination of the prayer for Queen Adelaide. Many years elapsed before those who were impressed with Beethoven's music ventured to enjoy it sufficiently to discover what a large part of it is a riot of whimsical fun. As to Ibsen, I remember a performance of The Wild Duck, at which the late Clement Scott pointed out triumphantly that the play was so absurd that even the champions of Ibsen could not help laughing at it. It had not occurred to him that Ibsen could laugh like other men. Not until an author has become so familiar that we are quite at our ease with him, and are up to his tricks of manner, do we cease to imagine that he is, relatively to older writers, terribly serious.

Still, the utmost allowance we can make for this difference does not persuade us that Dickens took the improvidence and futility of Micawber as Ibsen took the improvidence and futility of Hjalmar Ekdal. The difference is plain in the works of Dickens himself; for the Dickens of the second half of the nineteenth century (the Ibsen half) is a different man from the Dickens of the first half. From Hard Times and Little Dorrit to Our Mutual Friend every one of Dickens's books lays a heavy burden on our conscience without flattering us with any hopes of a happy ending. But from The Pickwick Papers to Bleak House you can read and laugh and cry and go happy to bed after forgetting yourself in a jolly book. I have pointed out elsewhere how Charles Lever, after producing a series of books in which the old manner of rollicking through life as if all its follies and failures were splendid jokes, and all its conventional enjoyments and attachments delightful and sincere, suddenly supplied the highly appreciative Dickens (as editor of All the Year Round) with a quite new sort of novel, called A Day's Ride: A Life's Romance, which affected both Dickens and the public very unpleasantly by the bitter but tonic flavor we now know as Ibsenism; for the hero began as that uproarious old joke, the boaster who, being a coward, is led into all sorts of dangerous situations, like Bob Acres and Mr Winkle, and then unexpectedly made them laugh very much on the wrong side of their mouths, exactly as if he were a hero by Ibsen, Strindberg, Turgenieff, Tolstoy, Gorki, Tchekov or Brieux. And here there was no question of the author being taken too gloomily. His readers, full of Charles O'Malley and Mickey Free, were approaching the work with the most unsuspicious confidence in its entire jollity. The shock to the security of their senseless laughter caught them utterly unprepared; and they resented it accordingly.

Now that a reaction against realism has set in, and the old jolly ways are coming into fashion again, it is perhaps not so easy as it once was to conceive the extraordinary fascination of this mirthless comedy, this tragedy that stripped the soul naked instead of bedizening it in heroic trappings. But if you have not experienced this fascination yourself, and cannot conceive it, you may take my word for it that it exists, and operates with such power that it puts Shakespear himself out of countenance. And even for those who are in full reaction against it, it can hardly be possible to go back from the death of Hedwig Ekdal to the death of Little Nell otherwise than as a grown man goes down on all fours and pretends to be a bear for the amusement of his children. Nor need we regret this: there are noble compensations for our increase of wisdom and sorrow. After Hedwig you may not be able to cry over Little Nell, but at least you can read Little Dorrit without calling it twaddle, as some of its first critics did. The jests do not become poorer as they mature into earnest. It was not through joyless poverty of soul that Shelley never laughed, but through an enormous apprehension and realization of the gravity of things that seemed mere fun to other men. If there is no Swiveller and no Trabbs's boy in The Pilgrim's Progress, and if Mr Badman is drawn as Ibsen would have drawn him and not as Sheridan would have seen him, it does not follow that there is less strength (and joy is a quality of strength) in Bunyan than in Sheridan and Dickens. After all, the salvation of the world depends on the men who will not take evil good-humoredly, and whose laughter destroys the fool instead of encouraging him. 'Rightly to be great,' said Shakespear when he had come to the end of mere buffoonery, 'is greatly to find quarrel in a straw.' The English cry of 'Amuse us – take things easily – dress up the world prettily for us' seems mere cowardice to the strong souls that dare look facts in the face; and just so far as people cast off levity and idolatry they find themselves able to bear the company of Bunyan and Shelley, of Ibsen and Strindberg and the great Russian realists, and unable to tolerate the sort of laughter that African tribes cannot restrain when a man is flogged or an animal trapped and wounded. They are gaining strength and wisdom; gaining, in short, that sort of life which we call the life everlasting, a sense of which is worth, for pure well-being alone, all the brutish jollities of Tom Cringle and Humphrey Clinker, and even of Falstaff, Pecksniff and Micawber.

THE TECHNICAL NOVELTY IN
IBSEN'S PLAYS

IT is a striking and melancholy example of the preoccupation of critics with phrases and formulas to which they have given life by taking them into the tissue of their own living minds, and which therefore seem and feel vital and important to them whilst they are to everybody else the deadest and dreariest rubbish (this is the great secret of academic dryasdust), that to this day they remain blind to a new technical factor in the art of popular stage-play making which every considerable playwright has been thrusting under their noses night after night for a whole generation. This technical factor in the play is the discussion. Formerly you had in what was called a well-made play an exposition in the first act, a situation in the second and unravelling in the third. Now you have exposition, situation and discussion; and the discussion is the test of the playwright. The critics protest in vain. They declare that discussions are not dramatic, and that art should not be didactic. Neither the playwrights nor the public take the smallest notice of them. The discussion conquered Europe in Ibsen's Doll's House; and now the serious playwright recognizes in the discussion not only the main test of his highest powers, but also the real centre of his play's interest. Sometimes he even takes every possible step to assure the public beforehand that his play will be fitted with that newest improvement.

This was inevitable if the drama was ever again to be raised above the childish demand for fables without morals. Children have a settled arbitrary morality: therefore to them moralizing is nothing but an intolerable platitudinizing. The morality of the grown-up is also very largely a settled morality, either purely conventional and of no ethical significance, like the rule of the road or the rule that when you ask for a yard of ribbon the shopkeeper shall give you thirty-six inches and not interpret the word yard as he pleases, or else too obvious in its ethics to leave any room for discussion: for instance, that if the boots keeps you waiting too long for your shaving water you must not plunge your razor into his throat in your irritation, no matter how great an effort of self-control your forbearance may cost you.

Now when a play is only a story of how a villain tries to separate an honest young pair of betrothed lovers; to gain the hand of the woman by calumny; and to ruin the man by forgery, murder, false witness, and other commonplaces of the Newgate Calendar, the introduction of a discussion would clearly be ridiculous. There is nothing for sane people to discuss; and any attempt to Chadbandize on the wickedness of such crimes is at once resented as, in Milton's phrase, 'moral babble'.

But this sort of drama is soon exhausted by people who go often to the theatre. In twenty visits one can see every possible change rung on all the available plots and incidents out of which plays of this kind can be manufactured. The illusion of reality is soon lost: in fact it may be doubted whether any adult ever entertains it: it is only to very young children that the fairy queen is anything but an actress. But at the age when we cease to mistake the figures on the stage for *dramatis personae*, and know that they are actors and actresses, the charm of the performer begins to assert itself; and the child who would have been cruelly hurt by being told that the Fairy Queen was only Miss Smith dressed up to look like one, becomes the man who goes to the theatre expressly to see Miss Smith, and is fascinated by her skill or beauty to the point of delighting in plays which would be unendurable to him without her. Thus we get plays 'written round' popular performers, and popular performers who give value to otherwise useless plays by investing them with their own attractiveness. But all these enterprises are, commercially speaking,

desperately precarious. To begin with, the supply of performers whose attraction is so far independent of the play that
their inclusion in the cast sometimes makes the difference
between success and failure is too small to enable all our
theatres, or even many of them, to depend on their actors
rather than on their plays. And to finish with, no actor can
make bricks entirely without straw. From Grimaldi to Soth-
ern, Jefferson, and Henry Irving (not to mention living actors)
we have had players succeeding once in a lifetime in grafting
on to a play which would have perished without them some
figure imagined wholly by themselves; but none of them has
been able to repeat the feat, nor to save many of the plays in
which he has appeared from failure. In the long run nothing
can retain the interest of the playgoer after the theatre has
lost its illusion for his childhood, and its glamor for his
adolescence, but a constant supply of interesting plays; and
this is specially true in London, where the expense and
trouble of theatregoing have been raised to a point at which
it is surprising that sensible people of middle age go to the
theatre at all. As a matter of fact, they mostly stay at home.

Now an interesting play cannot in the nature of things
mean anything but a play in which problems of conduct and
character of personal importance to the audience are raised
and suggestively discussed. People have a thrifty sense of
taking away something from such plays: they not only have
had something for their money, but they retain that something as a permanent possession. Consequently none of the
commonplaces of the box office hold good of such plays. In
vain does the experienced acting manager declare that people
want to be amused and not preached at in the theatre; that
they will not stand long speeches; that a play must not contain
more than 18,000 words; that it must not begin before nine
nor last beyond eleven; that there must be no politics and no
religion in it; that breach of these golden rules will drive
people to the variety theatres; that there must be a woman of
bad character, played by a very attractive actress, in the piece;

and so on and so forth. All these counsels are valid for plays in which there is nothing to discuss. They may be disregarded by the playwright who is a moralist and a debater as well as a dramatist. From him, within the inevitable limits set by the clock and by the physical endurance of the human frame, people will stand anything as soon as they are matured enough and cultivated enough to be susceptible to the appeal of his particular form of art. The difficulty at present is that mature and cultivated people do not go to the theatre, just as they do not read penny novelets; and when an attempt is made to cater for them they do not respond to it in time, partly because they have not the habit of playgoing, and partly because it takes too long for them to find out that the new theatre is not like all the other theatres. But when they do at last find their way there, the attraction is not the firing of blank cartridges at one another by actors, nor the pretence of falling down dead that ends the stage combat, nor the simulation of erotic thrills by a pair of stage lovers, nor any of the other tomfooleries called action, but the exhibition and discussion of the character and conduct of stage figures who are made to appear real by the art of the playwright and the performers.

This, then, is the extension of the old dramatic form effected by Ibsen. Up to a certain point in the last act, A Doll's House is a play that might be turned into a very ordinary French drama by the excision of a few lines, and the substitution of a sentimental happy ending for the famous last scene: indeed the very first thing the theatrical wiseacres did with it was to effect exactly this transformation, with the result that the play thus pithed had no success and attracted no notice worth mentioning. But at just that point in the last act, the heroine very unexpectedly (by the wiseacres) stops her emotional acting and says: 'We must sit down and discuss all this that has been happening between us.' And it was by this new technical feature, this addition of a new movement, as musicians would say, to the dramatic form, that A Doll's

House conquered Europe and founded a new school of dramatic art.

Since that time the discussion has expanded far beyond the limits of the last ten minutes of an otherwise 'well-made' play. The disadvantage of putting the discussion at the end was not only that it came when the audience was fatigued, but that it was necessary to see the play over again, so as to follow the earlier acts in the light of the final discussion, before it became fully intelligible. The practical utility of this book is due to the fact that unless the spectator at an Ibsen play has read the pages referring to it beforehand, it is hardly possible for him to get its bearings at a first hearing if he approaches it, as most spectators still do, with conventional idealist prepossessions. Accordingly, we now have plays, including some of my own, which begin with discussion and end with action, and others in which the discussion inter-penetrates the action from beginning to end. When Ibsen invaded England, discussion had vanished from the stage; and women could not write plays. Within twenty years women were writing better plays than men; and these plays were passionate arguments from beginning to end. The action of such plays consists of a case to be argued. If the case is uninteresting or stale or badly conducted or obviously trumped up, the play is a bad one. If it is important and novel and convincing, or at least disturbing, the play is a good one. But anyhow the play in which there is no argument and no case no longer counts as serious drama. It may still please the child in us as Punch and Judy does; but nobody nowadays pretends to regard the well-made play as anything more than a commercial product which is not in question when modern schools of serious drama are under discussion. Indeed within ten years of the production of A Doll's House in London, audiences had become so derisive of the more obvious and hackneyed features of the methods of Sardou that it became dangerous to resort to them; and playwrights who persisted in 'constructing' plays in the old French manner lost ground not for lack of ideas, but because their technique was unbearably out of fashion.

In the new plays, the drama arises through a conflict of unsettled ideals rather than through vulgar attachments, rapacities, generosities, resentments, ambitions, misunderstandings, oddities and so forth as to which no moral question is raised. The conflict is not between clear right and wrong: the villain is as conscientious as the hero, if not more so: in fact, the question which makes the play interesting (when it *is* interesting) is which is the villain and which the hero. Or, to put it another way, there are no villains and no heroes. This strikes the critics mainly as a departure from dramatic art; but it is really the inevitable return to nature which ends all the merely technical fashions. Now the natural is mainly the everyday; and its climaxes must be, if not everyday, at least everylife, if they are to have any importance for the spectator. Crimes, fights, big legacies, fires, shipwrecks, battles and thunderbolts are mistakes in a play, even when they can be effectively simulated. No doubt they may acquire dramatic interest by putting a character through the test of an emergency; but the test is likely to be too obviously theatrical, because, as the playwright cannot in the nature of things have much experience of such catastrophes, he is forced to substitute a set of conventions or conjectures for the feelings they really produce.

In short, pure accidents are not dramatic: they are only anecdotic. They may be sensational, impressive, provocative, ruinous, curious or a dozen other things; but they have no specifically dramatic interest. There is no drama in being knocked down or run over. The catastrophe in Hamlet would not be in the least dramatic had Polonius fallen downstairs and broken his neck, Claudius succumbed to delirium tremens, Hamlet forgotten to breathe in the intensity of his philosophic speculation, Ophelia died of Danish measles, Laertes been shot by the palace sentry, and Rosencrantz and Guildenstern drowned in the North Sea. Even as it is, the

Queen, who poisons herself by accident, has an air of being polished off to get her out of the way; her death is the one dramatic failure of the piece. Bushels of good paper have been inked in vain by writers who imagined they could produce a tragedy by killing everyone in the last act accidentally. As a matter of fact no accident, however sanguinary, can produce a moment of real drama, though a difference of opinion between husband and wife as to living in town or country might be the beginning of an appalling tragedy or a capital comedy.

It may be said that everything is an accident; that Othello's character is an accident, Iago's character another accident, and the fact that they happened to come together in the Venetian service an even more accidental accident. Also that Torvald Helmer might just as likely have married Mrs Nickleby as Nora. Granting this trifling for what it is worth, the fact remains that marriage is no more an accident than birth or death: that is, it is expected to happen to everybody. And if every man has a good deal of Torvald Helmer in him, and every woman a good deal of Nora, neither their characters nor their meeting and marrying are accidents. Othello, though entertaining, pitiful and resonant with the thrills a master of language can produce by mere artistic sonority is certainly much more accidental than A Doll's House; but it is correspondingly less important and interesting to us. It has been kept alive, not by its manufactured misunderstandings and stolen handkerchiefs and the like, nor even by its orchestral verse, but by its exhibition and discussion of human nature, marriage, and jealousy; and it would be a prodigiously better play if it were a serious discussion of the highly interesting problem of how a simple Moorish soldier would get on with a 'supersubtle' Venetian lady of fashion if he married her. As it is, the play turns on a mistake; and though a mistake can produce a murder, which is the vulgar substitute for a tragedy, it cannot produce a real tragedy in the modern sense. Reflective people are not more interested in the Chamber of

Horrors than in their own homes, nor in murderers, victims and villains than in themselves; and the moment a man has acquired sufficient reflective power to cease gaping at waxworks, he is on his way to losing interest in Othello, Desdemona, and Iago exactly to the extent to which they become interesting to the police. Cassio's weakness for drink comes much nearer home to most of us than Othello's strangling and throat cutting, or Iago's theatrical confidence trick. The proof is that Shakespear's professional colleagues, who exploited all his sensational devices, and piled up torture on murder and incest on adultery until they had far out-Heroded Herod, are now unmemorable and unplayable. Shakespear survives because he coolly treated the sensational horrors of his borrowed plots as inorganic theatrical accessories, using them simply as pretexts for dramatizing human character as it exists in the normal world. In enjoying and discussing his plays we unconsciously discount the combats and murders; commentators are never so astray (and consequently so ingenious) as when they take Hamlet seriously as a madman, Macbeth as a homicidal Highlander, and impish humorists like Richard and Iago as lurid villains of the Renascence. The plays in which these figures appear could be changed into comedies without altering a hair of their beards. Shakespear, had anyone been intelligent enough to tax him with this, would perhaps have said that most crimes are accidents that happen to people exactly like ourselves, and that Macbeth, under propitious circumstances, would have made an exemplary rector of Stratford, a real criminal being a defective monster, a human accident, useful on the stage for minor parts such as Don Johns, second murderers, and the like. Anyhow, the fact remains that Shakespear survives by what he has in common with Ibsen, and not by what he has in common with Webster and the rest. Hamlet's surprise at finding that he 'lacks gall' to behave in the idealistically conventional manner, and that no extremity of rhetoric about the duty of revenging 'a dear father slain' and exterminating the 'bloody bawdy villain' who murdered him seems to make any difference in their domestic relations in the palace in Elsinore, still keeps us talking about him and going to the theatre to listen to him, whilst the older Hamlets, who never had any Ibsenist hesitations, and shammed madness, and entangled the courtiers in the arras and burnt them, and stuck hard to the theatrical school of the fat boy in Pickwick ('I wants to make your flesh creep'), are as dead as John Shakespear's mutton.

We have progressed so rapidly on this point under the impulse given to the drama by Ibsen that it seems strange now to contrast him favorably with Shakespear on the ground that he avoided the old catastrophes which left the stage strewn with the dead at the end of an Elizabethan tragedy. For perhaps the most plausible reproach levelled at Ibsen by modern critics of his own school is just that survival of the old school in him which makes the death rate so high in his last acts. Do Oswald Alving, Hedvig Ekdal, Rosmer and Rebecca, Hedda Gabler, Solness, Eyolf, Borkman, Rubeck and Irene die dramatically natural deaths, or are they slaughtered in the classic and Shakespearean manner, partly because the audience expects blood for its money, partly because it is difficult to make people attend seriously to anything except by startling them with some violent calamity? It is so easy to make out a case for either view that I shall not argue the point. The post-Ibsen playwrights apparently think that Ibsen's homicides and suicides were forced. In Tchekov's Cherry Orchard, for example, where the sentimental ideals of our amiable, cultured, Schumann-playing propertied class are reduced to dust and ashes by a hand not less deadly than Ibsen's because it is so much more caressing, nothing more violent happens than that the family cannot afford to keep up its old house. In Granville-Barker's plays, the campaign against our society is carried on with all Ibsen's implacability; but the one suicide (in Waste) is unhistorical; for neither Parnell nor Dilke, who were the actual cases in point of the waste which was the subject of the play, killed himself. I myself have been reproached because the characters in my plays 'talk but do nothing', meaning that they do not commit felonies. As a matter of fact we have come to see that it is no true *dénouement* to cut the Gordian knot as Alexander did with a stroke of the sword. If people's souls are tied up by law and public opinion it is much more tragic to leave them to wither in these bonds than to end their misery and relieve the salutary compunction of the audience by outbreaks of violence. Judge Brack was, on the whole, right when he said that people dont do such things. If they did, the idealists would be brought to their senses very quickly indeed.

But in Ibsen's plays the catastrophe, even when it seems forced, and when the ending of the play would be more tragic without it, is never an accident; and the play never exists for its sake. His nearest to an accident is the death of little Eyolf, who falls off a pier and is drowned. But this instance only reminds us that there is one good dramatic use for an accident – it can awaken people. When England wept over the deaths of little Nell and Paul Dombey, the strong soul of Ruskin was moved to scorn; to novelists who were at a loss to make their books sell he offered the formula: When at a loss, kill a child. But Ibsen did not kill little Eyolf to manufacture pathos. The surest way to achieve a thoroughly bad performance of Little Eyolf is to conceive it as a sentimental tale of a drowned darling. Its drama lies in the awakening of Allmers and his wife to the despicable quality and detestable rancors of the life they have been idealizing as blissful and poetic. They are so sunk in their dream that the awakening can be effected only by a violent shock. And that is just the one dramatically useful thing an accident can do. It can shock. Hence the accident that befalls Eyolf.

As to the deaths in Ibsen's last acts, they are a sweeping up of the remains of dramatically finished people. Solness's fall from the tower is as obviously symbolic as Phaeton's fall from the chariot of the sun. Ibsen's dead bodies are those of the exhausted or destroyed: he does not kill Hilda, for instance, as Shakespear killed Juliet. He is ruthless enough with Hedvig and Eyolf because he wants to use their deaths to expose their parents; but if he had written Hamlet nobody would have been killed in the last act except perhaps Horatio, whose correct nullity might have provoked Fortinbras to let some of the moral sawdust out of him with his sword. For Shakespearean deaths in Ibsen you must go back to Lady Inger and the plays of his nonage, with which this book is not concerned.

The drama was born of old from the union of two desires: the desire to have a dance and the desire to hear a story. The dance became a rant, the story became a situation. When Ibsen began to make plays, the art of the dramatist had shrunk into the art of contriving a situation. And it was held that the stranger the situation, the better the play. Ibsen saw that, on the contrary, the more familiar the situation, the more interesting the play. Shakespear had put ourselves on the stage but not our situations. Our uncles seldom murder our fathers, and cannot legally marry our mothers; we do not meet witches; our kings are not as a rule stabbed and succeeded by their stabbers; and when we raise money by bills we do not promise to pay pounds of our flesh. Ibsen supplies the want left by Shakespear. He gives us not only ourselves, but ourselves in our own situations. The things that happen to his stage figures are things that happen to us. One consequence is that his plays are much more important to us than Shakespear's. Another is that they are capable both of hurting us cruelly and of filling us with excited hopes of escape from idealistic tyrannies, and with visions of intenser life in the future.

Changes in technique follow inevitably from these changes in the subject matter of the play. When a dramatic poet can give you hopes and visions, such old maxims as that stage-craft is the art of preparation become boyish, and may be left to those unfortunate playwrights who, being unable to make anything really interesting happen on the stage, have to acquire the art of continually persuading the audience that it is going to happen presently. When he can stab people to the heart by shewing them the meanness or cruelty of something they did yesterday and intend to do tomorrow, all the old tricks to catch and hold their attention become the silliest of superfluities. The play called The Murder of Gonzago, which Hamlet makes the players act before his uncle, is artlessly constructed; but it produces a greater effect on Claudius than the Oedipus of Sophocles, because it is about himself. The writer who practises the art of Ibsen therefore discards all the old tricks of preparation, catastrophe, *dénouement* and so forth, without thinking about it, just as a modern rifleman never dreams of providing himself with powder horns, percussion caps, and wads: indeed he does not know the use of them. Ibsen substituted a terrible art of sharpshooting at the audience, trapping them, fencing with them, aiming always at the sorest spot in their consciences. Never mislead an audience, was an old rule. But the new school will trick the spectator into forming a meanly false judgment, and then convict him of it in the next act, often to his grievous mortification. When you despise something you ought to take off your hat to, or admire and imitate something you ought to loathe, you cannot resist the dramatist who knows how to touch these morbid spots in you and make you see that they are morbid. The dramatist knows that as long as he is teaching and saving his audience, he is as sure of their strained attention as a dentist is, or the Angel of the Annunciation. And though he may use all the magic of art to make you forget the pain he causes you or to enhance the joy of the hope and courage he awakens, he is never occupied in the old work of manufacturing interest and expectation with materials that have neither novelty, significance nor relevance to the experience or prospects of the spectators.

Hence a cry has arisen that the post-Ibsen play is not a play, and that its technique, not being the technique described by Aristotle, is not a technique at all. I will not enlarge on this: the fun poked at my friend Mr A. B. Walkley in the prologue of Fanny's First Play need not be repeated here. But I may remind him that the new technique is new only on the modern stage. It has been used by preachers and orators ever since speech was invented. It is the technique of playing upon the human conscience; and it has been practised by the playwright whenever the playwright has been capable of it. Rhetoric, irony, argument, paradox, epigram, parable, the rearrangement of haphazard facts into orderly and intelligent situations, these are both the oldest and the newest arts of the drama; and your plot construction and art of preparation are only the tricks of theatrical talent and the shifts of moral sterility, not the weapons of dramatic genius. In the theatre of Ibsen we are not flattered spectators killing an idle hour with an ingenious and amusing entertainment: we are 'guilty creatures sitting at a play'; and the technique of pastime is no more applicable than at a murder trial.

The technical novelties of the Ibsen and post-Ibsen plays are, then: first, the introduction of the discussion and its development until it so overspreads and interpenetrates the action that it finally assimilates it, making play and discussion practically identical; and, second, as a consequence of making the spectators themselves the persons of the drama, and the incidents of their own lives its incidents, the disuse of the old stage tricks by which audiences had to be induced to take an interest in unreal people and improbable circumstances, and the substitution of a forensic technique of recrimination, disillusion and penetration through ideals to the truth, with a free use of all the rhetorical and lyrical arts of the orator, the preacher, the pleader and the rhapsodist.

NEEDED: AN IBSEN THEATRE

IT must now be plain to my readers that the doctrine taught by Ibsen can never be driven home from the stage whilst his plays are presented to us in haphazard order at the commercial theatres. Indeed our commercial theatres are so well aware of this that they have from the first regarded Ibsen as hopelessly uncommercial; he might as well never have lived as far as they are concerned. Even the new advanced theatres which now deal freely with what I have called post-Ibsenist plays hardly meddle with him. Had it not been for the great national service disinterestedly rendered by Mr William Archer in giving us a complete translation of Ibsen's plays (a virtually unremunerated public service which I hope the State will recognize fitly), Ibsen would be less known in England than Swedenborg. By losing his vital contribution to modern thought we are losing ground relatively to the countries which, like Germany, have made his works familiar to their playgoers. But even in Germany, Ibsen's meaning is seen only by glimpses. What we need is a theatre devoted primarily to Ibsen as the Bayreuth Festspielhaus is devoted to Wagner. I have shewn how the plays, as they succeed one another, are parts of a continuous discussion; how the difficulty left by one is dealt with in the next; how Mrs Alving is a reply to your hasty remark that Nora Helmer ought to be ashamed of herself for leaving her husband; how Gregers Werle warns you not to be as great a fool in your admiration of Lona Hessel as of Patient Grisel. The plays should, like Wagner's Ring, be performed in cycles; so that Ibsen may hunt you down from position to position until you are finally cornered.

The larger truth of the matter is that modern European literature and music now form a Bible far surpassing in

importance to us the ancient Hebrew Bible that has served us
so long. The notion that inspiration is something that happened thousands of years ago, and was then finished and
done with, never to occur again, in other words, the theory
that God retired from business at that period and has not
since been heard from, is as silly as it is blasphemous. He
who does not believe that revelation is continuous does not
believe in revelation at all, however familiar his parrot's
tongue and pewsleepy ear may be with the word. There
comes a time when the formula 'Also sprach Zarathustra'
succeeds to the formula 'Thus saith the Lord', and when the
parable of the doll's house is more to our purpose than the
parable of the prodigal son. When Bunyan published The
Pilgrim's Progress, his first difficulty was with the literal
people who said, 'There is no such individual in the directory
as Christian, and no such place in the gazetteer as the City of
Destruction: therefore you are a liar.' Bunyan replied by citing
the parables; asking, in effect, whether the story of the wise
and foolish virgins is also a lie. A couple of centuries or so
later, when I myself wrote a play for the Salvation Army to
shew them that the dramatic method might be used for their
gospel as effectively as the lyric or orchestral method, I was
told that unless I could guarantee that the persons in my play
actually existed, and the incidents had actually occurred, I,
like Bunyan, would be regarded by the elderly soldiers in the
army as no better than Ananias. As it was useless for me to
try to make these simple souls understand that in real life
truth is revealed by parables and falsehood supported by
facts, I had to leave the army to its oratorical metaphors and
to its popular songs about heartbroken women waiting for
the footsteps of their drunken husbands, and hearing instead
the joyous step of the converted man whose newly found
salvation will dry all their tears. I had not the heart to suggest
that these happy pairs were as little authentic as The Second
Mrs Tanqueray; for I spied behind the army's confusion of
truth with mere fact the old doubt whether anything good

can come out of the theatre, a doubt as inveterate and neither more nor less justifiable than the doubt of our Secularists whether anything good can come out of the gospels.

But I think Ibsen has proved the right of the drama to take scriptural rank, and his own right to canonical rank as one of the major prophets of the modern Bible. The sooner we recognize that rank and give up the idea of trying to make a fashionable entertainment of his plays the better. It ends in our not performing them at all, and remaining in barbarous and dangerous ignorance of the case against idealism. We want a frankly doctrinal theatre. There is no more reason for making a doctrinal theatre inartistic than for putting a cathedral organ out of tune: indeed all experience shews that doctrine alone nerves us to the effort called for by the greatest art. I therefore suggest that even the sciolists and voluptuaries who care for nothing in art but its luxuries and its executive feats are as strongly interested in the establishment of such a theatre as those for whom the What is always more important than the How, if only because the How cannot become really magical until such magic is indispensable to the revelation of an all-important What.

I do not suggest that the Ibsen theatre should confine itself to Ibsen any more than the Established Church confines itself to Jeremiah. The post-Ibsenists could also be expounded there; and Strindberg should have his place, were it only as Devil's Advocate. But performances should be in the order of academic courses, designed so as to take audiences over the whole ground as Ibsen and his successors took them; so that the exposition may be consecutive. Otherwise the doctrine will not be interesting, and the audiences will not come regularly. The efforts now being made to regenerate the drama are often wasted through lack of doctrinal conviction and consequent want of system, the net result being an irresolute halting between the doctrinal and the merely entertaining.

For this sort of enterprise an endowment is necessary,

because commercial capital is not content in a theatre with reasonable interest; it demands great gains even at the cost of great hazards. Besides, nobody will endow mere pleasure, whereas doctrine can always command endowment. It is the foolish disclaiming of doctrine that keeps dramatic art unendowed. When we ask for an endowed theatre we always take the greatest pains to assure everybody that we do not mean anything unpleasantly serious and that our endowed theatre will be as bright and cheery (meaning as low and common) as the commercial theatres. As a result of which we get no endowment. When we have the sense to profit by this lesson and promise that our endowed theatre will be an important place, and that it will make people of low tastes and tribal or commercial ideas horribly uncomfortable by its efforts to bring conviction of sin to them, we shall get endowment as easily as the religious people who are not foolishly ashamed to ask for what they want.

THE PERFECT WAGNERITE

A COMMENTARY ON THE NIBLUNG'S RING

PREFACE TO THE FOURTH EDITION

MUCH water, some of it deeply stained with blood, has passed under the bridges since this book was first published twenty-four years ago. Musically Wagner is now more old-fashioned than Handel and Bach, Mozart and Beethoven, whose fashions have perished though their music remains; whilst his own fashion has been worn to rags by young composers in their first efforts to draw the bow of Ulysses. Finally, it has been discarded as Homerically impossible; and England, after two centuries of imitative negligibility, has suddenly flung into the field a cohort of composers whose methods have made a technical revolution in musical composition so complete that the conductor does not dare to correct the most cacophonous errors in band parts lest the composer should have intended them, and looks in vain for key signatures because young men no longer write in keys but just mark their notes flat or sharp as they come. One can imagine Wagner trying to conduct the latest British tone poem, and exclaiming in desperation, 'Is this music?' just as his own contemporaries did when they were confronted with the 'false relations' in the score of Tristan. It is true that most of the modern developments, as far as they are really developments and not merely experimental eccentricities, are implicit in Parsifal. Indeed, for that matter, they are implicit in Bach: still, the first man to be scandalized by a new departure is usually he that found the path for it; and I cannot feel sure that Wagner would have encouraged Messrs Bax, Ireland, Cyril Scott, Holst, Goossens, Vaughan Williams, Frank Bridge, Boughton, Holbrooke, Howells and the rest (imagine being able to remember off-hand so many names of British composers turning out serious music in native styles of their own!!!) any more than Haydn encouraged Beethoven.

179

Wagner, after his 1855 London season as conductor of the Philharmonic, would not have believed that such a thing could happen in England. Had he been told that within two years a British baby Elgar would arrive who would attain classic rank as a European composer, he would hardly have kept his temper. Yet all this has happened very much as it happened before in Shakespear's time; and the English people at large are just as unconcerned about it, and indeed unconscious of it, as they were then.

Also the English have taken, as I said in this book they might, to Wagner singing and acting; and there is now no question of going to Bayreuth or importing German singers when we wish to hear The Ring or Parsifal; for much better performances of both can be heard now from English companies in England than Wagner ever heard at Bayreuth; and even a transpontine theatre like the Old Vic. thinks no more of doing Tannhäuser than it would have thought of doing Black-Eyed Susan half a century ago.

Another change has outmoded my description of the Bayreuth Festival Playhouse as an ultra-modern theatre. Bayreuth has a pictorial stage framed by a proscenium, and the framed picture stage is not now in the latest fashion. When the monarchy and the theatre were restored in England simultaneously on the accession of Charles II, the representation of Shakespear's plays as he planned them was made impossible by the introduction of pictorial scenery and of the proscenium with its two curtains, the act drop and the final green baize, to divide the plays into acts and hide the stage for intervals during which elaborate scenes were built up on it. His plays had to be chopped into fragments; divided into acts; re-written and provided with new endings to make effective 'curtains', in which condition they were intolerably tedious except as mere pedestals for irresistibly attractive actors and actresses.

Thus the pictorial stage not only murdered Shakespear, and buried the old Athenian drama, but dictated the form of opera (which grew up with it) and changed the form of the spoken drama. Wagner submitted to it as inevitable; but when he conceived the performances of The Ring, and planned a theatre for them, he made a desperate effort to elaborate its machinery so as to enable complete changes of scene to be made without stopping the performance and keeping the audience staring idly for fifteen minutes at a dropped curtain, or scrambling to and from their seats to fill up the time by smoking cigarets and drinking. One of his devices was to envelop the stage in mists produced by what was called a steam curtain, which looked exactly like what it really was, and made the theatre smell like a laundry. By its aid The Rhine Gold was performed without a break instead of in three acts with long intervals between each.

One had to admit at Bayreuth that here was the utmost perfection of the pictorial stage, and that its machinery could go no further. Nevertheless, having seen it at its best, fresh from Wagner's own influence, I must also admit that my favorite way of enjoying a performance of The Ring is to sit at the back of a box, comfortable on two chairs, feet up, and listen without looking. The truth is, a man whose imagination cannot serve him better than the most costly devices of the imitative scenepainter, should not go to the theatre, and as a matter of fact does not. In planning his Bayreuth theatre, Wagner was elaborating what he had better have scrapped altogether.

But as this did not occur to him, he allowed his technical plan of The Ring to be so governed by pictorial visions that it is as unreasonable to ask Bayreuth to scrap the Wagner tradition as it would be to ask the Théâtre Français to scrap the Molière tradition. Only, I must now treat that tradition as old-fashioned, whereas when this book was first published it was the latest development. What has happened since in England is that an Englishman, Mr Harley Granville-Barker, developing certain experiments made from time to time by Mr William Poel, another Englishman, inaugurated twentieth-century Shakespear by a series of performances in which the plays were given with unprecedented artistic splendor without the omission of a single decently presentable line, undivided into acts, without the old pictorial scenery, and with, as a result, a blessed revelation of Shakespear as the Prince of Entertainers instead of the most dreaded of bores, and a degree of illusion which the pictorial theatre had not only failed to attain, but had sedulously destroyed, nowhere more effectively than (save only in certain scenes of pure ritual in Parsifal) at Bayreuth.

Almost simultaneously with Mr Granville-Barker's revolutionary restoration of Shakespear, the pictorial stage triumphantly announced that at the English Bayreuth, which is the Shakespear Memorial Theatre at Stratford-on-Avon, the play of Coriolanus had been, by a climax of Procrustean adaptation, cut down to a performance lasting only one hour, in which state it was humbly hoped that the public would steel itself to bear it just once or twice for the sake of our national playwright. That was too much. Mr Bridges Adams, who had started with Mr Granville-Barker, took the new method to Stratford, where the former victims of the pictorial stage now find to their amazement that three hours of unabbreviated Shakespear fly faster than one hour of Procrusty Coriolanus. And at the Old Vic. in London, where the reform was adopted by Mr Atkins, Shakespear now draws better than would-be popular melodrama.

Thus have Englishmen left Wagner behind as to methods, and made obsolete all that part of this book which presents him as a pioneer. I must add that nobody who knows the snobbish contempt in which most Englishmen hold one another will be surprised when I mention that in England the exploits of Poel, Granville-Barker, Bridges Adams, Atkins and the English designers and painters who have worked for them, are modestly attributed to Herr Reinhardt, their eminent German contemporary. The only Englishman who is given any credit by his countrymen is Mr Gordon Craig, a fascinating propagandist who still loves the stage picture better than the stage play, and, living in the glamor of the Continent, seldom meddles with the actual theatre except to wipe his boots on it and on all the art that grows on its boards.

As to the sociological aspect of The Ring, which is unaffected by the rapid ageing of its technical aspect as a musical composition and a theatrical spectacle, it seems to challenge the so-called Great War to invalidate it if it can. Gross as the catastrophe has been, it has not shaken Bayreuth. But postwar contemplation of The Ring must not make us forget that all the progress Wagner saw was from the revolutions of 1848, when he was with the barricaders, to the Imperialist climax of 1871, when he sang:

> Hail, hail, our Caesar!
> Royal William!
> Rock and ward of German freedom!

What would he have said had he lived to see 1917 in Russia and 1918 in Germany, with England singing 'Hang, hang that Kaiser!' and Germany sympathizing to such an extent that the grandson of Wagner's William had to seek safety in Holland? Rhine maidens walking out with British Tommies, Senegalese negroes in Goethe's house, Marx enthroned in Russia, pistolled Romanoffs, fugitive Hapsburgs, exiled Hohenzollerns marking the ruins of empires with no more chance of restoration than the Stuarts and Bourbons: such a Götterdämmerung, in short, as in its craziness can be fitted into no allegory until its upshot becomes plainer than it now is: all this has so changed the political atmosphere in which Wagner lived, and in which this book was written, that it says much for the comprehensiveness of his grasp of things that his allegory should still be valid and important. Indeed the war was more a great tearing off of masks than a change of face: the main difference is that Alberic is richer, and his slaves hungrier and harder worked when they are so lucky as to have any work to do. The Ring ends with everybody dead except three mermaids; and though the war went far enough in that conclusive direction to suggest that the next war may possibly kill even the mermaids with 'depth charges', the curtain is not yet down on our drama, and we have to carry on as best we can. If we succeed, this book may have to pass into yet another edition: if not, the world itself will have to be re-edited.

AYOT ST LAWRENCE, 1922

PREFACE TO THE THIRD EDITION

In 1907 The Perfect Wagnerite was translated into German by my friend Siegfried Trebitsch. On reading through his version in manuscript I was struck by the inadequacy of the merely negative explanation given by me of the irrelevance of Night Falls on The Gods (Die Götterdämmerung) to the general philosophic scheme of The Ring. That explanation was correct as far as it went; but, put as I had put it, it seemed to me to suggest that the operatic character of Night Falls on The Gods was the result of indifference or forgetfulness produced by the lapse of twenty-five years between the first projection of The Ring and its completion. Now it is clear that in whatever other ways Wagner may have changed, he never became careless and never became indifferent. I therefore inserted in the first German edition a new section in which I shewed how the revolutionary history of Western Europe from the Liberal explosion of 1848 to the confused attempt at a popular and *quasi* Socialist military and municipal administration by the Commune of Paris in 1871 (that is to say, from the literary beginning of The Niblung's Ring by Wagner to the long-delayed musical completion of Night Falls on The Gods) had demonstrated practically that the passing away of the present capitalistic order was going to be a much more complicated business than it appears in Wagner's dramatization.

Since 1907, then, the German edition has been more complete than the English one. I now, after six years' pure procrastination, for which I have no excuse except preoccupation with other work, add the German extension to the English text. It begins on page 266, and ends on page 273. Otherwise the book remains as it was.

I have sometimes been asked why anyone should read a philosophic treatise merely to find out the story of The Ring.

185

I take this opportunity to reply publicly that there is, as far as I know, no reason why anyone should take any trouble in the matter at all unless they want to, and that the degree of trouble must be determined by the degree of want, which, again, will be determined by the wanter's capacity. But this I will say. Even for the purposes of the idlest Bayreuth tourist the story of The Ring must be told as Wagner's score tells it if it is to be of any real use to the visitor who cannot understand what the singers are saying. Anyone can, without knowing a bar of the score, string the events narrated in The Ring together in the order of their occurrence on the stage, add the names of the *dramatis personae* and a description of the scenes, and offer the result as a guide to The Ring. But such a mechanical account of the affair will hinder more than it will help. It will pass over as trivial, or even omit altogether, points to which Wagner has given immense weight and consequence, either by the length or intensity of his direct musical treatment or by the recurrence of themes connected with them; and it will rhetorically emphasize or spread itself descriptively over the more obvious matters which speak for themselves to the spectator and occupy little space and less depth in the musical fabric. People primed with such accounts sit waiting to see the bear or the dragon or the rainbow, or the transformation of Alberic into a snake and a toad, or the magic fire or the swimming feats of the Rhine daughters, and are bored because these exciting spectacles are so unconscionably delayed whilst Wotan, Fricka, Brynhild, Erda, Alberic, and Loki discuss things of which the 'synopsis' gives no hint.

Now the story as it is told in this book has its centres of gravity placed exactly where Wagner has placed them in his score. What Wagner has made much of, I have made much of; and I have explained why he made much of it. What he passed lightly over, I have passed lightly over. There is a good deal in The Ring which is on the surface of the score: nobody with ears and eyes can miss its significance at the performance. But there is also a good deal that was at the back of Wagner's mind, and that determined what I have called the centres of gravity; and this, which is neither in the score nor in the stage action, being assumed by Wagner to be part of the common consciousness of mankind, is what I have chiefly attended to. For this, obvious as it was to Wagner, and as it is to anyone who has reflected on human history and destiny in the light of a competent knowledge of modern capitalistic civilization, is an absolute blank to many persons who are highly susceptible to the musical qualities of Wagner's music and poetry, but have never reflected on human destiny at all, and have been brought up in polite ignorance of the infernal depths our human society descended to in the nineteenth century. Clearly none of your synopses or popular guides or lists of musical themes would be of the slightest use here. That, I take it, is why this little book remains, after some fifteen years, still in demand, and why I have found it necessary to complete it in this edition by a chapter dealing neither with music nor poetry, but with European history. For it was in that massive material, and not in mere crotchets and quavers, that Wagner found the stuff for his masterpiece.

G. B. S.

Ayot St Lawrence, 1913

PREFACE TO THE SECOND EDITION

THE preparation of a Second Edition of this booklet is quite the most unexpected literary task that has ever been set me. When it first appeared I was ungrateful enough to remonstrate with its publisher for printing, as I thought, more copies than the most sanguine Wagnerite could ever hope to sell. But the result proved that exactly one person buys a copy on every day in the year, including Sundays; and so, in the process of the suns, a reprint has become necessary.

Save a few verbal slips of no importance, I have found nothing to alter in this edition. As usual, the only protests the book has elicited are protests, not against the opinions it expresses, but against the facts it records. There are people who cannot bear to be told that their hero was associated with a famous Anarchist in a rebellion; that he was proclaimed as 'wanted' by the police; that he wrote revolutionary pamphlets; and that his picture of Niblunghome under the reign of Alberic is a poetic vision of unregulated industrial capitalism as it was made known in Germany in the middle of the nineteenth century by Engels's Condition of the Laboring Classes in England. They frantically deny these facts, and then declare that I have connected them with Wagner in a paroxysm of senseless perversity. I am sorry I have hurt them; and I appeal to charitable publishers to bring out a new life of Wagner, which shall describe him as a court musician of unquestioned fashion and orthodoxy, and a pillar of the most exclusive Dresden circles. Such a work would, I believe, have a large sale, and be read with satisfaction and reassurance by many lovers of Wagner's music.

As to my much demurred-to relegation of Night Falls on The Gods to the category of grand opera, I have nothing to add or withdraw. Such a classification is to me as much a matter of fact as the Dresden rising or the police proclamation; but I shall not pretend that it is a matter of such fact as everybody's judgment can grapple with. People who prefer grand opera to serious music-drama naturally resent my placing a very grand opera below a very serious music-drama. The ordinary lover of Shakespear would equally demur to my placing his popular catchpenny plays, of which As You Like It is an avowed type, below true Shakespearean plays like Measure for Measure. I cannot help that. Popular dramas and operas may have overwhelming merits as enchanting make-believes; but a poet's sincerest vision of the world must always take precedence of his prettiest fool's paradise.

As many English Wagnerites seem to be still under the impression that Wagner composed Rienzi in his youth, Tannhäuser and Lohengrin in his middle age, and The Ring in his later years, may I again remind them that The Ring was the result of a political convulsion which occurred when Wagner was only thirty-six, and that the poem was completed when he was forty, with thirty more years of work before him? It is as much a first essay in political philosophy as Die Feen is a first essay in romantic opera. The attempt to recover its spirit twenty years later, when the music of Night Falls on the Gods was added, was an attempt to revive the barricades of Dresden in the Temple of the Grail. Only those who have never had any political enthusiasms to survive can believe that such an attempt could succeed.

G. B. S.

LONDON, 1901

PREFACE TO THE FIRST EDITION

THIS book is a commentary on The Niblung's Ring, Richard Wagner's chief work. I offer it to those enthusiastic admirers of Wagner who are unable to follow his ideas, and do not in the least understand the dilemma of Wotan, though they are filled with indignation at the irreverence of the Philistines who frankly avow that they find the remarks of the god too often tedious and nonsensical. Now to be devoted to Wagner merely as a dog is devoted to his master, sharing a few elementary ideas, appetites and emotions with him, and, for the rest, reverencing his superiority without understanding it, is no true Wagnerism. Yet nothing better is possible without a stock of ideas common to master and disciple. Unfortunately, the ideas of the revolutionary Wagner of 1848 are taught neither by the education nor the experience of English and American gentleman-amateurs, who are almost always political mugwumps, and hardly ever associate with revolutionists. The earlier attempts to translate his numerous pamphlets and essays into English resulted in ludicrous mixtures of pure nonsense with the absurdest distortions of his ideas into the ideas of the translators. We now have a translation which is a masterpiece of interpretation and an eminent addition to our literature; but that is not because its author, Mr Ashton Ellis, knows the German dictionary better than his predecessors. He is simply in possession of Wagner's ideas, which were to them inconceivable.

All I pretend to do in this book is to impart the ideas which are most likely to be lacking in the conventional Englishman's equipment. I came by them myself much as Wagner did, having learnt more about music than about anything else in my youth, and sown my political wild oats subsequently in the revolutionary school. This combination is not common in

England; and as I seem, so far, to be the only publicly articulate result of it, I venture to add my commentary to what has already been written by musicians who are no revolutionists, and revolutionists who are no musicians.

G. B. S.

PITFOLD, HINDHEAD, 1898

PRELIMINARY ENCOURAGEMENTS

A FEW of these will be welcome to the ordinary citizen visiting the theatre to satisfy his curiosity, or his desire to be in the fashion, by witnessing a representation of Richard Wagner's famous tetralogy, The Niblung's Ring.

First, The Ring, with all its gods and giants and dwarfs, its water-maidens and Valkyries, its wishing-cap, magic ring, enchanted sword, and miraculous treasure, is a drama of today, and not of a remote and fabulous antiquity. It could not have been written before the second half of the nineteenth century, because it deals with events which were only then consummating themselves. Unless the spectator recognizes in it an image of the life he is himself fighting his way through, it must needs appear to him a monstrous development of the Christmas pantomimes, spun out here and there into intolerable lengths of dull conversation by the principal baritone. Fortunately, even from this point of view, The Ring is full of extraordinarily attractive episodes, both orchestral and dramatic. The nature music alone – music of river and rainbow, fire and forest – is enough to bribe people with any love of the country in them to endure the passages of political philosophy in the sure hope of a prettier page to come. Everybody, too, can enjoy the love music, the hammer and anvil music, the clumping of the giants, the tune of the young woodsman's horn, the trilling of the bird, the dragon music and nightmare music and thunder and lightning music, the profusion of simple melody, the sensuous charm of the orchestration: in short, the vast extent of common ground between The Ring and the ordinary music we use for play and pleasure. Hence it is that the four separate music-plays of which it is built have become popular throughout Europe as operas. We shall presently see that one of them, Night Falls on The Gods, actually is an opera.

It is generally understood, however, that there is an inner ring of superior persons to whom the whole work has a most urgent and searching philosophic and social significance. I profess to be such a superior person; and I write this pamphlet for the assistance of those who wish to be introduced to the work on equal terms with that inner circle of adepts.

My second encouragement is addressed to modest citizens who may suppose themselves to be disqualified from enjoying The Ring by their technical ignorance of music. They may dismiss all such misgivings speedily and confidently. If the sound of music has any power to move them, they will find that Wagner exacts nothing further. There is not a single bar of 'classical music' in The Ring – not a note in it that has any other point than the single direct point of giving musical expression to the drama. In classical music there are, as the analytical programs tell us, first subjects and second subjects, free fantasias, recapitulations, and codas; there are fugues, with counter-subjects, strettos, and pedal points; there are passacaglias on ground basses, canons ad hypo-diapente, and other ingenuities, which have, after all, stood or fallen by their prettiness as much as the simplest folktune. Wagner is never driving at anything of this sort any more than Shakespear in his plays is driving at such ingenuities of verse-making as sonnets, triolets and the like. And this is why he is so easy for the natural musician who has had no academic teaching. The professors, when Wagner's music is played to them, exclaim at once 'What is this? Is it aria, or recitative? Is there no cabaletta to it – not even a full close? Why was that discord not prepared; and why does he not resolve it correctly? How dare he indulge in those scandalous and illicit transitions into a key that has not one note in common with the key he has just left? Listen to those false relations! What does he want with six drums and eight horns when Mozart worked miracles with two of each? The man is no musician.' The layman neither knows nor cares about any of these things. If Wagner were to turn aside from his straightforward dramatic purpose to propitiate the professors with correct exercises in sonata form, his music would at once become unintelligible to the unsophisticated spectator, upon whom the familiar and dreaded 'classical' sensation would descend like the influenza. Nothing of the kind need be dreaded. The unskilled, untaught musician may approach Wagner boldly; for there is no possibility of a misunderstanding between them: the Ring music is perfectly single and simple. It is the adept musician of the old school who has everything to unlearn; and him I leave, unpitied, to his fate.

THE NIBLUNG'S RING

The Ring consists of four plays, intended to be performed on four successive evenings, entitled The Rhine Gold (a prologue to the other three), The Valkyrie, Siegfried, and Night Falls on The Gods; or, in the original German, Das Rheingold, Die Walküre, Siegfried and Die Götterdämmerung.

THE RHINE GOLD

Let me assume for a moment that you are a young and good-looking woman. Try to imagine yourself in that character at Klondyke five years ago. The place is teeming with gold. If you are content to leave the gold alone, as the wise leave flowers without plucking them, enjoying with perfect naïveté its color and glitter and preciousness, no human being will ever be the worse for your knowledge of it; and whilst you remain in that frame of mind the golden age will endure.

Now suppose a man comes along: a man who has no sense of the golden age, nor any power of living in the present: a man with common desires, cupidities, ambitions, just like most of the men you know. Suppose you reveal to that man the fact that if he will only pluck this gold up, and turn it into money, millions of men, driven by the invisible whip of hunger, will toil underground and overground night and day to pile up more and more gold for him until he is master of the world! You will find that the prospect will not tempt him so much as you might imagine, because it involves some distasteful trouble to himself to start with, and because there is something else within his reach involving no distasteful toil, which he desires more passionately; and that is yourself. So long as he is preoccupied with love of you, the gold, and all that it implies, will escape him; the golden age will endure. Not until he forswears love will he stretch out his hand to the gold, and found the Plutonic empire for himself. But the choice between love and gold may not rest altogether with him. He may be an ugly, ungracious, unamiable person, whose affections may seem merely ludicrous and despicable to you. In that case, you may repulse him, and most bitterly humiliate and disappoint him. What is left to him then but to curse the love he can never win, and turn remorselessly to the gold? With that, he will make short work of your golden age, and leave you lamenting its lost thoughtlessness and sweetness.

In due time the gold of Klondyke will find its way to the great cities of the world. But the old dilemma will keep continually reproducing itself. The man who will turn his back on love, and upon all the fruitful, creative, life-pursuing activities into which the loftiest human energy can develop it, and will set himself single-heartedly to gather gold in an exultant dream of wielding its Plutonic powers, will find the treasure yielding quickly to his touch. But few men will make this sacrifice voluntarily. Not until the Plutonic power is so strongly set up that the higher human impulses are suppressed as rebellious, and even the mere appetites are denied, starved, and insulted when they cannot purchase their satisfaction with gold, are the energetic spirits driven to build their lives upon riches. How inevitable that course has become to us is plain enough to those who have the power of understanding what they see as they look at the plutocratic societies of our modern capitals.

FIRST SCENE

Here, then, is the subject of the first scene of The Rhine Gold. As you sit waiting for the curtain to rise, you suddenly catch the booming ground-tone of a mighty river. It becomes plainer, clearer: you get nearer to the surface, and catch the green light and the flights of bubbles. Then the curtain goes up and you see what you heard – the depths of the Rhine, with three strange fairy fishes, half water-maidens, singing and enjoying themselves exuberantly. They are not singing barcarolles or ballads about the Lorely and her fated lovers, but simply trolling any nonsense that comes into their heads in time to the dancing of the water and the rhythm of their swimming. It is the golden age; and the attraction of this spot for the Rhine maidens is a lump of the Rhine gold, which they value, in an entirely uncommercial way, for its bodily beauty and splendor. Just at present it is eclipsed, because the sun is not striking down through the water.

Presently there comes a poor devil of a dwarf stealing along the slippery rocks of the river bed, a creature with energy enough to make him strong of body and fierce of passion, but with a brutish narrowness of intelligence and selfishness of imagination: too stupid to see that his own welfare can only be compassed as part of the welfare of the world, too full of brute force not to grab vigorously at his own gain. Such dwarfs are quite common in London. He comes now with a fruitful impulse in him, in search of what he lacks in himself, beauty, lightness of heart, imagination, music. The Rhine maidens, representing all these to him, fill him with hope and longing; and he never considers that he has nothing to offer that they could possibly desire, being by natural limitation incapable of seeing anything from anyone else's point of view. With perfect simplicity, he offers himself as a sweetheart to them. But they are thoughtless, elemental, only half real things, much like modern young ladies. That the poor dwarf is repulsive to their sense of physical beauty and their romantic conception of heroism, that he is ugly and awkward, greedy and ridiculous, disposes for them of his claim to live and love. They mock him atrociously, pretending to fall in love with him at first sight, and then slipping away and making game of him, heaping ridicule and disgust on the poor wretch until he is beside himself with mortification and rage. They forget him when the water begins to glitter in the sun, and the gold to reflect its glory. They break into ecstatic worship of their treasure; and though they know the parable of Klondyke quite well, they have no fear that the gold will be wrenched away by the dwarf, since it will yield to no one who has not forsworn love for it, and it is in pursuit of love that he has come to them. They forget that they have poisoned that desire in him by their mockery and denial of it, and that he now knows that life will give him nothing that he cannot wrest from it by the Plutonic power. It is just as if some poor, rough, vulgar, coarse fellow were to offer to take his part in aristocratic society, and be snubbed into the knowledge that only as a millionaire could he ever hope to bring that society to his feet and buy himself a beautiful and refined wife. His choice is forced on him. He forswears love as thousands of us forswear it everyday; and in a moment the gold is in his grasp, and he disappears in the depths, leaving the water-fairies vainly screaming 'Stop thief!', whilst the river seems to plunge into darkness and sink from us as we rise to the cloud regions above.

And now, what forces are there in the world to resist Alberic, our dwarf, in his new character of sworn plutocrat? He is soon at work wielding the power of the gold. For his gain, hordes of his fellow-creatures are thenceforth condemned to slave miserably, overground and underground, lashed to their work by the invisible whip of starvation. They never see him, any more than the victims of our 'dangerous trades' ever see the shareholders whose power is nevertheless everywhere, driving them to destruction. The very wealth they create with their labor becomes an additional force to impoverish them; for as fast as they make it it slips from their hands into the hands of their master, and makes him mightier than ever. You can see the process for yourself in every civilized country today, where millions of people toil in want and disease to heap up more wealth for our Alberics, laying up nothing for themselves, except sometimes horrible and agonizing disease and the certainty of premature death. All this part of the story is frightfully real, frightfully present, frightfully modern; and its effects on our social life are so ghastly and ruinous that we no longer know enough of happiness to be discomposed by it. It is only the poet, with his vision of what life might be, to whom these things are unendurable. If we were a race of poets we would make an end of them before the end of this miserable century. Being a race of moral dwarfs instead, we think them highly respectable, comfortable and proper, and allow them to breed and multiply their evil in all directions. If there were no higher power in the world to work against Alberic, the end of it would be utter destruction.

Such a force there is, however; and it is called Godhead. The mysterious thing we call life organizes itself into all living shapes, bird, beast, beetle and fish, rising to the human marvel in cunning dwarfs and in laborious muscular giants, capable, these last, of enduring toil, willing to buy love and life, not with suicidal curses and renunciations, but with patient manual drudgery in the service of higher powers. And these higher powers are called into existence by the same self-organization of life still more wonderfully into rare persons who may by comparison be called gods, creatures capable of thought, whose aims extend far beyond the satisfaction of their bodily appetites and personal affections, since they perceive that it is only by the establishment of a social order founded on common bonds of moral faith that the world can rise from mere savagery. But how is this order to be set up by Godhead in a world of stupid giants, since these thoughtless ones pursue only their narrower personal ends and can by no means understand the aims of a god? Godhead, face to face with Stupidity, must compromise. Unable to enforce on the world the pure law of thought, it must resort to a mechanical law of commandments to be enforced by brute punishments and the destruction of the disobedient. And however carefully these laws are framed to represent the highest thoughts of the framers at the moment of their promulgation, before a day has elapsed that thought has grown and widened by the ceaseless evolution of life; and lo! yesterday's law already fallen out with today's thought. Yet if the high givers of that law themselves set the example of breaking it before it is a week old, they destroy all its authority with their subjects, and so break the weapon they have forged to rule them for their own good. They must therefore maintain at all costs the sanctity of the law, even when it has ceased to represent their thought; so that at last they get entangled in a network of ordinances which they no longer believe in, and yet have made so sacred by custom and so terrible by punishment, that they cannot themselves escape from them. Thus Godhead's resort to law finally costs it half its integrity – as if a spiritual king, to gain temporal power, had plucked out one of his eyes – and it finally begins secretly to long for the advent of some power higher than itself which will destroy its artificial empire of law, and establish a true republic of free thought.

This is by no means the only difficulty in the dominion of Law. The brute force for its execution must be purchased; and the mass of its subjects must be persuaded to respect the authority which employs this force. But how is such respect to be implanted in them if they are unable to comprehend the thought of the lawgiver? Clearly, only by associating the legislative power with such displays of splendor and majesty as will impress their senses and awe their imaginations. The god turned lawgiver, in short, must be crowned Pontiff and King. Since he cannot be known to the common folk as their superior in wisdom, he must be known to them as their superior in riches, as the dweller in castles, the wearer of gold and purple, the eater of mighty feasts, the commander of armies, and the wielder of powers of life and death, of salvation and damnation after death. Something may be done in this way without corruption whilst the golden age still endures. Your gods may not prevail with the dwarf's; but they may go to these honest giants who will give a day's work for a day's pay, and induce them to build for Godhead a mighty fortress, complete with hall and chapel, tower and bell, for the sake of the homesteads that will grow up in security round that church-castle. This only, however, whilst the golden age lasts. The moment the Plutonic power is let loose, and the loveless Alberic comes into the field with his corrupting millions, the gods are face to face with destruction; since Alberic, able with invisible hunger-whip to force the labor of the dwarfs and to buy the services of the giants, can outshine all the temporal shows and splendors of the golden age, and make himself master of the world, unless the gods, with their bigger brains, can capture his gold. This, the dilemma of the Church today, is the situation created by the exploit of Alberic in the depths of the Rhine.

SECOND SCENE

From the bed of the river we rise into cloudy regions, and finally come out into the clear in a meadow, where Wotan, the god of gods, and his consort Fricka lie sleeping. Wotan, you will observe, has lost one eye and you will presently learn that he plucked it out voluntarily as the price to be paid for his alliance with Fricka, who in return has brought to him as her dowry all the powers of Law. The meadow is on the brink of a ravine, beyond which, towering on distant heights, stands Godhome, a mighty castle, newly built as a house of state for the one-eyed god and his all-ruling wife. Wotan has not yet seen this castle except in his dreams: two giants have just built it for him whilst he slept; and the reality is before him for the first time when Fricka wakes him. In that majestic burg he is to rule with her and through her over the humble giants, who have eyes to gape at the glorious castles their own hands have built from his design, but no brains to design castles for themselves, or to comprehend divinity. As a god, he is to be great, secure, and mighty; but he is also to be passionless, affectionless, wholly impartial; for Godhead, if it is to live with law, must have no weaknesses, no respect for persons. All such sweet littlenesses must be left to the humble stupid giants to make their toil sweet to them; and the god must, after all, pay for Olympian power the same price the dwarf has paid for Plutonic power.

Wotan has forgotten this in his dreams of greatness. Not so Fricka. What she is thinking of is this price that Wotan has consented to pay, in token whereof he has promised this day to hand over to the giants Fricka's sister, the goddess Freia, with her golden love-apples. When Fricka reproaches Wotan with having selfishly forgotten this, she finds that he, like herself, is not prepared to go through with his bargain, and that he is trusting to another great world-force, the Lie (a European Power, as Lassalle said), to help him to trick the giants out of their reward. But this force does not dwell in Wotan himself, but in another, a god over whom he has triumphed, one Loki, the god of Intellect, Argument, Imagination, Illusion, and Reason. Loki has promised to deliver him from his contract, and to cheat the giants for him; but he has not arrived to keep his word: indeed, as Fricka bitterly points out, why should not the Lie fail Wotan, since such failure is the very essence of him?

The giants come soon enough; and Freia flies to Wotan for protection against them. Their purposes are quite honest; and they have no doubt of the god's faith. There stands their part of the contract fulfilled, stone on stone, port and pinnacle all faithfully finished from Wotan's design by their mighty labor. They have come undoubtingly for their agreed wage. Then there happens what is to them an incredible, inconceivable thing. The god begins to shuffle. There are no moments in life more tragic than those in which the humble common man, the manual worker, leaving with implicit trust all high affairs to his betters, and reverencing them wholly as worthy of that trust, even to the extent of accepting as his rightful function the saving of them from all roughening and coarsening drudgeries, first discovers that they are corrupt, greedy, unjust and treacherous. The shock drives a ray of prophetic light into one giant's mind, and gives him a momentary eloquence. In that moment he rises above his stupid giant-hood, and earnestly warns the Son of Light that all his power and eminence of priesthood, godhood, and kingship must stand or fall with the unbearable cold greatness of the incorruptible lawgiver. But Wotan, whose assumed character of lawgiver is altogether false to his real passionate nature, despises the rebuke; and the giant's ray of insight is lost in the murk of his virtuous indignation.

In the midst of the wrangle, Loki comes at last, excusing himself for being late on the ground that he has been detained by a matter of importance which he has promised to lay before Wotan. When pressed to give his mind to the business immediately in hand, and to extricate Wotan from his dilemma, he has nothing to say except that the giants are evidently altogether in the right. The castle has been duly built: he has tried every stone of it, and found the work first-rate: there is nothing to be done but pay the price agreed upon by handing over Freia to the giants. The gods are furious; and Wotan passionately declares that he only con-sented to the bargain on Loki's promise to find a way for him out of it. But Loki says no: he has promised to find a way out if any such may exist, but not to make a way if there is no way. He has wandered over the whole earth in search of some treasure great enough to buy Freia back from the giants; but in all the world he has found nothing for which Man will give up Woman. And this, by the way, reminds him of the matter he had promised to lay before Wotan. The Rhine maidens have complained to him of Alberic's theft of their gold: and he mentions it as a curious exception to his universal law of the unpurchasable preciousness of love, that this gold-robber has forsworn love for the sake of the fabulous riches of the Plutonic empire and the mastery of the world through its power.

No sooner is the tale told than the giants stoop lower than the dwarf. Alberic forswore love only when it was denied to him and made the instrument for cruelly murdering his self-respect. But the giants, with love within their reach, with Freia and her golden apples in their hands, offer to give her up for the treasure of Alberic. Observe, it is the treasure alone that they desire. They have no fierce dreams of dominion over their superiors, or of moulding the world to any conceptions of their own. They are neither clever nor ambitious: they simply covet money. Alberic's gold: that is their demand, or else Freia, as agreed upon, whom they now carry off as hostage, leaving Wotan to consider their ultimatum.

Freia gone, the gods begin to wither and age: her golden apples, which they so lightly bargained away, they now find to be a matter of life and death to them; for not even the gods can live on Law and Godhead alone, be their castles ever so splendid. Loki alone is unaffected: the Lie, with all its cunning wonders, its glistenings and shiftings and mirages, is a mere appearance: it has no body and needs no food. What is Wotan to do? Loki sees the answer clearly enough; he must bluntly rob Alberic. There is nothing to prevent him except moral scruple; for Alberic, after all, is a poor, dim, dwarfed, credulous creature whom a god can outsee and a lie can outwit. Down, then, Wotan and Loki plunge into the mine where Alberic's slaves are piling up wealth for him under the invisible whip.

THIRD SCENE

This gloomy place need not be a mine: it might just as well be a match-factory, with yellow phosphorus, phossy jaw, a large dividend, and plenty of clergymen shareholders. Or it might be a whitelead factory, or a chemical works, or a pottery, or a railway shunting yard, or a tailoring shop, or a little gin-sodden laundry, or a bakehouse, or a big shop, or any other of the places where human life and welfare are daily sacrificed in order that some greedy foolish creature may be able to hymn exultantly to his Plutonic idol:

> Thou mak'st me eat whilst others starve,
> And sing while others do lament:
> Such unto me Thy blessings are,
> As if I were Thine only care.

In the mine, which resounds with the clinking anvils of the dwarfs toiling miserably to heap up treasure for their master, Alberic has set his brother Mime – more familiarly, Mimmy – to make him a helmet. Mimmy dimly sees that there is some magic in this helmet, and tries to keep it; but Alberic wrests it from him, and shews him, to his cost, that it is the veil of the invisible whip, and that he who wears it can appear in what shape he will, or disappear from view altogether. This helmet is a very common article in our streets, where it generally takes the form of a tall hat. It makes a man invisible as a shareholder, and changes him into various shapes, such as a pious Christian, a subscriber to hospitals, a benefactor of the poor, a model husband and father, a shrewd, practical, independent Englishman, and what not, when he is really a pitiful parasite on the commonwealth, consuming a great deal, and producing nothing, feeling nothing, knowing nothing, believing nothing, and doing nothing except what all the rest do, and that only because he is afraid not to do it, or at least pretend to do it.

When Wotan and Loki arrive, Loki claims Alberic as an old acquaintance. But the dwarf has no faith in these civil strangers: Greed instinctively mistrusts Intellect, even in the garb of Poetry and the company of Godhead, whilst envying the brilliancy of the one and the dignity of the other. Alberic breaks out at them with a terrible boast of the power now within his grasp. He paints for them the world as it will be when his dominion over it is complete, when the soft airs and green mosses of its valleys shall be changed into smoke, slag and filth; when slavery, disease and squalor, soothed by drunkenness and mastered by the policeman's baton, shall become the foundation of society; and when nothing shall escape ruin except such pretty places and pretty women as he may like to buy for the slaking of his own lusts. In that kingdom of evil he sees that there will be no power but his own. These gods, with their moralities and legalities and intellectual subtlety, will go under and be starved out of existence. He bids Wotan and Loki beware of it; and his 'Hab' Acht!' is hoarse, horrible, and sinister. Wotan is revolted to the very depths of his being: he cannot stifle the execration that bursts from him. But Loki is unaffected: he has no moral passion; indignation is as absurd to him as enthusiasm. He finds it exquisitely amusing – having a touch of the comic spirit in him – that the dwarf, in stirring up the moral fervour of Wotan, has removed his last moral scruple about becoming a thief. Wotan will now rob the dwarf without remorse; for is it not positively his highest duty to take this power out of such evil hands and use it himself in the interests of Godhead? On the loftiest moral grounds, he lets Loki do his worst.

A little cunningly disguised flattery makes short work of Alberic. Loki pretends to be afraid of him; and he swallows that bait unhesitatingly. But how, inquires Loki, is he to guard against the hatred of his million slaves? Will they not steal from him, whilst he sleeps, the magic ring, the symbol of his power, which he has forged from the gold of the Rhine? 'You think yourself very clever,' sneers Alberic, and then begins to boast of the enchantments of the magic helmet. Loki refuses to believe in such marvels without witnessing them. Alberic, only too glad to shew off his powers, puts on the helmet and transforms himself into a monstrous serpent. Loki gratifies him by pretending to be frightened out of his wits, but ventures to remark that it would be better still if the helmet could transform its owner into some tiny creature that could hide and spy in the smallest cranny. Alberic promptly transforms himself into a toad. In an instant Wotan's foot is on him; Loki tears away the helmet; they pinion him, and drag him away a prisoner up through the earth to the meadow by the castle.

FOURTH SCENE

There, to pay for his freedom, he has to summon his slaves from the depths to place all the treasure they have heaped up for him at the feet of Wotan. Then he demands his liberty; but Wotan must have the ring as well. And here the dwarf, like the giant before him, feels the very foundations of the world shake beneath him at the discovery of his own base cupidity in a higher power. That evil should, in its loveless desperation, create malign powers which Godhead could not create, seems but natural justice to him. But that Godhead should steal those malign powers from evil, and wield them itself, is a monstrous perversion; and his appeal to Wotan to forego it is almost terrible in its conviction of wrong. It is of no avail. Wotan falls back again on virtuous indignation. He reminds Alberic that he stole the gold from the Rhine daughters, and takes the attitude of the just judge compelling a restitution of stolen goods. Alberic, knowing perfectly well that the judge is taking the goods to put them in his own pocket, has the ring torn from his finger, and is once more as poor as he was when he came slipping and stumbling among the slimy rocks in the bed of the Rhine.

This is the way of the world. In older times, when the Christian laborer was drained dry by the knightly spendthrift, and the spendthrift was drained by the Jewish usurer, Church and State, religion and law, seized on the Jew and drained him as a Christian duty. When the forces of lovelessness and greed had built up our own sordid capitalist systems, driven by invisible proprietorship, robbing the poor, defacing the earth, and forcing themselves as a universal curse even on the generous and humane, then religion and law and intellect, which would never themselves have discovered such systems, their natural bent being towards welfare, economy and life instead of towards corruption, waste and death, nevertheless did not scruple to seize by fraud and force these powers of evil on pretence of using them for good. And it inevitably happens that when the Church, the Law, and all the Talents have made common cause to rob the people, the Church is far more vitally harmed by that unfaithfulness to itself than its more mechanical confederates; so that finally they turn on their discredited ally and rob the Church, with the cheerful co-operation of Loki, as in France and Italy for instance.

The twin giants come back with their hostage, in whose presence Godhead blooms again. The gold is ready for them; but now that the moment has come for parting with Freia the gold does not seem so tempting; and they are sorely loth to let her go. Not unless there is gold enough to utterly hide her from them – not until the heap has grown so that they can see nothing but gold – until money has come between them and every human feeling, will they part with her. There is not gold enough to accomplish this: however cunningly Loki spreads it, the glint of Freia's hair is still visible to Giant Fafnir, and the magic helmet must go on the heap to shut it out. Even then Fafnir's brother, Fasolt, can catch a beam from her eye through a chink, and is rendered incapable thereby of forswearing her. There is nothing to stop that chink but the ring; and Wotan is as greedily bent on keeping that as Alberic himself was; nor can the other gods persuade him that Freia is worth it, since for the highest god, love is not the highest good, but only the universal delight that bribes all living things to travail with renewed life. Life itself, with its accomplished marvels and its infinite potentialities, is the only force that Godhead can worship. Wotan does not yield until he is reached by the voice of the fruitful earth, that before he or the dwarfs or the giants or the Law or the Lie or any of these things were, had the seed of them all in her bosom, and the seed perhaps of something higher even than himself, that shall one day supersede him and cut the tangles and alliances and compromises that already have cost him one of his eyes. When Erda, the First Mother of life, rises from her sleeping-place in the heart of the earth, and warns him to yield the ring, he obeys her; the ring is added to the heap of gold; and all sense of Freia is cut off from the giants.

But now what Law is left to these two poor stupid laborers whereby one shall yield to the other any of the treasures for which they have each paid the whole price in surrendering Freia? They look by mere habit to the god to judge for them; but he, with his heart stirring towards higher forces than himself, turns with disgust from these lower forces. They settle it as two wolves might; and Fafnir batters his brother dead with his staff. It is a horrible thing to see and hear, to anyone who knows how much blood has been shed in the world in just that way by its brutalized toilers, honest fellows enough until their betters betrayed them. Fafnir goes off with his booty. It is quite useless to him. He has neither the cunning nor the ambition to establish the Plutonic empire with it. Merely to prevent others from getting it is the only purpose it brings him. He piles it in a cave; transforms himself into a dragon by the helmet; and devotes his life to guarding it, as much a slave to it as a jailor is to his prisoner. He had much better have thrown it all back into the Rhine and transformed himself into the shortest-lived animal that enjoys at least a brief run in the sunshine. His case, however, is far too common to be surprising. The world is overstocked with persons who sacrifice all their affections, and madly trample and batter down their fellows to obtain riches of which, when they get them, they are unable to make the smallest use, and to which they become the most miserable slaves.

The gods soon forget Fafnir in their rejoicing over Freia. Donner, the Thunder god, springs to a rocky summit and calls the clouds as a shepherd calls his flocks. They come at his summons; and he and the castle are hidden by their black legions. Froh, the Rainbow god, hastens to his side.

At the stroke of Donner's hammer the black murk is riven in all directions by darting ribbons of lightning; and as the air clears, the castle is seen in its fullest splendor, accessible now by the rainbow bridge which Froh has cast across the ravine. In the glory of this moment Wotan has a great thought. With all his aspirations to establish a reign of noble thought, of righteousness, order, and justice, he has found that day that there is no race yet in the world that quite spontaneously, naturally and unconsciously realizes his ideal. He himself has found how far short Godhead falls of the thing it conceives. He, the greatest of gods, has been unable to control his fate: he has been forced against his will to choose between evils, to make disgraceful bargains, to break them still more disgracefully, and even then to see the price of his disgrace slip through his fingers. His consort has cost him half his vision; his castle has cost him his affections; and the attempt to retain both has cost him his honor. On every side he is shackled and bound, dependent on the laws of Fricka and on the lies of Loki, forced to traffic with dwarfs for handicraft and with giants for strength, and to pay them both in false coin. After all, a god is a pitiful thing. But the fertility of the First Mother is not yet exhausted. The life that came from her has ever climbed up to a higher and higher organization. From toad and serpent to dwarf, from bear and elephant to giant, from dwarf and giant to a god with thoughts, with comprehension of the world, with ideals. Why should it stop there? Why should it not rise from the god to the Hero? to the creature in whom the god's unavailing thought shall have become effective will and life, who shall make his way straight to truth and reality over the laws of Fricka and the lies of Loki with a strength that overcomes giants and a cunning that outwits dwarfs? Yes: Erda, the First Mother, must travail again, and breed him a race of heroes to deliver the world and himself from his limited powers and disgraceful bargains. This is the vision that flashes on him as he turns to the rainbow bridge and calls his wife to come and dwell with him in Valhalla, the home of the gods.

They are all overcome with Valhalla's glory except Loki. He is behind the scenes of this joint reign of the Divine and the Legal. He despises these gods with their ideals and their golden apples. 'I am ashamed,' he says, 'to have dealings with these futile creatures.' And so he follows them to the rainbow bridge. But as they set foot on it, from the river below rises the wailing of the Rhine daughters for their lost gold. 'You down there in the water,' cries Loki with brutal irony, 'you used to bask in the glitter of your gold: henceforth you shall bask in the splendor of the gods.' And they reply that the truth is in the depths and the darkness, and that what blazes on high there is falsehood. And with that the gods pass into their glorious stronghold.

WAGNER AS REVOLUTIONIST

BEFORE leaving this explanation of The Rhine Gold, I must have a word or two about it with the reader.

It is the least popular of the sections of The Ring. The reason is that its dramatic moments lie quite outside the consciousness of people whose joys and sorrows are all domestic and personal, and whose religions and political ideas are purely conventional and superstitious. To them it is a struggle between half a dozen fairy-tale personages for a ring, involving hours of scolding and cheating, and one long scene in a dark, gruesome mine, with gloomy, ugly music, and not a glimpse of a handsome young man or pretty woman. Only those of wider consciousness can follow it breathlessly, seeing in it the whole tragedy of human history and the whole horror of the dilemmas from which the world is shrinking today. At Bayreuth I have seen a party of English tourists, after enduring agonies of boredom from Alberic, rise in the middle of the third scene, and almost force their way out of the dark theatre into the sunlit pinewood without. And I have seen people who were deeply affected by the scene driven almost beside themselves by this disturbance. But it was a very natural thing for the unfortunate tourists to do, since in this Rhine Gold prologue there is no interval between the acts for escape. Roughly speaking, people who have no general ideas, no touch of the concern of the philosopher and statesman for the race, cannot enjoy The Rhine Gold as a drama. They may find compensations in some exceedingly pretty music, at times even grand and glorious, which will enable them to escape occasionally from the struggle between Alberic and Wotan; but if their capacity for music should be as limited as their comprehension of the world, they had better stay away.

And now, attentive Reader, we have reached the point at which some foolish person is sure to interrupt us by declaring that The Rhine Gold is what they call 'a work of art' pure and simple, and that Wagner never dreamt of shareholders, tall hats, whitelead factories, and industrial and political questions looked at from the socialistic and humanitarian points of view. We need not discuss these impertinences; it is easier to silence them with the facts of Wagner's life. In 1843 he obtained the position of conductor of the Opera at Dresden at a salary of £225 a year, with a pension. This was a first-rate permanent appointment in the service of the Saxon State, carrying an assured professional position and livelihood with it. In 1848, the year of revolutions, the discontented middle class, unable to rouse the Church-and-State governments of the day from their bondage to custom, caste and law by appeals to morality or constitutional agitation for Liberal reforms, made common cause with the starving wage-working class, and resorted to armed rebellion, which reached Dresden in 1849. Had Wagner been the mere musical epicure and political mugwump that the term 'artist' seems to suggest to so many critics and amateurs – that is, a creature in their own lazy likeness – he need have taken no more part in the political struggles of his day than Bishop took in the English Reform agitation of 1832, or Sterndale Bennett in the Chartist or Free Trade movements. What he did do was first to make a desperate appeal to the King to cast off his bonds and answer the need of the time by taking true kingship on himself and leading his people to the redress of their intolerable wrongs (fancy the poor monarch's feelings!), and then, when the crash came, to take his side with the right and the poor against the rich and the wrong. When the insurrection was defeated, three leaders of it were especially marked down for vengeance: August Roeckel, an old friend of Wagner's to whom he wrote a well-known series of letters; Michael Bakoonin, afterwards a famous apostle of revolutionary Anarchism; and Wagner himself. Wagner escaped to

Switzerland: Roeckel and Bakoonin suffered long terms of imprisonment. Wagner was of course utterly ruined, pecuniarily and socially (to his own intense relief and satisfaction); and his exile lasted twelve years. His first idea was to get his Tannhäuser produced in Paris. With the notion of explaining himself to the Parisians he wrote a pamphlet entitled Art and Revolution, a glance through which will shew how thoroughly the socialistic side of the revolution had his sympathy, and how completely he had got free from the influence of the established churches of his day. For three years he kept pouring forth pamphlets – some of them elaborate treatises in size and intellectual rank, but still essentially the pamphlets and manifestoes of a born agitator – on social evolution, religion, life, art and the influence of riches. In 1853 the poem of The Ring was privately printed; and in 1854, five years after the Dresden insurrection, The Rhine Gold score was completed to the last drum tap.

These facts are on official record in Germany, where the proclamation summing up Wagner as 'a politically dangerous person' may be consulted to this day. The pamphlets are now accessible to English readers in the translation of Mr Ashton Ellis. This being so, any person who, having perhaps heard that I am a Socialist, attempts to persuade you that my interpretation of The Rhine Gold is only 'my socialism' read into the works of a dilettantist who borrowed an idle tale from an old saga to make an opera book with, may safely be dismissed from your consideration as an ignoramus.

If you are now satisfied that The Rhine Gold is an allegory, do not forget that an allegory is never quite consistent except when it is written by someone without dramatic faculty, in which case it is unreadable. There is only one way of dramatizing an idea; and that is by putting on the stage a human being possessed by that idea, yet none the less a human being with all the human impulses which make him akin and therefore interesting to us. Bunyan, in his Pilgrim's Progress, does not, like his unread imitators, attempt to personify Christianity and Valour: he dramatizes for you the life of the Christian and the Valiant Man. Just so, though I have shewn that Wotan is Godhead and Kingship, and Loki Logic and Imagination without living Will (Brain without Heart, to put it vulgarly); yet in the drama Wotan is a religiously moral man, and Loki a witty, ingenious, imaginative and cynical one. As to Fricka, who stands for State Law, she does not assume her allegorical character in The Rhine Gold at all, but is simply Wotan's wife and Freia's sister: nay, she contradicts her allegorical self by conniving at all Wotan's rogueries. That, of course, is just what State Law would do; but we must not save the credit of the allegory by a quip. Not until she reappears in the next play (The Valkyrie) does her function in the allegorical scheme become plain.

One preconception will bewilder the spectator hopelessly unless he has been warned against it or is naturally free from it. In the old-fashioned orders of creation, the supernatural personages are invariably conceived as greater than man, for good or evil. In the modern humanitarian order as adopted by Wagner, Man is the highest. In The Rhine Gold, it is pretended that there are as yet no men on the earth. There are dwarfs, giants, and gods. The danger is that you will jump to the conclusion that the gods, at least, are a higher order than the human order. On the contrary, the world is waiting for Man to redeem it from the lame and cramped government of the gods. Once grasp that; and the allegory becomes simple enough. Really, of course, the dwarfs, giants, and gods are dramatizations of the three main orders of men: to wit, the instinctive, predatory, lustful, greedy people; the patient, toiling, stupid, respectful, money-worshipping people; and the intellectual, moral, talented people who devise and administer States and Churches. History shews us only one order higher than the highest of these: namely, the order of Heroes.

Now it is quite clear – though you have perhaps never thought of it – that if the next generation of Englishmen

consisted wholly of Julius Caesars, all our political, ecclesiastical, and moral institutions would vanish, and the less
perishable of their appurtenances be classed with Stonehenge
and the cromlechs and round towers as inexplicable relics of
a bygone social order. Julius Caesars would no more trouble
themselves about such contrivances as our codes and
churches than a Fellow of the Royal Society will touch his hat
to the squire and listen to the village curate's sermons. This
is precisely what must happen some day if life continues
thrusting towards higher and higher organizations as it has
hitherto done. As most of our English professional men are
to Australian bushmen, so, we must suppose, will the average
man of some future day be to Julius Caesar. Let any man of
middle age, pondering this prospect, consider what has
happened within a single generation to the articles of faith
his father regarded as eternal, nay, to the very scepticism and
blasphemies of his youth (Bishop Colenso's criticism of the
Pentateuch, for example!); and he will begin to realize how
much of our barbarous Theology and Law the man of the
future will do without. Bakoonin, the Dresden revolutionary
leader with whom Wagner went out in 1949, put forward
later on a program, often quoted with foolish horror, for the
abolition of all institutions, religious, political, juridical,
financial, legal, academic and so on, so as to leave the will of
man free to find its own way. All the loftiest spirits of that
time were burning to raise Man up, to give him self-respect,
to shake him out of his habit of grovelling before the ideals
created by his own imagination, of attributing the good that
sprang from the ceaseless energy of the life within himself to
some superior power in the clouds, and of making a fetish of
self-sacrifice to justify his own cowardice.

Farther on in The Ring we shall see the Hero arrive and
make an end of dwarfs, giants, and gods. Meanwhile, let us
not forget that godhood means to Wagner infirmity and
compromise, and manhood strength and integrity. Above all,
we must understand – for it is the key to much that we are to

see – that the god, since his desire is toward a higher and fuller life, must long in his inmost soul for the advent of that greater power whose first work, though this he does not see as yet, must be his own undoing.

In the midst of all these far-reaching ideas, it is amusing to find Wagner still full of his ingrained theatrical professionalism, and introducing effects which now seem old-fashioned and stagey with as much energy and earnestness as if they were his loftiest inspirations. When Wotan wrests the ring from Alberic, the dwarf delivers a lurid and blood-curdling stage curse, calling down on its every future possessor care, fear and death. The musical phrase accompanying this outburst was a veritable harmonic and melodic bogey to mid-century ears, though time has now robbed it of its terrors. It sounds again when Fafnir slays Fasolt, and on every subsequent occasion when the ring brings death to its holder. This episode must justify itself purely as a piece of stage sensationalism. On deeper ground it is superfluous and confusing, as the ruin to which the pursuit of riches leads needs no curse to explain it; nor is there any sense in investing Alberic with providential powers in the matter.

THE VALKYRIE

BEFORE the curtain rises on The Valkyrie, let us see what has happened since it fell on The Rhine Gold. The persons of the drama will tell us presently; but as we probably do not understand German, that may not help us.

Wotan is still ruling the world in glory from his giant-built castle with his wife Fricka. But he has no security for the continuance of his reign, since Alberic may at any moment contrive to recover the ring, the full power of which he can wield because he has forsworn love. Such forswearing is not possible to Wotan; love, though not his highest need, is a higher than gold – otherwise he would be no god. Besides, as we have seen, his power has been established in the world by and as a system of laws enforced by penalties. These he must consent to be bound by himself; for a god who broke his own laws would betray the fact that legality and conformity are not the highest rule of conduct – a discovery fatal to his supremacy as Pontiff and Lawgiver. Hence he may not wrest the ring unlawfully from Fafnir, even if he could bring himself to forswear love.

In this insecurity he has hit on the idea of forming a heroic bodyguard. He has trained his love children as war-maidens (Valkyries) whose duty it is to sweep through battle-fields and bear away to Valhalla the souls of the bravest who fall there. Thus reinforced by a host of warriors, he has thoroughly indoctrinated them, Loki helping him as dialectician-in-chief, with the conventional system of law and duty, supernatural religion and self-sacrificing idealism, which they believe to be the essence of his godhood, but which is really only the machinery of the love of necessary power which is his mortal weakness. This process secures their fanatical devotion to his system of government; but he knows perfectly well that such systems, in spite of their moral pretensions, serve selfish and ambitious tyrants better than benevolent despots, and that, if once Alberic gets the ring back, he will easily out-Valhalla Valhalla, if not buy it over as a going concern. The only chance of permanent security, then, is the appearance in the world of a hero who, without any illicit prompting from Wotan, will destroy Alberic and wrest the ring from Fafnir. There will then, he believes, be no further cause for anxiety, since he does not yet conceive Heroism as a force hostile to Godhead. In his longing for a rescuer, it does not occur to him that when the Hero comes, his first exploit must be to sweep the gods and their ordinances from the path of the heroic will.

Indeed, he feels that in his own Godhead is the germ of such Heroism, and that from himself the Hero must spring. He takes to wandering, mostly in search of love, from Fricka and Valhalla. He seeks the First Mother; and through her womb, eternally fertile, the inner true thought that made him first a god is reborn as his daughter, uncorrupted by his ambition, unfettered by his machinery of power and his alliances with Fricka and Loki. This daughter, the Valkyrie Brynhild, is his true will, his real self (as he thinks): to her he may say what he must not say to anyone, since in speaking to her he but speaks to himself. 'Was keinem in Worten ich künde,' he says to her, 'unausgesprochen bleib es ewig: mit mir nur rath' ich, red' ich zu dir.'

But from Brynhild no hero can spring until there is a man of Wotan's race to breed with her. Wotan wanders further; and a mortal woman bears him twins: a son and a daughter. He separates them by letting the girl fall into the hands of a forest tribe which in due time gives her as wife to a fierce chief, one Hunding. With the son he himself leads the life of a wolf, and teaches him the only power a god can teach, the power of doing without happiness. When he has given him this terrible training, he abandons him, and goes to the bridal feast of his daughter Sieglinda and Hunding. In the blue cloak of the Wanderer, wearing the broad hat that flaps over the socket of his forfeited eye, he appears in Hunding's house, the middle pillar of which is a mighty tree. Into that tree, without a word, he strikes a sword up to the hilt, so that only the might of a hero can withdraw it. Then he goes out as silently as he came, blind to the truth that no weapon from the armory of Godhead can serve the turn of the true Human Hero. Neither Hunding nor any of his guests can move the sword; and there it stays awaiting the destined hand. That is the history of the generations between The Rhine Gold and The Valkyrie.

THE FIRST ACT

This time, as we sit looking expectantly at the curtain, we hear, not the deep booming of the Rhine, but the patter of forest downpour, accompanied by the mutter of a storm which soon gathers into a roar and culminates in crashing thunderbolts. As it passes off, the curtain rises; and there is no mistaking whose forest habitation we are in; for the central pillar is a mighty tree, and the place fit for the dwelling of a fierce chief. The door opens; and an exhausted man reels in; an adept from the school of unhappiness. Sieglinda finds him lying on the hearth. He explains that he has been in a fight; that his weapons, not being as strong as his arms, were broken; and that he had to fly. He desires some drink and a moment's rest; then he will go; for he is an unlucky person, and does not want to bring his ill-luck on the woman who is succoring him. But she, it appears, is also unhappy; and a strong sympathy springs up between them. When her husband arrives, he observes not only this sympathy, but a resemblance between them, a gleam of the snake in their eyes. They sit down to table; and the stranger tells them his unlucky story. He is the son of Wotan, who is known to him only as Wolfing, of the race of the Volsungs. The earliest thing he remembers is returning from a hunt with his father to find their home destroyed, his mother murdered, and his twin-sister carried off. This was the work of a tribe called the Neidings, upon whom he and Wolfing thenceforth waged implacable war until the day when his father disappeared, leaving no trace of himself but an empty wolfskin. The young Volsung was thus cast alone upon the world, finding most hands against him, and bringing no good luck even to his friends. His latest exploit has been the slaying of certain brothers who were forcing their sister to wed against her will. The result has been the slaughter of the woman by her brothers' clansmen, and his own narrow escape by flight.

His luck on this occasion is even worse than he supposes; for Hunding, by whose hearth he has taken refuge, is clansman to the slain brothers and is bound to avenge them. He tells the Volsung that in the morning, weapons or no weapons, he must fight for his life. Then he orders the woman to bed, and follows her himself, taking his spear with him.

The unlucky stranger, left brooding by the hearth, has nothing to console himself with but an old promise of his father's that he shall find a weapon to his hand when he most needs one. The last flicker of the dying fire strikes on the golden hilt of the sword that sticks in the tree; but he does not see it; and the embers sink into blackness. Then the woman returns. Hunding is safely asleep: she has drugged him. She tells the story of the one-eyed man who appeared at her forced marriage, and of the sword. She has always felt, she says, that her miseries will end in the arms of the hero who shall succeed in drawing it forth. The stranger, diffident as he is about his luck, has no misgivings as to his strength and destiny. He gives her his affection at once, and abandons himself to the charm of the night and the season; for it is the beginning of Spring. They soon learn from their confidences that she is his stolen twin-sister. He is transported to find that the heroic race of the Volsungs need neither perish nor be corrupted by a lower strain. Hailing the sword by the name of Nothung (or Needed), he plucks it from the tree as her bride-gift, and then, crying 'Both bride and sister be of thy brother; and blossom the blood of the Volsungs!' clasps her as the mate the Spring has brought him.

THE SECOND ACT

So far, Wotan's plan seems prospering. In the mountains he calls his war-maiden Brynhild, the child borne to him by the First Mother, and bids her see to it that Hunding shall fall in the approaching combat. But he is reckoning without his consort, Fricka. What will she, the Law, say to the lawless pair who have heaped incest on adultery? A hero may have defied the law, and put his own will in its place; but can a god hold him guiltless, when the whole power of the gods can enforce itself only by law? Fricka, shuddering with horror, outraged in every instinct, comes clamoring for punishment. Wotan pleads the general necessity of encouraging heroism in order to keep up the Valhalla bodyguard; but his remonstrances only bring upon him torrents of reproaches for his own unfaithfulness to the law in roaming through the world and begetting war-maidens, 'wolf-cubs', and the like. He is hopelessly beaten in the argument. Fricka is absolutely right when she declares that the ending of the gods began when he brought this wolf-hero into the world; and now, to save their very existence, she pitilessly demands his destruction. Wotan has no power to refuse; it is Fricka's mechanical force, and not his thought, that really rules the world. He has to recall Brynhild; take back his former instructions; and ordain that Hunding shall slay the Volsung.

But now comes another difficulty. Brynhild is the inner thought and will of Godhead, the aspiration from the high life to the higher that is its divine element, and only becomes separated from it when its resort to kingship and priestcraft for the sake of temporal power has made it false to itself. Hitherto, Brynhild, as Valkyrie or hero chooser, has obeyed Wotan implicitly, taking her work as the holiest and bravest in his kingdom; and now he tells her what he could not tell Fricka – what indeed he could not tell to Brynhild, were she not, as she says, his own will – the whole story of Alberic and of that inspiration about the raising up of a hero. She thoroughly approves of the inspiration; but when the story ends in the assumption that she too must obey Fricka, and help Fricka's vassal, Hunding, to undo the great work and strike the hero down, she for the first time hesitates to accept his command. In his fury and despair he overawes her by the most terrible threats of his anger; and she submits.

Then comes the Volsung Siegmund, following his sister bride, who has fled into the mountains in a revulsion of horror at having allowed herself to bring her hero to shame. Whilst she is lying exhausted and senseless in his arms, Brynhild appears to him and solemnly warns him that he must presently leave the earth with her. He asks whither he must follow her. To Valhalla, to take his place there among the heroes. He asks, shall he find his father there? Yes. Shall he find a wife there? Yes: he will be waited on by beautiful wish-maidens. Shall he meet his sister there? No. Then, says Siegmund, I will not come with you. She tries to make him understand that he cannot help himself. Being a hero, he will not be so persuaded: he has his father's sword, and does not fear Hunding. But when she tells him that she comes from his father, and that the sword of a god will not avail in the hands of a hero, he accepts his fate, but will shape it with his own hand, both for himself and his sister, by slaying her, and then killing himself with the last stroke of the sword. And thereafter he will go to Hell, rather than to Valhalla.

How now can Brynhild, being what she is, choose her side freely in a conflict between this hero and the vassal of Fricka? By instinct she at once throws Wotan's command to the winds, and bids Siegmund nerve himself for the combat with Hunding, in which she pledges him the protection of her shield. The horn of Hunding is soon heard; and Siegmund's spirits rise to fighting pitch at once. The two meet; and the

Valkyrie's shield is held before the hero. But when he delivers his sword-stroke at his foe, the weapon shivers on the spear of Wotan, who suddenly appears between them and the first of the race of heroes falls with the weapon of the Law's vassal through his breast. Brynhild snatches the fragments of the broken sword, and flies, carrying off the woman with her on her war-horse; and Wotan, in terrible wrath, slays Hunding with a wave of his hand, and starts in pursuit of his disobedient daughter.

THE THIRD ACT

On a rocky peak, four of the Valkyries are waiting for the rest. The absent ones soon arrive, galloping through the air with slain heroes, gathered from the battle-field, hanging over their saddles. Only Brynhild, who comes last, has for her spoil a live woman. When her eight sisters learn that she has defied Wotan, they dare not help her; and Brynhild has to rouse Sieglinda to make an effort to save herself, by reminding her that she bears in her the seed of a hero, and must face everything, endure anything, sooner than let that seed miscarry. Sieglinda, in a transport of exaltation, takes the fragments of the sword and flies into the forest. Then Wotan comes; the sisters fly in terror at his command; and he is left alone with Brynhild.

Here, then, we have the first of the inevitable moments which Wotan did not foresee. Godhead has now established its dominion over the world by a mighty Church, compelling obedience through its ally, the Law, with its formidable State organization of force of arms and cunning of brain. It has submitted to this alliance to keep the Plutonic power in check – built it up primarily for the sake of that soul in itself which cares only to make the highest better and the best higher; and now here is that very soul separated from it and working for the destruction of its indispensable ally, the lawgiving State. How is the rebel to be disarmed? Slain it cannot be by

Godhead, since it is still Godhead's own very dearest soul. But hidden, stifled, silenced it must be; or it will wreck the State and leave the Church defenceless. Not until it passes completely away from Godhead, and is reborn as the soul of the hero, can it work anything but the confusion and destruction of the existing order. How is the world to be protected against it in the meantime? Clearly Loki's help is needed here: it is the Lie that must, on the highest principles, hide the Truth. Let Loki surround this mountain top with the appearance of a consuming fire; and who will dare penetrate to Brynhild? It is true that if any man will walk boldly into that fire, he will discover it at once to be a lie, an illusion, a mirage through which he might carry a sack of gunpowder without being a penny the worse. Therefore let the fire seem so terrible that only the hero, when in the fulness of time he appears upon earth, will venture through it; and the problem is solved. Wotan, with a breaking heart, takes leave of Brynhild; throws her into a deep sleep; covers her with her long warshield; summons Loki, who comes in the shape of a wall of fire surrounding the mountain peak; and turns his back on Brynhild for ever.

The allegory here is happily not so glaringly obvious to the younger generations of our educated classes as it was forty years ago. In those days, any child who expressed a doubt as to the absolute truth of the Church's teaching, even to the extent of asking why Joshua told the sun to stand still instead of telling the earth to cease turning, or of pointing out that a whale's throat would hardly have been large enough to swallow Jonah, was unhesitatingly told that if it harbored such doubts it would spend all eternity after its death in horrible torments in a lake of burning brimstone. It is difficult to write or read this nowadays without laughing; yet no doubt millions of ignorant and credulous people are still teaching their children that. When Wagner himself was a little child, the fact that hell was a fiction devised for the intimidation and subjection of the masses was a well-kept secret of the thinking and governing classes. At that time the fires of Loki were a very real terror to all except persons of exceptional force of character and intrepidity of thought. Even thirty years after Wagner had printed the verses of The Ring for private circulation, we find him excusing himself from perfectly explicit denial of current superstitions, by reminding his readers that it would expose him to prosecution. In England, so many of our respectable voters are still grovelling in a gloomy devil worship, of which the fires of Loki are the main bulwark, that no Government has yet had the conscience or the courage to repeal our monstrous laws against 'blasphemy'.

SIEGFRIED

SIEGLINDA, when she flies into the forest with the hero's son unborn in her womb, and the broken pieces of his sword in her hand, finds shelter in the smithy of a dwarf, where she brings forth her child and dies. This dwarf is no other than Mimmy, the brother of Alberic, the same who made for him the magic helmet. His aim in life is to gain possession of the helmet, the ring and the treasure, and through them to obtain that Plutonic mastery of the world under the beginnings of which he himself writhed during Alberic's brief reign. Mimmy is a blinking, shambling, ancient creature, too weak and timid to dream of taking arms himself to despoil Fafnir who still, transformed to a monstrous serpent, broods on the gold in a hole in the rocks. Mimmy needs the help of a hero for that; and he has craft enough to know that it is quite possible, and indeed much in the ordinary way of the world, for senile avarice and craft to set youth and bravery to work to win empire for it. He knows the pedigree of the child left on his hands, and nurses it to manhood with great care.

His plans are too well rewarded for his comfort. The boy Siegfried, having no god to instruct him in the art of unhappiness, inherits none of his father's ill luck, and all his father's hardihood. The fear against which Siegmund set his face like flint, and the woe which he wore down, are unknown to the son. The father was faithful and grateful: the son knows no law but his own humor; detests the ugly dwarf who has nursed him; chafes furiously under his claims for some return for his tender care; and is, in short, a totally unmoral person, a born anarchist, the ideal of Bakoonin, an anticipation of the 'overman' of Nietzsche. He is enormously strong, full of life and fun, dangerous and destructive to what he dislikes, and affectionate to what he likes; so that it is fortunate that his

227

likes and dislikes are sane and healthy. Altogether an inspir-
iting young forester, a son of the morning, in whom the
heroic race has come out into the sunshine from the clouds of
his grandfather's majestic entanglements with law, and the
night of his father's tragic struggle with it.

THE FIRST ACT

Mimmy's smithy is a cave, in which he hides from the light
like the eyeless fish of the American caverns. Before the
curtain rises the music already tells us that we are groping in
darkness. When it does rise Mimmy is in difficulties. He is
trying to make a sword for his nursling, who is now big
enough to take the field against Fafnir. Mimmy can make
mischievous swords; but it is not with dwarfmade weapons
that heroic man will hew the way of his own will through
religions and governments and plutocracies and all the other
devices of the kingdom of the fears of the unheroic. As fast as
Mimmy makes swords, Siegfried Bakoonin smashes them,
and then takes the poor old swordsmith by the scruff of the
neck and chastises him wrathfully. The particular day on
which the curtain rises begins with one of these trying
domestic incidents. Mimmy has just done his best with a
new sword of surpassing excellence. Siegfried returns home
in rare spirits with a wild bear, to the extreme terror of the
wretched dwarf. When the bear is dismissed, the new sword
is produced. It is promptly smashed, as usual, with, also, the
usual effects on the temper of Siegfried, who is quite
boundless in his criticisms of the smith's boasted skill, and
declares that he would smash the sword's maker too if he
were not too disgusting to be handled.

Mimmy falls back on his stock defence; a string of maudlin
reminders of the care with which he has nursed the little boy
into manhood. Siegfried replies candidly that the strangest
thing about all this care is that instead of making him grateful,
it inspires him with a lively desire to wring the dwarf's neck.

Only, he admits that he always comes back to his Mimmy, though he loathes him more than any living thing in the forest. On this admission the dwarf attempts to build a theory of filial instinct. He explains that he is Siegfried's father, and that this is why Siegfried cannot do without him. But Siegfried has learned from his forest companions, the birds and foxes and wolves, that mothers as well as fathers go to the making of children. Mimmy, on the desperate ground that man is neither bird nor fox, declares that he is Siegfried's father and mother both. He is promptly denounced as a filthy liar, because the birds and foxes are exactly like their parents, whereas Siegfried, having often watched his own image in the water, can testify that he is no more like Mimmy than a toad is like a trout. Then, to place the conversation on a plane of entire frankness, he throttles Mimmy until he is speechless. When the dwarf recovers, he is so daunted that he tells Siegfried the truth about his birth, and for testimony thereof produces the pieces of the sword that broke upon Wotan's spear. Siegfried instantly orders him to repair the sword on pain of an unmerciful thrashing, and rushes off into the forest, rejoicing in the discovery that he is no kin of Mimmy's, and need have no more to do with him when the sword is mended.

Poor Mimmy is now in a worse plight than ever; for he has long ago found that the sword utterly defies his skill: the steel will yield neither to his hammer nor to his furnace. Just then there walks into his cave a Wanderer, in a blue mantle, spear in hand, with one eye concealed by the brim of his wide hat. Mimmy, not by nature hospitable, tries to drive him away; but the Wanderer announces himself as a wise man, who can tell his host, in emergency, what it most concerns him to know. Mimmy, taking this offer in high dudgeon, because it implies that his visitor's wits are better than his own, offers to tell the wise one something that *he* does not know: to wit, the way to the door. The imperturbable Wanderer's reply is to sit down and challenge the dwarf to a trial of wit. He wagers his head against Mimmy's that he will answer any three questions the dwarf can put to him.

Now here were Mimmy's opportunity, had he only the wit to ask what he wants to know, instead of pretending to know everything already. It is above all things needful to him at this moment to find out how that sword can be mended; and there has just dropped in upon him in his need the one person who can tell him. In such circumstances a wise man would hasten to shew to his visitor his three deepest ignorances, and ask him to dispel them. The dwarf, being a crafty fool, desiring only to detect ignorance in his guest, asks him for information on the three points on which he is proudest of being thoroughly well instructed himself. His three questions are: Who dwell under the earth? Who dwell on the earth? and Who dwell in the cloudy heights above? The Wanderer, in reply, tells him of the dwarfs and of Alberic; of the earth, and the giants Fasolt and Fafnir; of the gods and of Wotan: himself, as Mimmy now recognizes with awe.

Next, it is Mimmy's turn to face three questions. What is that race, dearest to Wotan, against which Wotan has nevertheless done his worst? Mimmy can answer that: he knows the Volsungs, the race of heroes born of Wotan's infidelities to Fricka, and can tell the Wanderer the whole story of the twins and their son Siegfried. Wotan compliments him on his knowledge, and asks further with what sword Siegfried will slay Fafnir? Mimmy can answer that too: he has the whole history of the sword at his fingers' ends. Wotan hails him as the knowingest of the knowing, and then hurls at him the question he should himself have asked: Who will mend the sword? Mimmy, his head forfeited, confesses with loud lamentations that he cannot answer. The Wanderer reads him an appropriate little lecture on the folly of being too clever to ask what he wants to know, and informs him that a smith to whom fear is unknown will mend Nothung. To this smith he leaves the forfeited head of his host, and wanders off into the forest. Then Mimmy's nerves give way completely. He shakes like a man in delirium tremens, and has a horrible nightmare, in the supreme convulsion of which Siegfried, returning from the forest, presently finds him.

A curious and amusing conversation follows. Siegfried himself does not know fear, and is impatient to acquire it as an accomplishment. Mimmy is all fear: the world for him is a phantasmagoria of terrors. It is not that he is afraid of being eaten by bears in the forest, or of burning his fingers in the forge fire. A lively objection to being destroyed or maimed does not make a man a coward: on the contrary, it is the beginning of a brave man's wisdom. But in Mimmy, fear is not the effect of danger: it is a natural quality of him which no security can allay. He is like many a poor newspaper editor, who dares not print the truth, however simple, even when it is obvious to himself and all his readers. Not that anything unpleasant would happen to him if he did – not, indeed, that he could fail to become a distinguished and influential leader of opinion by fearlessly pursuing such a course, but solely because he lives in a world of imaginary terrors, rooted in a modest and gentlemanly mistrust of his own strength and worth, and consequently of the value of his opinion. Just so is Mimmy afraid of anything that can do him any good, especially of the light and the fresh air. He is also convinced that anybody who is not sufficiently steeped in fear to be constantly on his guard must perish immediately on his first sally into the world. To preserve Siegfried for the enterprise to which he has destined him he makes a grotesque attempt to teach him fear. He appeals to his experience of the terrors of the forest, of its dark places, of its threatening noises, its stealthy ambushes, its sinister flickering lights, its heart-tightening ecstasies of dread.

All this has no other effect than to fill Siegfried with wonder and curiosity; for the forest is a place of delight for him. He is as eager to experience Mimmy's terrors as a schoolboy to feel what an electric shock is like. Then Mimmy has the happy idea of describing Fafnir to him as a likely person to

231

give him an exemplary fright. Siegfried jumps at the idea, and, since Mimmy cannot mend the sword for him, proposes to set to work then and there to mend it for himself. Mimmy shakes his head, and bids him see now how his youthful laziness and frowardness have found him out – how he would not learn the smith's craft from Professor Mimmy, and therefore does not know how even to begin mending the sword. Siegfried Bakoonin's retort is simple and crushing. He points out that the net result of Mimmy's academic skill is that he can neither make a decent sword himself nor even set one to rights when it is damaged. Reckless of the remonstrances of the scandalized professor, he seizes a file, and in a few moments utterly destroys the fragments of the sword by rasping them into a heap of steel filings. Then he puts the filings into a crucible; buries it in the coals; and sets to at the bellows with the shouting exultation of the anarchist who destroys only to clear the ground for creation. When the steel is melted he runs it into a mould; and lo! a sword-blade in the rough. Mimmy, amazed at the success of this violation of all the rules of his craft, hails Siegfried as the mightiest of smiths, professing himself barely worthy to be his cook and scullion; and forthwith proceeds to poison some soup for him so that he may murder him safely when Fafnir is slain. Meanwhile Siegfried forges and tempers and hammers and rivets, uproariously singing the while as nonsensically as the Rhine daughters themselves. Finally he assails the anvil on which Mimmy's swords have been shattered, and cleaves it with a mighty stroke of the newly forged Nothung.

THE SECOND ACT

In the darkest hour before the dawn of that night, we find ourselves before the cave of Fafnir; and there we find Alberic, who can find nothing better to do with himself than to watch the haunt of the dragon, and eat his heart out in vain longing for the gold and the ring. The wretched Fafnir, once an honest giant, can only make himself terrible enough to keep his gold by remaining a venomous reptile. Why he should not become an honest giant again, and clear out of his cavern, leaving the gold and the ring and the rest of it for anyone fool enough to take them at such a price, is the first question that would occur to anyone except a civilized man, who would be too accustomed to that sort of mania to be at all surprised at it.

To Alberic in the night comes the Wanderer, whom the dwarf, recognizing his despoiler of old, abuses as a shameless thief, taunting him with the helpless way in which all his boasted power is tied up with the laws and bargains recorded on the haft of his spear, which, says Alberic truly, would crumble like chaff in his hands if he dared use it for his own real ends. Wotan, having already had to kill his own son with it, knows that very well; but it troubles him no more; for he is now at last rising to abhorrence of his own artificial power, and looking to the coming hero, not for its consolidation but its destruction. When Alberic breaks out again with his still unquenched hope of one day destroying the gods and ruling the world through the ring, Wotan is no longer shocked. He tells Alberic that Brother Mime approaches with a hero whom Godhead can neither help nor hinder. Alberic may try his luck against him without disturbance from Valhalla. Perhaps, he suggests, if Alberic warns Fafnir, and offers to deal with the hero for him, Fafnir may give him the ring. They accordingly wake up the dragon, who condescends to enter into bellowing conversation, but is proof against their proposition, strong in the magic of property. 'I have and hold,' he says, 'leave me to sleep.' Wotan, with a wise laugh, turns to Alberic. 'That shot missed,' he says, 'no use abusing me for it. And now let me tell you one thing. All things happen according to their nature; and *you* can't alter them.' And so he leaves him. Alberic, raging with the sense that his old enemy has been laughing at him, and yet prophetically convinced that the last word will not be with the god, hides himself as the day breaks, and his brother approaches with Siegfried.

Mimmy makes a final attempt to frighten Siegfried by discoursing of the dragon's terrible jaws, poisonous breath, corrosive spittle and deadly, stinging tail. Siegfried is not interested in the tail; he wants to know whether the dragon has a heart, being confident of his ability to stick Nothung into it if it exists. Reassured on this point, he drives Mimmy away, and stretches himself under the trees, listening to the morning chatter of the birds. One of them has a great deal to say to him; but he cannot understand it; and after vainly trying to carry on the conversation with a reed which he cuts, he takes to entertaining the bird with tunes on his horn, asking it to send him a loving mate such as all the other creatures of the forest have. His tunes wake up the dragon; and Siegfried makes merry over the grim mate the bird has sent him. Fafnir is highly scandalized by the irreverence of the young Bakoonin. He loses his temper; fights; and is forthwith slain, to his own great astonishment.

In such conflicts one learns to interpret the messages of Nature a little. When Siegfried, stung by the dragon's vitriolic blood, pops his finger into his mouth and tastes it, he understands what the bird is saying to him, and, instructed by it concerning the treasures within his reach, goes into the cave to secure the gold, the ring and the wishing cap. Then Mimmy returns, and is confronted by Alberic. The two quarrel furiously over the sharing of the booty they have not yet secured, until Siegfried comes from the cave with the ring and the helmet, not much impressed by the heap of gold, and disappointed because he has not yet learned to fear.

He has, however, learnt to read the thoughts of such a creature as poor Mimmy, who, intending to overwhelm him with flattery and fondness, only succeeds in making such a self-revelation of murderous envy that Siegfried smites him with Nothung and slays him, to the keen satisfaction of the hidden Alberic. Caring nothing for the gold, which he leaves to the care of the slain, disappointed in his fancy for learning fear, and longing for a mate, he casts himself wearily down, and again appeals to his friend the bird, who tells him of a woman sleeping on a mountain peak within a fortress of fire that only the fearless can penetrate. Siegfried is up in a moment with all the tumult of spring in his veins, and follows the flight of the bird as it pilots him to the fiery mountain.

THE THIRD ACT

To the foot of the mountain comes also the Wanderer, now nearing his doom. He calls up the First Mother from the depths of the earth, and begs counsel from her. She bids him confer with the Norns (the Fates). But they are of no use to him; what he seeks is some foreknowledge of the way of the Will in its perpetual strife with these helpless Fates who can only spin the net of circumstance and environment round the feet of men. Why not, says Erda then, go to the daughter I bore you, and take counsel with her? He has to explain how he has cut himself off from her, and set the fires of Loki between the world and her counsel. In that case the First Mother cannot help him; such a separation is part of the bewilderment that is ever the first outcome of her eternal work of thrusting the life energy of the world to higher and higher organization. She can shew him no way of escape from the destruction he foresees. Then from the innermost of him breaks the confession that he rejoices in his doom, and now himself exults in passing away with all his ordinances and alliances, with the spear-sceptre which he has only wielded on condition of slaying his dearest children with it, with the kingdom, the power and the glory which will never again boast themselves as 'world without end'. And so he dismisses Erda to her sleep in the heart of the earth as the forest bird draws near, piloting the slain son's son to his goal.

Now it is an excellent thing to triumph in the victory of the new order and the passing away of the old; but if you happen to be part of the old order yourself, you must none the less fight for your life. It seems hardly possible that the British army at the battle of Waterloo did not include at least one Englishman intelligent enough to hope, for the sake of his country and humanity, that Napoleon might defeat the allied sovereigns; but such an Englishman would kill a French cuirassier rather than be killed by him just as energetically as the silliest soldier ever encouraged, by people who ought to know better, to call his ignorance, ferocity and folly, patriotism and duty. Outworn life may have become mere error; but it still claims the right to die a natural death, and will raise its hand against the millennium itself in self defence if it tries to come by the short cut of murder. Wotan finds this out when he comes face to face with Siegfried, who is brought to a standstill at the foot of the mountain by the disappearance of the bird. Meeting the Wanderer there, he asks him the way to the mountain where a woman sleeps surrounded by fire. The Wanderer questions him, and extracts his story from him, breaking into fatherly delight when Siegfried, describing the mending of the sword, remarks that all he knew about the business was that the broken bits of Nothung would be of no use to him unless he made a new sword out of them right over again from the beginning. But the Wanderer's interest is by no means reciprocated by Siegfried. His majesty and elderly dignity are thrown away on the young anarchist, who, unwilling to waste time talking, bluntly bids him either shew him the way to the mountain, or else 'shut his muzzle'. Wotan is a little hurt. 'Patience, my lad,' he says, 'if you were an old man I should treat you with respect.' 'That would be a precious notion,' says Siegfried. 'All my life long I was bothered and hampered by an old man until I swept him out of my way. I will sweep you in the same fashion if you don't let me pass. Why do you wear such a big hat; and what has happened to one of your eyes? was it knocked out by somebody whose way you obstructed?' To which Wotan replies allegorically that the eye that is gone – the eye that his marriage with Fricka cost him – is now looking at him out of Siegfried's head. At this, Siegfried gives up the Wanderer as a lunatic, and renews his threats of personal violence. Then Wotan throws off the mask of the Wanderer; uplifts the world-governing spear; and puts forth all his divine awe and grandeur as the guardian of the mountain, round the crest of which the fires of Loki now break into a red background for the majesty of the god. But all this is lost on Siegfried Bakoonin. 'Aha!' he cries, as the spear is levelled against his breast, 'I have found my father's foe'; and the spear falls in two pieces under the stroke of Nothung. 'Up then,' says Wotan, 'I cannot withhold you,' and disappears forever from the eye of man. The fires roll down the mountain; but Siegfried goes at them as exultantly as he went at the forging of the sword or the heart of the dragon, and shoulders his way through them, joyously sounding his horn to the accompaniment of their crackling and seething. And never a hair of his head is singed. Those frightful flames which have scared mankind for centuries from the Truth have not heat enough in them to make a child shut its eyes. They are mere phantasmagoria, highly creditable to Loki's imaginative stage-management; but nothing ever has perished or will perish eternally in them except the Churches which have been so poor and faithless as to trade for their power on the lies of a romancer.

BACK TO OPERA AGAIN

And now, O Nibelungen Spectator, pluck up; for all allegories come to an end somewhere; and the hour of your release from these explanations is at hand. The rest of what you are going to see is opera, and nothing but opera. Before many bars have been played, Siegfried and the wakened Brynhild, newly become tenor and soprano, will sing a concerted cadenza; plunge on from that to a magnificent love duet; and end with a precipitous *allegro a capella*, driven headlong to its end by the impetuous semiquaver triplets of the famous finales to the first act of Don Giovanni or the coda to the Leonore overture, with a specifically contrapuntal theme, *points d'orgue*, and a high C for the soprano all complete.

What is more, the work which follows, entitled Night Falls on The Gods, is a thorough grand opera. In it you shall see what you have so far missed, the opera chorus in full parade on the stage, not presuming to interfere with the prima donna as she sings her death song over the footlights. Nay, that chorus will have its own chance when it first appears, with a good roaring strain in C major, not, after all, so very different from, or at all less absurd than the choruses of courtiers in La Favorita or 'Per te immenso giubilo' in Lucia. The harmony is no doubt a little developed, Wagner augmenting his fifths with a G sharp where Donizetti would have put his fingers in his ears and screamed for G natural. But it is an opera chorus all the same; and along with it we have theatrical grandiosities that recall Meyerbeer and Verdi: *pezzi d'insieme* for all the principals in a row, vengeful conjurations for trios of them, romantic death song for the tenor: in short, all manner of operatic conventions.

Now it is probable that some of us will have been so talked by the more superstitious Bayreuth pilgrims into regarding Die Götterdämmerung as the mighty climax to a mighty epic, more Wagnerian than all the other three sections put together, as not to dare notice this startling atavism, especially if we find the trio-conjurations more exhilarating than the metaphysical discourses of Wotan in the three true music dramas of The Ring. There is, however, no real atavism involved. Die Götterdämmerung, though the last of The Ring dramas in order of performance, was the first in order of conception, and was indeed the root from which all the others sprang.

The history of the matter is as follows. All Wagner's works prior to The Ring are operas. The last of them, Lohengrin, is perhaps the best known of modern operas. As performed in its entirety at Bayreuth, it is even more operatic than it appears at Covent Garden, because it happens that its most old-fashioned features, notably some of the big set concerted pieces for principals and chorus (*pezzi d'insieme* as I have called them above), are harder to perform than the more modern and characteristically Wagnerian sections, and for that reason were cut out in preparing the abbreviated fashionable version. Thus Lohengrin came upon the ordinary operatic stage as a more advanced departure from current operatic models than its composer had made it. Still, it is unmistakably an opera, with chorus, concerted pieces, grand finales and a heroine who, if she does not sing florid variations with flute obbligato, is none the less a very perceptible prima donna. In everything but musical technique the change from Lohengrin to The Rhine Gold is quite revolutionary.

The explanation is that Night Falls on The Gods came in between them, although its music was not finished until twenty years after that of The Rhine Gold, and thus belongs to a later and more masterful phase of Wagner's harmonic style. It first came into Wagner's head as an opera to be entitled 'Siegfried's Death', founded on the old Niblung Sagas, which offered to Wagner the same material for an effective theatrical tragedy as they did to Ibsen. Ibsen's Vikings in Helgeland is, in kind, what 'Siegfried's Death' was originally intended to be: that is, a heroic piece for the theatre, without the metaphysical or allegorical complications of The Ring. Indeed, the ultimate catastrophe of the Saga cannot by any perversion of ingenuity be adapted to the perfectly clear allegorical design of The Rhine Gold, The Valkyrie and Siegfried.

SIEGFRIED AS PROTESTANT

THE philosophically fertile element in the original project of 'Siegfried's Death' was the conception of Siegfried himself as a type of the healthy man raised to perfect confidence in his own impulses by an intense and joyous vitality which is above fear, sickliness of conscience, malice, and the make-shifts and moral crutches of law and order which accompany them. Such a character appears extraordinarily fascinating and exhilarating to our guilty and conscience-ridden generations, however little they may understand him. The world has always delighted in the man who is delivered from conscience. From Punch and Don Juan down to Robert Macaire, Jeremy Diddler and the pantomime clown, he has always drawn large audiences; but hitherto he has been decorously given to the devil at the end. Indeed eternal punishment is sometimes deemed too high a compliment to his nature. When the late Lord Lytton, in his Strange Story, introduced a character personifying the joyousness of intense vitality, he felt bound to deny him the immortal soul which was at the time conceded even to the humblest characters in fiction, and to accept mischievousness, cruelty and utter incapacity for sympathy as the inevitable consequence of his magnificent bodily and mental health.

In short, though men felt all the charm of abounding life and abandonment to its impulses, they dared not, in their deep self-mistrust, conceive it otherwise than as a force making for evil – one which must lead to universal ruin unless checked and literally mortified by self-renunciation in obedience to super-human guidance, or at least to some reasoned system of morals. When it became apparent to the cleverest of them that no such superhuman guidance existed, and that their secularist systems had all the fictitiousness of 'revelation' without its poetry, there was no escaping the conclusion that all the good that man had done must be put down to his arbitrary will as well as all the evil he had done; and it was also obvious that if progress were a reality, his beneficent impulses must be gaining on his destructive ones. It was under the influence of these ideas that we began to hear about the joy of life where we had formerly heard about the grace of God or the Age of Reason, and that the boldest spirits began to raise the question whether churches and laws and the like were not doing a great deal more harm than good by their action in limiting the freedom of the human will. Four hundred years ago, when belief in God and in revelation was general throughout Europe, a similar wave of thought led the strongest-hearted peoples to affirm that every man's private judgment was a more trustworthy interpreter of God and revelation than the Church. This was called Protestantism; and though the Protestants were not strong enough for their creed, and soon set up a Church of their own, yet the movement, on the whole, has justified the direction it took. Nowadays the supernatural element in Protestantism has perished; and if every man's private judgment is still to be justified as the most trustworthy interpreter of the will of Humanity (which is not a more extreme proposition than the old one about the will of God) Protestantism must take a fresh step in advance, and become Anarchism. Which it has accordingly done, Anarchism being one of the notable new creeds of the eighteenth and nineteenth centuries.

The weak place which experience finds out in the Anarchist theory is its reliance on the progress already achieved by 'Man'. There is no such thing as Man in the world: what we have to deal with is a multitude of men, some of them great rascals, some of them great statesmen, others both, with a vast majority capable of managing their personal affairs, but not of comprehending social organization, or grappling with the problems created by their association in enormous numbers. If 'Man' means this majority, then 'Man' has made no progress; he has, on the contrary, resisted it. He will not even pay the cost of

existing institutions; the requisite money has to be filched from
him by 'indirect taxation'. Such people, like Wagner's giants,
must be governed by laws; and their assent to such government
must be secured by deliberately filling them with prejudices
and practising on their imaginations by pageantry and artificial eminences and dignities. The government is of course
established by the few who are capable of government, though,
its mechanism once complete, it may be, and generally is,
carried on unintelligently by people who are incapable of it, the
capable people repairing it from time to time when it gets too
far behind the continuous advance or decay of civilization. All
these capable people are thus in the position of Wotan, forced
to maintain as sacred, and themselves submit to, laws which
they privately know to be obsolescent makeshifts, and to affect
the deepest veneration for creeds and ideals which they ridicule among themselves with cynical scepticism. No individual
Siegfried can rescue them from this bondage and hypocrisy; in
fact, the individual Siegfried has come often enough, only to
find himself confronted with the alternative of governing those
who are not Siegfrieds or risking destruction at their hands.
And this dilemma will persist until Wotan's inspiration comes
to our governors, and they see that their business is not the
devising of laws and institutions to prop up the weaknesses of
mobs and secure the survival of the unfittest, but the breeding
of men whose wills and intelligences may be depended on to
produce spontaneously the social wellbeing our clumsy laws
now aim at and miss. The majority of men at present in Europe
have no business to be alive; and no serious progress will be
made until we address ourselves earnestly and scientifically to
the task of producing trustworthy human material for society.
In short, it is necessary to breed a race of men in whom the life-
giving impulses predominate, before the New Protestantism
becomes politically practicable.[1]

The most inevitable dramatic conception, then, of the
nineteenth century is that of a perfectly naïve hero upsetting
religion, law and order in all directions, and establishing in

their place the unfettered action of Humanity doing exactly what it likes, and producing order instead of confusion thereby because it likes to do what is necessary for the good of the race. This conception, already incipient in Adam Smith's Wealth of Nations, was certain at last to reach some great artist, and be embodied by him in a masterpiece. It was also certain that if that master happened to be a German, he should take delight in describing his hero as the Free Willer of Necessity, thereby beyond measure exasperating Englishmen with a congenital incapacity for metaphysics.

PANACEA QUACKERY, OTHERWISE IDEALISM

Unfortunately, human enlightenment does not progress by nicer and nicer adjustments, but by violent corrective reactions which invariably send us clean over our saddle and would bring us to the ground on the other side if the next reaction did not send us back again with equally excessive zeal. Ecclesiasticism and Constitutionalism sends us one way, Protestantism and Anarchism the other; Order rescues us from confusion and lands us in Tyranny; Liberty then saves the situation and is presently found to be as great a nuisance as Despotism. A scientifically balanced application of these forces, theoretically possible, is practically incompatible with human passion. Besides, we have the same weakness in morals as in medicine: we cannot be cured of running after panaceas, or, as they are called in the sphere of morals, ideals. One generation sets up duty, renunciation, self-sacrifice as a panacea. The next generation, especially the women, wake up at the age of forty or thereabouts to the fact that their lives have been wasted in the worship of this ideal, and, what is still more aggravating, that the elders who imposed it on them did so in a fit of satiety with their own experiments in the other direction. Then that defrauded generation foams at the mouth at the very mention of duty, and sets up the alternative panacea of love, their deprivation of which seems to them to have been the most cruel and mischievous feature of their slavery to duty. It is useless to warn them that this reaction, if prescribed as a panacea, will prove as great a failure as all the other reactions have done; for they do not recognize its identity with any reaction that ever occurred before. Take for instance the hackneyed historic example of the austerity of the Commonwealth being followed by the licence of the Restoration. You cannot persuade any moral enthusiast to accept this as a pure oscillation from action to reaction. If he is a Puritan he looks upon the Restoration as a national disaster: if he is an artist he regards it as the salvation of the country from gloom, devil worship and starvation of the affections. The Puritan is ready to try the Commonwealth again with a few modern improvements: the Amateur is equally ready to try the Restoration with modern enlightenments. And so for the present we must be content to proceed by reactions, hoping that each will establish some permanently practical and beneficial reform or moral habit that will survive the correction of its excesses by the next reaction.

DRAMATIC ORIGIN OF WOTAN

We can now see how a single drama in which Wotan does not appear, and of which Siegfried is the hero, expanded itself into a great fourfold drama of which Wotan is the hero. You cannot dramatize a reaction by personifying the reacting force only, any more than Archimedes could lift the world without a fulcrum for his lever. You must also personify the established power against which the new force is reacting; and in the conflict between them you get your drama, conflict being the essential ingredient in all drama. Siegfried, as the hero of Die Götterdämmerung, is only the *primo tenore robusto* of an opera book, deferring his death, after he has been stabbed in the last act, to sing rapturous love strains to the heroine exactly like Edgardo in Donizetti's Lucia. In order to make him intelligible in the wider significance which his joyous, fearless, conscienceless heroism soon assumed in Wagner's imagination, it was necessary to provide him with a much vaster dramatic antagonist than the operatic villain Hagen. Hence Wagner had to create Wotan as the anvil for Siegfried's hammer; and since there was no room for Wotan in the original opera book, Wagner had to work back to a preliminary drama reaching primarily to the very beginnings of human society. And since, on this world-embracing scale, it was clear that Siegfried must come into conflict with many baser and stupider forces than those lofty ones of supernatural religion and political constitutionalism typified by Wotan and his wife Fricka, these minor antagonists had to be dramatized also in the persons of Alberic, Mime, Fafnir, Loki, and the rest. None of these appear in Night Falls on The Gods save Alberic, whose weird dream-colloquy with Hagen, effective as it is, is as purely theatrical as the scene of the Ghost in Hamlet, or the statue in Don Giovanni. Cut the conference of the Norns and the visit of Valtrauta to Brynhild out of Night Falls on The Gods, and the drama remains coherent and complete without them. Retain them, and the play becomes connected by conversational references with the three music dramas; but the connection establishes no philosophic coherence, no real identity between the operatic Brynhild of the Gibichung episode (presently to be related) and the daughter of Wotan and the First Mother.

THE LOVE PANACEA

We shall now find that at the point where The Ring changes from music drama into opera, it also ceases to be philosophic, and becomes didactic. The philosophic part is a dramatic symbol of the world as Wagner observed it. In the didactic part the philosophy degenerates into the prescription of a romantic nostrum for all human ills. Wagner, only mortal after all, succumbed to the panacea mania when his philosophy was exhausted, like any of the rest of us.

The panacea is by no means an original one. Wagner was anticipated in the year 1819 by a young country gentleman from Sussex named Shelley, in a work of extraordinary artistic power and splendor. Prometheus Unbound is an English attempt at a Ring; and when it is taken into account that the author was only 27, whereas Wagner was 40 when he completed the poem of The Ring, our vulgar patriotism may find an envious satisfaction in insisting upon the comparison. Both works set forth the same conflict between humanity and its gods and governments, issuing in the redemption of man from their tyranny by the growth of his will into perfect strength and self-confidence; and both finish by a lapse into panacea-mongering didacticism by the holding up of Love as the remedy for all evils and the solvent of all social difficulties.

The differences between Prometheus Unbound and The Ring are as interesting as the likenesses. Shelley, caught in the pugnacity of his youth and the first impetuosity of his prodigious artistic power by the first fierce attack of the New Reformation, gave no quarter to the antagonist of his hero. His Wotan, whom he calls Jupiter, is the almighty fiend into whom the Englishman's God had degenerated during two centuries of ignorant Bible worship and shameless commercialism. He is Alberic, Fafnir, Loki and the ambitious side of Wotan all rolled into one melodramatic demon who is finally torn from his throne and hurled shrieking into the abyss by a spirit representing that conception of Eternal Law which has been replaced since by the conception of Evolution. Wagner, an older, more experienced man than the Shelley of 1819, understood Wotan and pardoned him, separating him tenderly from all the compromising alliances to which Shelley fiercely held him; making the truth and heroism which overthrow him the children of his inmost heart; and representing him as finally acquiescing in and working for his own supersession and annihilation. Shelley, in his later works, is seen progressing towards the same tolerance, justice, and humility of spirit, as he advanced towards the middle age he never reached. But there is no progress from Shelley to Wagner as regards the panacea, except that in Wagner there is a certain shadow of night and death come on it; nay, even a clear opinion that the supreme good of love is that it so completely satisfies the desire for life that after it the Will to Live ceases to trouble us, and we are at last content to achieve the highest happiness of death.

This reduction of the panacea to absurdity was not forced upon Shelley, because the love which acts as a universal solvent in his Prometheus Unbound is a sentiment of affectionate benevolence which has nothing to do with sexual passion. It might, and in fact does, exist in the absence of any sexual interest whatever. The words mercy and kindness connote it less ambiguously than the word love. But Wagner sought always for some point of contact between his ideas and the physical senses, so that people might not only think or imagine them in the eighteenth-century fashion, but see them on the stage, hear them from the orchestra, and feel them through the infection of passionate emotion. Dr Johnson kicking the stone to confute Berkeley is not more bent on common-sense concreteness than Wagner: on all occasions he insists on the need for sensuous apprehension to give reality to abstract comprehension, maintaining, in fact, that reality has no other meaning. Now he could apply this process to poetic love only by following it back to its alleged origin in sexual passion, the emotional phenomena of which he has expressed in music with a frankness and forcible naturalism which would possibly have scandalized Shelley. The love duet in the first act of The Valkyrie is brought to a point at which the conventions of our society demand the precipitate fall of the curtain; whilst the prelude to Tristan and Isolde is such an astonishingly intense and faithful translation into music of the emotions which accompany the union of a pair of lovers that it is questionable whether the great popularity of this piece at our orchestral concerts really means that our audiences are entirely catholic in their respect for life in all its beneficently creative functions, or whether they simply enjoy the music without understanding it.

But however offensive and inhuman may be the superstition which brands such exaltations of natural passion as shameful and indecorous, there is at least as much common sense in disparaging love as in setting it up as a panacea. Even the mercy and loving-kindness of Shelley do not hold good as a universal law of conduct: Shelley himself makes extremely short work of Jupiter, just as Siegfried does of Fafnir, Mime and Wotan; and the fact that Prometheus is saved from doing the destructive part of his work by the intervention of that very nebulous personification of Eternity called Demogorgon does not in the least save the situation, because, flatly, there is no such person as Demogorgon, and if Prometheus does not pull down Jupiter himself, no one else will. It would be exasperating, if it were not so funny, to see these poets leading their heroes through blood and destruction to the conclusion that, as Browning's David puts it (David of all people!), 'All's Love; yet all's Law.'

Certainly it is clear enough that such love as that implied by Siegfried's first taste of fear as he cuts through the mailed coat of the sleeping figure on the mountain, and discovers that it is a woman; by her fierce revolt against being touched by him when his terror gives way to ardor; by his manly transports of victory; and by the womanly mixture of rapture and horror with which she abandons herself to the passion which has seized on them both, is an experience which it is much better, like the vast majority of us, never to have passed through, than to allow it to play more than a recreative holiday part in our lives. It did not play a very large part in Wagner's own laborious life, and does not occupy more than two scenes of The Ring. Tristan and Isolde, wholly devoted to it, is a poem of destruction and death. The Mastersingers, a work full of health, fun and happiness, contains not a single bar of love music that can be described as passionate: the hero of it is a widower who cobbles shoes, writes verses, and contents himself with looking on at the sweetheartings of his customers. Parsifal makes an end of it altogether. The truth is that the love panacea in Night Falls on The Gods and in the last act of Siegfried is a survival of the first crude operatic conception of the story, modified by an anticipation of Wagner's later, though not latest, conception of love as the fulfiller of our Will to Live and consequently our reconciler to night and death.

NOT LOVE, BUT LIFE

The only faith which any reasonable disciple can gain from The Ring is not in love, but in life itself as a tireless power which is continually driving onward and upward – not, please observe, being beckoned or drawn by Das ewig Weibliche or any other external sentimentality, but growing from within, by its own inexplicable energy, into ever higher and higher forms of organization, the strengths and the needs of which are continually superseding the institutions which were made to fit our former requirements. When your Bakoonins call out for the demolition of all these venerable institutions, there is no need to fly into a panic and lock them up in prison whilst your parliament is bit by bit doing exactly what they advised you to do. When your Siegfrieds melt down the old weapons into new ones, and with disrespectful words chop in twain the antiquated constable's staves in the hands of their elders, the end of the world is no nearer than it was before. If human nature, which is the highest organization of life reached on this planet, is really degenerating, then human society will decay; and no panic-begotten penal measures can possibly save it: we must, like Prometheus, set to work to make new men instead of vainly torturing old ones. On the other hand, if the energy of life is still carrying human nature to higher and higher levels, then the more young people shock their elders and deride and discard their pet institutions the better for the hopes of the world, since the apparent growth of anarchy is only the measure of the rate of improvement. History, as far as we are capable of history (which is not saying much as yet), shews that all changes from crudity of social organization to complexity, and from mechanical agencies in government to living ones, seems anarchic at first sight. No doubt it is natural to a snail to think that any evolution which threatens to do away with shells will result in general death from exposure. Nevertheless, the most elaborately housed beings today are born not only without houses on their backs but without even fur or feathers to clothe them.

ANARCHISM NO PANACEA

One word of warning to those who may find themselves attracted by Siegfried's Anarchism, or, if they prefer a term with more respectable associations, his neo-Protestantism. Anarchism, as a panacea, is just as hopeless as any other panacea, and will still be so even if we breed a race of perfectly benevolent men. It is true that in the sphere of thought, Anarchism is an inevitable condition of progressive evolution. A nation without Freethinkers – that is, without intellectual Anarchists – will share the fate of China. It is also true that our criminal law, based on a conception of crime and punishment which is nothing but our vindictiveness and cruelty in a virtuous disguise, is an unmitigated and abominable nuisance, bound to be beaten out of us finally by the mere weight of our experience of its evil and uselessness. But it will not be replaced by anarchy. Applied to the industrial or political machinery of modern society, anarchy must always reduce itself speedily to absurdity. Even the modified form of anarchy on which modern civilization is based: that is, the abandonment of industry, in the name of individual liberty, to the upshot of competition for personal gain between private capitalists, is a disastrous failure, and is, by the mere necessities of the case, giving way to ordered Socialism. For the economic rationale of this, I must refer disciples of Siegfried to a tract from my hand published by the Fabian Society and entitled The Impossibilities of Anarchism, which explains why, owing to the physical constitution of our globe, society cannot effectively organize the production of its food, clothes, and housing, nor distribute them fairly and economically on any anarchic plan: nay, that without concerting our social action to a much higher degree than we do at present we can never get rid of the wasteful and iniquitous welter of a little riches and a great deal of poverty which current political humbug calls our prosperity and civilization. Liberty is an excellent thing: but it cannot begin until society has paid its daily debt to Nature by first earning its living. There is no liberty before that except the liberty to live at somebody else's expense, a liberty much sought after nowadays, since it is the criterion of gentility, but not wholesome from the point of view of the common weal.

SIEGFRIED CONCLUDED

In returning now to the adventures of Siegfried there is little more to be described except the finale of an opera. Siegfried, having passed unharmed through the fire, wakes Brynhild and goes through all the fancies and ecstasies of love at first sight in a duet which ends with an apostrophe to 'leuchtende Liebe, lachender Tod!', which has been romantically translated into 'Love that illumines, laughing at death', whereas it really identifies enlightening love and laughing death as involving each other so closely as to be virtually one and the same thing.

NIGHT FALLS ON THE GODS

DIE GÖTTERDÄMMERUNG begins with an elaborate prologue. The three Norns sit in the night on Brynhild's mountain top spinning their thread of destiny, and telling the story of Wotan's sacrifice of his eye, and of his breaking off a bough from the World Ash to make a haft for his spear, also how the tree withered after suffering that violence. They have also some fresher news to discuss. Wotan, on the breaking of his spear by Siegfried, has called all his heroes to cut down the withered World Ash and stack its faggots in a mighty pyre about Valhalla. Then, with his broken spear in his hand, he has seated himself in state in the great hall, with the Gods and Heroes assembled about him as if in council, solemnly waiting for the end. All this belongs to the old legendary materials with which Wagner began The Ring.

The tale is broken by the thread snapping in the hands of the third Norn; for the hour has arrived when man has taken his destiny in his own hands to shape it for himself, and no longer bows to circumstance, environment, necessity (which he now freely wills), and all the rest of the inevitables. So the Norns recognize that the world has no further use for them, and sink into the earth to return to the First Mother. Then the day dawns; and Siegfried and Brynhild come, and have another duet. He gives her his ring; and she gives him her horse. Away then he goes in search of more adventures; and she watches him from her crag until he disappears. The curtain falls; but we can still hear the trolling of his horn, and the merry clatter of his horse's shoes trotting gaily down the valley. The sound is lost in the grander rhythm of the Rhine as he reaches its banks. We hear again an echo of the lament of the Rhine maidens for the ravished gold; and then, finally, a new strain, which does not surge like the mighty flood of

252

the river, but has an unmistakable tramp of hardy men and a strong land flavor about it. And on this the opera curtain at last goes up – for please remember that all that has gone before is only the overture.

THE FIRST ACT

We now understand the new tramping strain. We are in the Rhineside hall of the Gibichungs, in the presence of King Gunther, his sister Gutruna, and Gunther's grim half-brother Hagen, the villain of the piece. Gunther is a fool, and has for Hagen's intelligence the respect a fool always has for the brains of a scoundrel. Feebly fishing for compliments, he appeals to Hagen to pronounce him a fine fellow and a glory to the race of Gibich. Hagen declares that it is impossible to contemplate him without envy, but thinks it a pity that he has not yet found a wife glorious enough for him. Gunther doubts whether so extraordinary a person can possibly exist. Hagen then tells him of Brynhild and her rampart of fire; also of Siegfried. Gunther takes this rather in bad part, since not only is he afraid of the fire, but Siegfried, according to Hagen, is not, and will therefore achieve this desirable match himself. But Hagen points out that since Siegfried is riding about in quest of adventures, he will certainly pay an early visit to the renowned chief of the Gibichungs. They can then give him a philtre which will make him fall in love with Gutruna and forget every other woman he has yet seen.

Gunther is transported with admiration of Hagen's cunning when he takes in this plan; and he has hardly assented to it when Siegfried, with operatic opportuneness, drops in just as Hagen expected, and is duly drugged into the heartiest love for Gutruna and total oblivion of Brynhild and his own past. When Gunther declares his longing for the bride who lies inaccessible within a palisade of flame, Siegfried at once offers to undertake the adventure for him. Hagen then explains to both of them that Siegfried can, after braving the fire, appear to Brynhild in the semblance of Gunther through the magic of the wishing cap (or Tarnhelm, as it is called throughout The Ring), the use of which Siegfried now learns for the first time. It is of course part of the bargain that Gunther shall give his sister to Siegfried in marriage. On that they swear blood-brotherhood; and at this opportunity the old operatic leaven breaks out amusingly in Wagner. With tremendous exordium of brass, the tenor and baritone go at it with a will, showing off the power of their voices, following each other in canonic imitation, singing together in thirds and sixths, and finishing with a lurid unison, quite in the manner of Ruy Gomez and Ernani, or Othello and Iago. Then without further ado Siegfried departs on his expedition, taking Gunther with him to the foot of the mountain, and leaving Hagen to guard the hall and sing a very fine solo which has often figured in the programs of the Richter concerts, explaining that his interest in the affair is that Siegfried will bring back the Ring, and that he, Hagen, will presently contrive to possess himself of that Ring and become Plutonic master of the world.

And now it will be asked how does Hagen know all about the Plutonic empire; and why was he able to tell Gunther about Brynhild and Siegfried, and to explain to Siegfried the trick of the Tarnhelm. The explanation is that though Hagen's mother was the mother of Gunther, his father was not the illustrious Gibich, but no less a person than our old friend Alberic, who, like Wotan, has begotten a son to do for him what he cannot do for himself.

In the above incidents, those gentle moralizers who find the serious philosophy of the music dramas too terrifying for them, may allegorize pleasingly on the philtre as the maddening chalice of passion which, once tasted, caused the respectable man to forget his lawfully wedded wife and plunge into adventures which eventually lead him headlong to destruction.

We now come upon a last relic of the tragedy of Wotan.

Returning to Brynhild's mountain, we find her visited by her sister Valkyrie Valtrauta, who has witnessed Wotan's solemn preparations with terror. She repeats to Brynhild the account already given by the Norns. Clinging in anguish to Wotan's knees, she has heard him mutter that were the ring returned to the daughters of the deep Rhine, both Gods and world would be redeemed from that stage curse of Alberic's in The Rhine Gold. On this she has rushed on her warhorse through the air to beg Brynhild to give the Rhine back its ring. But this is asking Woman to give up love for the sake of Church and State. She declares that she will see them both perish first; and Valtrauta returns to Valhalla in despair. Whilst Brynhild is watching the course of the black thundercloud that marks her sister's flight, the fires of Loki again flame high round the mountain; and the horn of Siegfried is heard as he makes his way through them. But the man who now appears wears the Tarnhelm: his voice is a strange voice; his figure is the unknown one of the king of the Gibichungs. He tears the ring from her finger, and, claiming her as his wife, drives her into the cave without pity for her agony of horror, and sets Nothung between them in token of his loyalty to the friend he is impersonating. No explanation of this highway robbery of the ring is offered. Clearly, this Siegfried is not the Siegfried of the previous drama.

THE SECOND ACT

In the second act we return to the hall of Gibich, where Hagen, in the last hours of that night, still sits, his spear in his hand, and his shield beside him. At his knees crouches a dwarfish spectre, his father Alberic, still full of his old grievances against Wotan, and urging his son in his dreams to win back the ring for him. This Hagen swears to do; and as the apparition of his father vanishes, the sun rises and Siegfried suddenly comes from the river bank tucking into his belt the Tarnhelm, which has transported him from the mountain like the enchanted carpet of the Arabian tales. He describes his adventures to Gutruna until Gunther's boat is seen approaching, when Hagen seizes a cowhorn and calls the tribesmen to welcome their chief and his bride. It is most exhilarating, this colloquy with the startled and hastily armed clan, ending with a thunderous chorus, the drums marking the time with mighty pulses from dominant to tonic, much as Rossini would have made them do if he had been a pupil of Beethoven's.

A terrible scene follows. Gunther leads his captive bride straight into the presence of Siegfried, whom she claims as her husband by the ring, which she is astonished to see on his finger: Gunther, as she supposes, having torn it from her the night before. Turning on Gunther, she says, 'Since you took that ring from me, and married me with it, tell him of your right to it; and make him give it back to you.' Gunther stammers, 'The ring! I gave him no ring – er – do you know him?' The rejoinder is obvious. 'Then where are you hiding the ring that you had from me?' Gunther's confusion enlightens her; and she calls Siegfried trickster and thief to his face. In vain he declares that he got the ring from no woman, but from a dragon whom he slew; for he is manifestly puzzled; and she, seizing her opportunity, accuses him before the clan of having played Gunther false with her.

Hereupon we have another grandiose operatic oath, Siegfried attesting his innocence on Hagen's spear, and Brynhild rushing to the footlights and thrusting him aside to attest his guilt, whilst the clansmen call upon their gods to send down lightnings and silence the perjured. The gods do not respond; and Siegfried, after whispering to Gunther that the Tarnhelm seems to have been only half effectual after all, laughs his way out of the general embarrassment and goes off merrily to prepare for his wedding, with his arm round Gutruna's waist, followed by the clan. Gunther, Hagen and Brynhild are left together to plot operatic vengeance. Brynhild, it appears, has enchanted Siegfried in such a fashion that no weapon can

256

hurt him. She has, however, omitted to protect his back, since it is impossible that he should ever turn that to a foe. They agree accordingly that on the morrow a great hunt shall take place, at which Hagen shall thrust his spear into the hero's vulnerable back. The blame is to be laid on the tusk of a wild boar. Gunther, being a fool, is remorseful about his oath of blood-brotherhood and about his sister's bereavement, without having the strength of mind to prevent the murder. The three burst into a herculean trio, similar in conception to that of the three conspirators in Un Ballo in Maschera; and the act concludes with a joyous strain heralding the appearance of Siegfried's wedding procession, with strewing of flowers, sacrificing to the gods, and carrying bride and bridegroom in triumph.

It will be seen that in this act we have lost all connection with the earlier drama. Brynhild is not only not the Brynhild of The Valkyrie, she is the Hiordis of Ibsen, a majestically savage woman, in whom jealousy and revenge are intensified to heroic proportions. That is the inevitable theatrical treatment of the murderous heroine of the Saga. Ibsen's aim in The Vikings was purely theatrical, and not, as in his later dramas, also philosophically symbolic. Wagner's aim in 'Siegfried's Death' was equally theatrical, and not, as it afterwards became in the dramas of which Siegfried's antagonist Wotan is the hero, likewise philosophically symbolic. The two master-dramatists therefore produce practically the same version of Brynhild. Thus on the second evening of The Ring we see Brynhild in the character of the truth-divining instinct in religion, cast into an enchanted slumber and surrounded by the fires of hell lest she should overthrow a Church corrupted by its alliance with government. On the fourth evening, we find her swearing a malicious lie to gratify her personal jealousy, and then plotting a treacherous murder with a fool and a scoundrel. In the original draft of Siegfried's Death, the incongruity is carried still further by the conclusion, at which the dead Brynhild, restored to her godhead by

Wotan, and again a Valkyrie, carries the slain Siegfried to Valhalla to live there happily ever after with its pious heroes.

As to Siegfried himself, he talks of women, both in this second act and the next, with the air of a man of the world. 'Their tantrums,' he says, 'are soon over.' Such speeches do not belong to the novice of the preceding drama, but to the original Siegfried's Tod, with its leading characters sketched on the ordinary romantic lines from the old Sagas, and not yet reminted as the original creations of Wagner's genius whose acquaintance we have made on the two previous evenings. The very title 'Siegfried's Death' survives as a strong theatrical point in the following passage. Gunther, in his rage and despair, cries, 'Save me, Hagen, save my honor and thy mother's who bore us both.' 'Nothing can save thee,' replies Hagen, 'neither brain nor hand, but *Siegfried's Death*.' And Gunther echoes with a shudder, '*Siegfried's Death!*'

A WAGNERIAN NEWSPAPER CONTROVERSY

The devotion which Wagner's work inspires has been illustrated lately in a public correspondence on this very point. A writer in The Daily Telegraph having commented on the falsehood uttered by Brynhild in accusing Siegfried of having betrayed Gunther with her, a correspondence in defence of the beloved heroine was opened in The Daily Chronicle. The imputation of falsehood to Brynhild was strongly resented and combated, in spite of the unanswerable evidence of the text. It was contended that Brynhild's statement must be taken as establishing the fact that she actually was ravished by somebody whom she believed to be Siegfried, and that since this somebody cannot have been Siegfried, he being as incapable of treachery to Gunther as she of falsehood, it must have been Gunther himself after a second exchange of personalities not mentioned in the text. The reply to this – if so obviously desperate a hypothesis needs a reply – is that the text is perfectly explicit as to Siegfried, disguised as

Gunther, passing the night with Brynhild with Nothung dividing them, and in the morning bringing her down the mountain *through the fire* (an impassable obstacle to Gunther) and there transporting himself in a single breath, by the Tarnhelm's magic, back to the hall of the Gibichungs, leaving the real Gunther to bring Brynhild down the river after him. One controversialist actually pleaded for the expedition occupying two nights, on the second of which the alleged outrage might have taken place. But the time is accounted for to the last minute; it all takes place during the single night watch of Hagen. There is no possible way out of the plain fact that Brynhild's accusation is to her own knowledge false; and the impossible ways just cited are only interesting as examples of the fanatical worship which Wagner and his creations have been able to inspire in minds of exceptional power and culture.

More plausible was the line taken by those who admitted the falsehood. Their contention was that when Wotan deprived Brynhild of her Godhead, he also deprived her of her former high moral attributes; so that Siegfried's kiss awakened an ordinary mortal jealous woman. But a goddess can become mortal and jealous without plunging at once into perjury and murder. Besides, this explanation involves the sacrifice of the whole significance of the allegory, and the reduction of The Ring to the plane of a child's conception of The Sleeping Beauty. Whoever does not understand that, in terms of The Ring philosophy, a change from godhead to humanity is a step higher and not a degradation, misses the whole point of The Ring. It is precisely because the truthfulness of Brynhild is proof against Wotan's spells that he has to contrive the fire palisade with Loki, to protect the fictions and conventions of Valhalla against her.

The only tolerable view is the one supported by the known history of The Ring, and also, for musicians of sufficiently fine judgment, by the evidence of the scores; of which more anon. As a matter of fact Wagner began, as I have said, with

'Siegfried's Death'. Then, wanting to develop the idea of Siegfried as neo-Protestant, he went on to 'The Young Siegfried'. As a Protestant cannot be dramatically projected without a pontifical antagonist, The Young Siegfried led to The Valkyrie, and that again to its preface The Rhine Gold (the preface is always written after the book is finished). Finally, of course, the whole was revised. The revision, if carried out strictly, would have involved the cutting out of Siegfried's Death, now become inconsistent and superfluous; and that would have involved, in turn, the facing of the fact that The Ring was no longer a Niblung epic, and really demanded modern costumes, tall hats for Tarnhelms, factories for Nibelheims, villas for Valhallas, and so on – in short, a complete confession of the extent to which the old Niblung epic had become the merest pretext and name directory in the course of Wagner's travail. But, as Wagner's most eminent English interpreter once put it to me at Bayreuth between the acts of Night Falls on The Gods, the master wanted to 'Lohengrinize' again after his long abstention from opera; and Siegfried's Death (first sketched in 1848, the year before the rising in Dresden and the subsequent events which so deepened Wagner's sense of life and the seriousness of art) gave him exactly the libretto he required for that outbreak of the old operatic Adam in him. So he changed it into Die Götterdämmerung, retaining the traditional plot of murder and jealousy, and with it, necessarily, his original second act, in spite of the incongruity of its Siegfried and Brynhild with the Siegfried and Brynhild of the allegory. As to the legendary matter about the world-ash and the destruction of Valhalla by Loki, it fitted in well enough; for though, allegorically, the blow by which Siegfried breaks the god's spear is the end of Wotan and of Valhalla, those who do not see the allegory, and take the story literally, like children, are sure to ask what becomes of Wotan after Siegfried gets past him up the mountain; and to this question the old tale told in Night Falls on The Gods is as good an answer as another. The very senselessness of the scenes of the Norns and of Valtrauta in relation to the three foregoing dramas, gives them a highly effective air of mystery; and no one ventures to challenge their consequentiality, because we are all more apt to pretend to understand great works of art than to confess that the meaning (if any) has escaped us. Valtrauta, however, betrays her irrelevance by explaining that the gods can be saved by the restoration of the ring to the Rhine daughters. This, considered as part of the previous allegory, is nonsense; so that even this scene, which has a more plausible air of organic connection with The Valkyrie than any other in Night Falls on The Gods, is as clearly part of a different and earlier conception as the episode which concludes it, in which Siegfried actually robs Brynhild of her ring, though he has no recollection of having given it to her. Night Falls on The Gods, in fact, was not even revised into any real coherence with the world-poem which sprang from it; and that is the authentic solution of all the controversies which have arisen over it.

THE THIRD ACT

The hunting party comes off duly. Siegfried strays from it and meets the Rhine maidens, who almost succeed in coaxing the ring from him. He pretends to be afraid of his wife; and they chaff him as to her beating him and so forth; but when they add that the ring is accursed and will bring death upon him, he discloses to them, as unconsciously as Julius Caesar disclosed it long ago, that secret of heroism, never to let your life be shaped by fear of its end.[1] So he keeps the ring; and they leave him to his fate. The hunting party now finds him; and they all sit down together to make a meal by the river side, Siegfried telling them meanwhile the story of his adventures. When he approaches the subject of Brynhild, as to whom his memory is a blank, Hagen pours an antidote to the love philtre into his drinking horn, whereupon, his memory returning, he proceeds to narrate the incident of the fiery mountain, to Gunther's intense mortification. Hagen then plunges his spear into the back of Siegfried, who falls dead on his shield, but gets up again, after the old operatic custom, to sing about thirty bars to his love before allowing himself to be finally carried off to the strains of the famous Trauermarsch.

The scene then changes to the hall of the Gibichungs by the Rhine. It is night; and Gutruna, unable to sleep, and haunted by all sorts of vague terrors, is waiting for the return of her husband, and wondering whether a ghostly figure she has seen gliding down to the river bank is Brynhild, whose room is empty. Then comes the cry of Hagen, returning with the hunting party to announce the death of Siegfried by the tusk of a wild boar. But Gutruna divines the truth; and Hagen does not deny it. Siegfried's body is brought in; Gunther claims the ring; Hagen will not suffer him to take it; they fight; and Gunther is slain. Hagen then attempts to take it; but the dead man's hand closes on it and raises itself threateningly. Then Brynhild comes; and a funeral pyre is raised whilst she declaims a prolonged scena, extremely moving and imposing, but yielding nothing to resolute intellectual criticism except a very powerful and elevated exploitation of theatrical pathos, psychologically identical with the scene of Cleopatra and the dead Antony in Shakespear's tragedy. Finally she flings a torch into the pyre, and rides her warhorse into the flames. The hall of the Gibichungs catches fire, as most halls would were a cremation attempted in the middle of the floor (I permit myself this gibe purposely to emphasize the excessive artificiality of the scene); but the Rhine overflows its banks to allow the three Rhine maidens to take the ring from Siegfried's finger, incidentally extinguishing the conflagration as it does so. Hagen attempts to snatch the ring from the maidens, who promptly drown him; and in the distant heavens the Gods and their castle are seen perishing in the fires of Loki as the curtain falls.

COLLAPSE OF THE ALLEGORY

In all this, it will be observed, there is nothing new. The musical fabric is enormously elaborate and gorgeous; but you cannot say, as you must in witnessing The Rhine Gold, The Valkyrie, and the first two acts of Siegfried, that you have never seen anything like it before, and that the inspiration is entirely original. Not only the action, but most of the poetry, might conceivably belong to an Elizabethan drama. The situation of Cleopatra and Antony is unconsciously reproduced without being bettered, or even equalled in point of majesty and musical expression. The loss of all simplicity and dignity, the impossibility of any credible scenic presentation of the incidents, and the extreme staginess of the conventions by which these impossibilities are got over, are no doubt covered from the popular eye by the overwhelming prestige of Die Götterdämmerung as part of so great a work as The Ring, and by the extraordinary storm of emotion and excitement which the music keeps up. But the very qualities that intoxicate the novice in music enlighten the adept. In spite of the fulness of the composer's technical accomplishment, the finished style and effortless mastery of harmony and instrumentation displayed, there is not a bar in the work which moves us as the same themes moved us in The Valkyrie, nor is anything but external splendor added to the life and humor of Siegfried.

In the original poem, Brynhild delays her self-immolation on the pyre of Siegfried to read the assembled choristers a homily on the efficacy of the Love panacea. 'My holiest wisdom's hoard,' she says, 'now I make known to the world. I believe not in property, nor money, nor godliness, nor hearth and high place, nor pomp and peerage, nor contract and custom, but in Love. Let that only prevail; and ye shall be blest in weal or woe.' Here the repudiations still smack of Bakoonin; but the savior is no longer the volition of the full-grown spirit of Man, the Free Willer of Necessity, sword in hand, but simply Love, and not even Shelleyan love, but vehement sexual passion. It is highly significant of the extent to which the uxorious commonplace lost its hold of Wagner (after disturbing his conscience, as he confesses to Roeckel, for years) that it disappears in the full score of Night Falls on The Gods, which was not completed until he was on the verge of producing Parsifal, twenty years after the publication of the poem. He cut the homily out, and composed the music of the final scene with a flagrant recklessness of the old intention. The rigorous logic with which representative musical themes are employed in the earlier dramas is here abandoned without scruple; and for the main theme at the conclusion he selects a rapturous passage sung by Sieglinda in the third act of The Valkyrie (p. 224, *ante*) when Brynhild inspires her with a sense of her high destiny as the mother of the unborn hero. There is no dramatic logic whatever in the recurrence of this theme to express the transport in which Brynhild immolates herself. There is of course an excuse for it, inasmuch as both women have an impulse of self-sacrifice for the sake of Siegfried; but this is really hardly more than an excuse; since the Valhalla theme might be attached to Alberic on the no worse ground that both he and Wotan are inspired by ambition, and that the ambition has the same object, the possession of the ring. The common sense of the matter is that the only themes which had fully retained their old hold on Wagner's intellectual conscience when he composed Night Falls on The Gods are those which are mere labels of external features, such as the Dragon, the Fire, the Water and so on. This particular theme of Sieglinda's is, in truth, of no great musical merit: it might easily be the pet climax of a popular sentimental ballad: in fact, the gushing effect which is its sole valuable quality is so cheaply attained that it is hardly going too far to call it the most trumpery phrase in the entire tetralogy. Yet, since it undoubtedly does gush very emphatically, Wagner chose, for convenience' sake, to work up this final scene with it rather than with the more distinguished, elaborate and beautiful themes connected with the love of Brynhild and Siegfried.

He would certainly not have thought this a matter of no consequence had he finished the whole work ten years earlier. It must always be borne in mind that the poem of The Ring was complete and printed in 1853, and represents the sociological ideas which, after germinating in the European atmosphere for many years, had been brought home to Wagner, who was intensely susceptible to such ideas, by the crash of 1849 at Dresden. Now no man whose mind is alive and active, as Wagner's was to the day of his death, can keep his political and spiritual opinions, much less his philosophic consciousness, at a standstill for a quarter of a century until he finishes an orchestral score. When Wagner first sketched Night Falls on The Gods he was 35. When he finished the score for the first Bayreuth festival in 1876 he had turned 60. No wonder he had lost his old grip of it and left it behind him. He even tampered with The Rhine Gold for the sake of theatrical effect when stage-managing it, making Wotan pick up and brandish a sword to give visible point to his sudden inspiration as to the raising up of a hero. The sword had first to be discovered by Fafnir among the Niblung treasures and thrown away by him as useless. There is no sense in this device; and its adoption shews the same recklessness as to the original intention which we find in the music of the last act of The Dusk of the Gods.[2]

WHY HE CHANGED HIS MIND

WAGNER, however, was not the man to allow his grip of a great philosophic theme to slacken, even in twenty-five years, had the theme stood the test of the world's experience. If the history of Germany from 1849 to 1876 had been the history of Siegfried and Wotan transposed into the key of actual life, Night Falls on The Gods would have been the logical consummation of The Rhine Gold and The Valkyrie instead of the operatic anachronism it actually is.

But, as a matter of fact, Siegfried did not arrive and Bismarck did. Roeckel faded into a prisoner whose imprisonment made no difference. Bakoonin broke up, not Valhalla, but The International, which petered out in an undignified quarrel between him and Karl Marx. The Siegfrieds of 1848 were hopeless political failures, whereas the Wotans and Alberics and Lokis were conspicuous political successes. Even the Mimes held their own as against Siegfried. With the single exception of Ferdinand Lassalle, there was no revolutionary leader who was not an obvious Impossibilist in practical politics; and Lassalle got himself killed in a romantic and quite indefensible duel after wrecking his health in a titanic oratorical campaign which convinced him that the great majority of the working classes were not ready to join him, and that the minority who were ready did not understand him. The International, founded in 1864 by Karl Marx in London, and mistaken for several years by nervous newspapers for a red spectre, was really only a turnip ghost. It achieved some beginnings of international Trade Unionism by inducing English workmen to send money to support strikes on the continent, and recalling English workers who had been taken across the North Sea to defeat such strikes; but on its revolutionary socialistic side it was a romantic figment. The suppression of the Paris Commune, one of the most tragic examples in history of the pitilessness with which capable practical administrators and soldiers are forced by the pressure of facts to destroy romantic amateurs and theatrical dreamers, made an end of melodramatic Socialism. It was as easy for Marx, with his literary talent, to hold up Thiers as the most execrable of living scoundrels, and to put upon Gallifet a brand indelible enough to ostracize him politically for ever, as it was for Victor Hugo to bombard Napoleon III from his paper battery in Jersey. It was also easy to hold up Félix Pyat and Delescluze as men of much loftier ideals than Thiers and Gallifet; but the one fact that could not be denied was that when it came to actual shooting, it was Gallifet who got Delescluze shot and not Delescluze who got Gallifet shot, and that when it came to administering the affairs of France, Thiers could in one way or another get it done, whilst Pyat could neither do it nor stop talking and allow somebody else to do it. True, the penalty of following Thiers was to be exploited by the landlord and capitalist; but then the penalty of following Pyat was to be shot like a mad dog, or at best sent to New Caledonia, quite unnecessarily and uselessly.

To put it in terms of Wagner's allegory, Alberic had got the ring back again, and was marrying into the best Valhalla families with it. He had thought better of his old threat to dethrone Wotan and Loki. He had found that Nibelheim was a very gloomy place, and that if he wanted to live handsomely and safely, he must not only allow Wotan and Loki to organize society for him, but pay them very handsomely for doing it. He needed splendor, military glory, loyalty, enthusiasm, and patriotism; and his greed and gluttony were wholly unable to create them, whereas Wotan and Loki carried them all to their most triumphant climax in Germany in 1871, when Wagner himself celebrated the event with his Kaiser-marsch, which sounded much more convincing than the Marseillaise or the Carmagnole.

How, after the Kaisermarsch, could Wagner go back to his idealization of Siegfried in 1853? How could he believe seriously in Siegfried slaying the dragon and charging through the mountain fire, when the immediate foreground was occupied by the Hôtel de Ville with Félix Pyat endlessly discussing the principles of Socialism whilst the shells of Thiers were already battering the Arc de Triomphe and ripping up the pavement of the Champs Elysées? Is it not clear that things had taken an altogether unexpected turn; that although The Ring may, like the famous Communist Manifesto of Marx and Engels, be an inspired guess at the historic laws and predestined end of our capitalistic-theocratic epoch, yet Wagner, like Marx, was too inexperienced in technical government and administration and too melodramatic in his hero-contra-villain conception of the class struggle, to foresee the actual process by which his generalization would work out, or the part to be played in it by the classes involved.

Let us go back for a moment to the point at which the Niblung legend first becomes irreconcilable with Wagner's allegory. Fafnir in the real world becomes a capitalist; but Fafnir in the allegory is a mere hoarder. His gold does not bring him in any revenue. It does not even support him: he has to go out and forage for food and drink. In fact, he is on the way to his drinking-pool when Siegfried kills him. And Siegfried himself has no more use for the gold than Fafnir: the only difference between them in this respect is that Siegfried does not waste his time watching a barren treasure that is useless to him, whereas Fafnir sacrifices his humanity and his life merely to prevent anybody else getting it. This contrast, true to human nature, is not true to modern economic development. The real Fafnir is not a miser: he seeks dividends, a comfortable life, and admission to the circles of Wotan and Loki. His only means of procuring these is to restore the gold to Alberic in exchange for scrip in Alberic's enterprises. Thus fortified with capital, Alberic exploits his fellow dwarfs as before, and also exploits Fafnir's fellow giants who have no capital. What is more, the competitive strategy and large-scaled enterprise the exploitation involves, and the self-respect and social esteem its success wins, effect a development in Alberic's own character which neither Marx nor Wagner appears to have foreseen. He discovers that to be a dull, greedy, narrow-minded money-grubber is not the way to make money on the modern scale; for though greed may suffice to turn tens into hundreds and even hundreds into thousands, to turn thousands into hundreds of thousands requires economic magnanimity and a will to power as well as to pelf. And to turn hundreds of thousands into millions, Alberic must make himself an earthly Providence for masses of workmen, creating towns, and governing markets. In the meantime, Fafnir, wallowing in the dividends he has done nothing to earn, may rot, intellectually and morally, from mere disuse of his energies and lack of incentive to excel; but the more impotent he becomes, the more dependent he is upon Alberic for his income, on Loki for his politics, and on Wotan for his respectability and safety from rebellion: Alberic, as the pursebearer, being, under Destiny, the real master of the situation. Consequently, though Alberic in 1850 may have been merely the vulgar Manchester factory-owner portrayed in Friedrich Engels' Condition of the Working Classes, in 1876 he was well on the way towards becoming exoterically a model philanthropic employer and esoterically a financier.

Now, without exaggerating the virtues of such gentlemen, it will be conceded by everybody except perhaps those veteran Social-Democrats who have made a cult of obsolescence under the name of Marxism, that the dominant sort of modern employer is not to be displaced and dismissed so lightly as Alberic in The Ring. Wotan is hardly less dependent on him than Fafnir: the War-Lord visits his works, acclaims them in stirring speeches, and imprisons his enemies; whilst Loki does his political jobs in Parliament, making wars and commercial treaties for him at command. And he owns and controls a new god, called The Press, which manufactures public opinion on his side, and organizes the persecution and suppression of Siegfried.

The end cannot come until Siegfried learns Alberic's trade and shoulders Alberic's burden. Not having as yet done so, he is still completely mastered by Alberic. He does not even rebel against him except when he is too stupid and ignorant, or too romantically impracticable, to see that Alberic's work, like Wotan's work and Loki's work, is necessary work, and that therefore Alberic can never be superseded by a warrior, but only by a capable man of business who is prepared to continue his work without a day's intermission. Even though the proletarians of all lands were to become 'class-conscious', and obey the call of Marx by uniting to rush the class struggle to a proletarian victory in which all capital should become common property, and all Monarchs, Millionaires, Landlords, and Capitalists become common citizens, the triumphant proletarians would have either to starve in anarchy next day or else do the political and industrial work which now gets itself done somehow under limited monarchs, despotic presidents, irresponsible financiers, and bourgeois parliaments. And in the meantime these magnates must defend their power and property with all their might against the revolutionary forces until these forces become positive, executive, administrative forces, instead of the conspiracies of protesting, moralizing, virtuously indignant amateurs who mistook Marx for a man of affairs and Thiers for a stage villain.

Now all this represents a development of which one gathers no forecast from Wagner or Marx. Both of them prophesied the end of our epoch, and, though in 1913 that epoch seemed so prosperous that the prophecy seemed ridiculously negligible, within ten years the centre had fallen out of Europe; and humane men could only shake their heads and shrug their shoulders when they were asked for another half-crown to help to save another ten million children from starvation.

Alberic had prospered so greatly that he had come to believe himself immortal; and his alliances with Wotan had brought his sons and daughters under the influences, dangerous to commerce, of feudal militarist ideals. The abyss in his path had been pointed out to him not only by Wagner and Marx, but by men who, instead of vainly consulting the oracle in the pages of Das Kapital, had sought new and safe paths by the light of contemporary history and practical administrative experience. But Alberic would neither believe that the old path led to the abyss nor explore the new paths; and the masses knew nothing of paths and much of poverty. So he went faster and faster, at last marching sword in hand with his feudal sons-in-law, blasting his way with cyclopean explosives, at which point he crashed into the abyss he had not believed in, bringing down the civilization of Central and Eastern Europe along with him, and leaving the Bolshevists (*ci-devant* Marxists), Social-Democrats, Republicans and amorphous revolutionaries generally to extricate it as best they could, and to learn in the process the truth of these last few pages.

But Wagner did not live to see this reduction of Alberic to absurdity. What he did see was the reduction of Siegfried to absurdity. Siegfried had done nothing that promised success in his struggle with Alberic; and Alberic had not yet outdone Siegfried in ineptitude by committing suicide. Now Wagner was compelled by his profession to be, compared with Siegfried, a practical man. It is possible to learn more of the world by producing a single opera, or even conducting a single orchestral rehearsal, than by ten years reading in the library of the British Museum. Wagner must have learnt between The Rhine Gold and the Kaisermarsch that there are yet several dramas to be interpolated in The Ring after The Valkyrie before the allegory can tell the whole story. If anyone doubts the extent to which Wagner's eyes had been opened to the administrative childishness and romantic conceit of the heroes of the revolutionary generation that served its

271

apprenticeship on the barricades of 1848–49, and perished on those of 1871 under Thiers' mitrailleuses, let him read Eine Kapitulation, that scandalous burlesque in which the poet and composer of Siegfried, with the levity of a schoolboy, mocked the French republicans who were doing in 1871 what he himself was exiled for doing in 1849. He had set the enthusiasm of the Dresden revolution to his own greatest music; but he set the enthusiasm of twenty years later in derision to the music of Rossini. There is no mistaking the tune he meant to suggest by his doggerel of Republik, Republik, Republik-lik-lik. The Overture to William Tell is there as plainly as if it were noted down in full score.

In the case of such a man as Wagner, you cannot explain this *volte-face* as mere jingoism produced by Germany's overwhelming victory in the Franco-Prussian war, nor as personal spite against the Parisians for the Tannhäuser fiasco. Wagner had more cause for personal spite against his own countrymen than he ever had against the Parisians: he was ten times bitterer against his respectable prosperity in Dresden than against his starvation in Paris. No doubt his outburst gratified the pettier feelings which great men have in common with small ones; but he was not a man to indulge in such gratifications or indeed to feel them as gratifications, if he had not become convinced of the administrative impotence of the agitators who were trying to wield Nothung, and who had done less for Wagner's own art than a single German king, and he, too, a mad one. Wagner had by that time done too much himself not to know that the world is ruled by deeds, not by good intentions, and that one efficient sinner is worth ten futile saints and martyrs.

I need not elaborate the point further in these pages. Like all men of genius, Wagner had exceptional sincerity, exceptional respect for facts, exceptional freedom from the hypnotic influence of sentimental popular movements, exceptional sense of the realities of political power as distinguished from the pretences and idolatries behind which the real masters of modern States pull their wires and train their guns. When he scored Night Falls on The Gods, he had accepted the failure of Siegfried and the triumph of the Wotan–Loki–Alberic trinity as a fact. He had given up dreaming of heroes, heroines and final solutions, and had conceived a new protagonist in Parsifal, whom he announced, not as a hero, but as a fool, armed, not with a sword which cut irresistibly, but with a spear which he held only on condition that he did not use it: one who, instead of exulting in the slaughter of a dragon, was ashamed of having shot a swan. The change in the conception of the Deliverer could hardly be more complete. It reflects the change which took place in Wagner's mind between the composition of The Rhine Gold and Night Falls on The Gods; and it explains why he found it so easy to drop the Ring allegory and fall back on Lohengrinizing.

WAGNER'S OWN EXPLANATION

AND now, having given my explanation of The Ring, can I give Wagner's explanation of it? If I could (and I can) I should not by any means accept it as conclusive. Nearly half a century has passed since the tetralogy was written; and in that time the purposes of many half instinctive acts of genius have become clearer to the common man than they were to the doers. Some years ago, in the course of an explanation of Ibsen's plays, I pointed out that it was by no means certain or even likely that Ibsen was as definitely conscious of his thesis as I. All the stupid people, and some critics who, though not stupid, had not themselves written what the Germans call 'tendency' works, saw nothing in this but a fantastic affectation of the extravagant self-conceit of knowing more about Ibsen than Ibsen himself. Fortunately, in taking exactly the same position now with regard to Wagner, I can claim his own authority to support me. 'How,' he wrote to Roeckel on the 23rd August 1856, 'can an artist expect that what he has felt intuitively should be perfectly realized by others, seeing that he himself feels in the presence of his work, if it is true Art, that he is confronted by a riddle, about which he, too, might have illusions, just as another might?'

The truth is, we are apt to deify men of genius, exactly as we deify the creative force of the universe, by attributing to logical design what is the result of blind instinct. What Wagner meant by 'true Art' is the operation of the artist's instinct, which is just as blind as any other instinct. Mozart, asked for an explanation of his works, said frankly 'How do I know?' Wagner, being a philosopher and critic as well as a composer, was always looking for moral explanations of what he had created; and he hit on several very striking ones, all different. In the same way one can conceive Henry the Eighth

274

speculating very brilliantly about the circulation of his own blood without getting as near the truth as Harvey did long after his death.

None the less, Wagner's own explanations are of exceptional interest. To begin with, there is a considerable portion of The Ring, especially the portraiture of our capitalistic industrial system from the socialist's point of view in the slavery of the Niblungs and the tyranny of Alberic, which is unmistakable, as it dramatizes that portion of human activity which lies well within the territory covered by our intellectual consciousness. All this is concrete Home Office business, so to speak: its meaning was as clear to Wagner as it is to us. Not so that part of the work which deals with the destiny of Wotan. And here, as it happened, Wagner's recollection of what he had been driving at was completely upset by his discovery, soon after the completion of The Ring poem, of Schopenhauer's famous treatise 'The World as Will and Representation.' So obsessed did he become with this masterpiece of philosophic art that he declared that it contained the intellectual demonstration of the conflict of human forces which he himself had demonstrated artistically in his great poem. 'I must confess,' he writes to Roeckel, 'to having arrived at a clear understanding of my own works of art through the help of another, who has provided me with the reasoned conceptions corresponding to my intuitive principles.'

Schopenhauer, however, had done nothing of the sort. Wagner's determination to prove that he had been a Schopenhauerite all along without knowing it only shews how completely the fascination of the great treatise on The Will had run away with his memory. It is easy to see how this happened. Wagner says of himself that 'seldom has there taken place in the soul of one and the same man so profound a division and estrangement between the intuitive or impulsive part of his nature and his consciously or reasonably formed ideas'. And since Schopenhauer's great contribution to modern thought was to educate us into clear consciousness of this distinction – a distinction familiar, in a fanciful way, to the Ages of Faith and Art before the Renascence, but afterwards swamped in the Rationalism of that movement – it was inevitable that Wagner should jump at Schopenhauer's metaphysiology (I use a word less likely to be mistaken than metaphysics) as the very thing for him. But metaphysiology is one thing, political philosophy another. The political philosophy of Siegfried is exactly contrary to the political philosophy of Schopenhauer, although the same clear meta-physiological distinction between the instinctive part of man (his Will) and his reasoning faculty (dramatized in The Ring as Loki) is insisted on in both. The difference is that to Schopenhauer the Will is the universal tormentor of man, the author of that great evil, Life; whilst reason is the divine gift that is finally to overcome this life-creating will and lead, through its abnegation, to cessation and peace, annihilation and Nirvana. This is the doctrine of Pessimism. Now Wagner was, when he wrote The Ring, a most sanguine revolutionary Meliorist, contemptuous of the reasoning faculty, which he typified in the shifty, unreal, delusive Loki, and full of faith in the life-giving Will, which he typified in the glorious Siegfried. Not until he read Schopenhauer did he become bent on proving that he had always been a Pessimist at heart, and that Loki was the most sensible and worthy adviser of Wotan in The Rhine Gold.

Sometimes he faces the change in his opinions frankly enough. 'My Niblung drama,' he writes to Roeckel, 'had taken form at a time when I had built up with my reason an optimistic world on Hellenic principles, believing that noth-ing was necessary for the realization of such a world but that men should wish it. I ingeniously set aside the problem why they did not wish it. I remember that it was with this definite creative purpose that I conceived the personality of Siegfried, with the intention of representing an existence free from pain.' But he appeals to his earlier works to shew that behind all these artificial optimistic ideas there was always with him an intuition of 'the sublime tragedy of renunciation, the negation of the will'. In trying to explain this, he is full of ideas philosophically, and full of the most amusing contradictions personally. Optimism, as an accidental excursion into the barren paths of reason on his own part, he calls 'Hellenic'. In others he denounces it as rank Judaism, the Jew having at that time become for him the whipping boy for all modern humanity. In a letter from London he expounds Schopenhauer to Roeckel with enthusiasm, preaching the renunciation of the Will to Live as the redemption from all error and vain pursuits: in the next letter he resumes the subject with unabated interest, and finishes by mentioning that on leaving London he went to Geneva and underwent 'a most beneficial course of hydropathy'. Seven months before this he had written as follows: 'Believe me, I too was once possessed by the idea of a country life. In order to become a radically healthy human being, I went two years ago to a Hydropathic Establishment, prepared to give up Art and everything if I could once more become a child of Nature. But, my good friend, I was obliged to laugh at my own naïveté when I found myself almost going mad. None of us will reach the promised land: we shall all die in the wilderness. Intellect is, as some one has said, a sort of disease: it is incurable.'

Roeckel knew his man of old, and evidently pressed him for explanations of the inconsistencies of The Ring with Night Falls on The Gods. Wagner defended himself with unfailing cleverness and occasional petulances, ranging from such pleas as 'I believe a true instinct has kept me from a too great definiteness; for it has been borne in on me that an absolute disclosure of the intention disturbs true insight,' to a volley of explanations and commentaries on the explanations. He gets excited and annoyed because Roeckel will not admire the Brynhild of Night Falls on The Gods; reinvents the Tarnhelm scene; and finally, the case being desperate, exclaims, 'It is wrong of you to challenge me to explain it in words: you must feel that something is being enacted that is not to be expressed in mere words.'

THE PESSIMIST AS AMORIST

Sometimes he gets very far away from Pessimism indeed, and recommends Roeckel to solace his captivity, not by conquering the will to live at liberty, but by 'the inspiring influences of the Beautiful'. The next moment he throws over even Art for Life. 'Where life ends,' he says, very wittily, 'Art begins. In youth we turn to Art, we know not why; and only when we have gone through with Art and come out on the other side, we learn to our cost that we have missed Life itself.' His only comfort is that he is beloved. And on the subject of love he lets himself loose in a manner that would have roused the bitterest scorn in Schopenhauer, though, as we have seen (p. 247), it is highly characteristic of Wagner. 'Love in its most perfect reality,' he says, 'is only possible between the sexes; it is only as man and woman that human beings can truly love. Every other manifestation of love can be traced back to that one absorbingly real feeling, of which all other affections are but an emanation, a connection, or an imitation. It is an error to look on this as only one of the forms in which love is revealed, as if there were other forms co-equal with it, or even superior to it. He who after the manner of metaphysicians prefers *unreality* to *reality*, and derives the concrete from the abstract – in short, puts the word before the fact – may be right in esteeming the idea of love as higher than the expression of love, and may affirm that actual love made manifest in feeling is nothing but the outward and visible sign of a pre-existent, non-sensuous, abstract love; and he will do well to despise that sensuous function in general. In any case it were safe to bet that such a man had never loved or been loved as human beings can love, or he would have understood that in despising this feeling, what he condemned was its sensual expression, the outcome of man's animal nature, and not true human love. The highest satisfaction and expression of the individual is only to be found in his complete absorption, and that is only possible through love. Now a human being is both *man* and *woman*: it is only when these two are united that the real human being exists; and thus it is only by love that man and woman attain to the full measure of humanity. But when nowadays we talk of a human being, such heartless block-heads are we that quite involuntarily we only think of man. It is only in the union of man and woman by love (sensuous and supersensuous) that the human being exists; and as the human being cannot rise to the conception of anything higher than his own existence – his own being – so the transcendent act of his life is this consummation of his humanity through love.'

It is clear after this utterance from the would-be Schopen-hauerian, that Wagner's explanations of his works for the most part explain nothing but the mood in which he happened to be on the day he advanced them, or the train of thought suggested to his very susceptible imagination and active mind by the points raised by his questioner. Especially in his private letters, where his outpourings are modified by his dramatic consciousness of the personality of his corre-spondent, do we find him taking all manner of positions, and putting forward all sorts of cases which must be taken as clever and suggestive special pleadings, and not as serious and permanent expositions of his works. These works must speak for themselves: if The Ring says one thing, and a letter written afterwards says that it said something else, The Ring must be taken to confute the letter just as conclusively as if the two had been written by different hands. However, nobody fairly well acquainted with Wagner's utterances as a whole will find any unaccountable contradictions in them. As in all men of his type, our manifold nature was so marked in him that he was like several different men rolled into one.

When he had exhausted himself in the character of the most pugnacious, aggressive and sanguine of reformers, he rested himself as a Pessimist and Nirvanist. In The Ring the quietism of Brynhild's 'Rest, rest, thou God', is sublime in its deep conviction; but you have only to turn back the pages to find the irrepressible bustle of Siegfried and the revelry of the clansmen expressed with equal zest. Wagner was not a Schopenhauerite every day in the week, nor even a Wagner-ite. His mind changes as often as his mood. On Monday nothing will ever induce him to return to quill-driving: on Tuesday he begins a new pamphlet. On Wednesday he is impatient of the misapprehensions of people who cannot see how impossible it is for him to preside as a conductor over platform performances of fragments of his works, which can only be understood when presented strictly according to his intention on the stage; on Thursday he gets up a concert of Wagnerian selections, and when it is over writes to his friends describing how profoundly both bandsmen and audience were impressed. On Friday he exults in the self-assertion of Siegfried's will against all moral ordinances, and is full of a revolutionary sense of 'the universal law of change and renewal'; on Saturday he has an attack of holiness, and asks, 'Can you conceive a moral action of which the root idea is not renunciation?' In short, Wagner can be quoted against himself almost without limit, much as Beethoven's adagios could be quoted against his scherzos if a dispute arose between two fools as to whether he was a melancholy man or a merry one.

THE MUSIC OF THE RING

To be able to follow the music of The Ring, all that is necessary is to become familiar enough with the brief musical phrases out of which it is built to recognize them and attach a certain definite significance to them, exactly as any ordinary Englishman recognizes and attaches a definite significance to the opening bars of 'God Save the Queen'. There is no difficulty here: every soldier is expected to learn and distinguish between different bugle calls and trumpet calls; and anyone who can do this can learn and distinguish between the representative themes or 'leading motives' (Leitmotifs) of The Ring. They are the easier to learn because they are repeated again and again; and the main ones are so emphatically impressed on the ear whilst the spectator is looking for the first time at the objects, or witnessing the first strong dramatic expression of the ideas they denote, that the requisite association is formed unconsciously. The themes are neither long, nor complicated, nor difficult. Whoever can pick up the flourish of a coach-horn, the note of a bird, the rhythm of the postman's knock or of a horse's gallop, will be at no loss in picking up the themes of The Ring. No doubt, when it comes to forming the necessary mental association with the theme, it may happen that the spectator may find his ear conquering the tune more easily than his mind conquers the thought. But for the most part the themes do not denote thoughts at all, but either emotions of a quite simple universal kind, or the sights, sounds and fancies common enough to be familiar to children. Indeed some of them are as frankly childish as any of the funny little orchestral interludes which, in Haydn's Creation, introduce the horse, the deer, or the worm. We have both the horse and the worm in The Ring, treated exactly in Haydn's manner, and with an effect not a whit less ridiculous

281

to superior people who decline to take it good-humoredly. Even the complaisance of good Wagnerites is occasionally rather overstrained by the way in which Brynhild's allusions to her charger Grani elicit from the band a little rum-ti-tum triplet which by itself is in no way suggestive of a horse, although a continuous rush of such triplets makes a very exciting musical gallop.

Other themes denote objects which cannot be imitatively suggested by music: for instance, music cannot suggest a ring, and cannot suggest gold, yet each of these has a representative theme which pervades the score in all directions. In the case of the gold the association is established by the very salient way in which the orchestra breaks into the pretty theme in the first act of The Rhine Gold at the moment when the sunrays strike down through the water and light up the glittering treasure, thitherto invisible. The reference of the strange little theme of the wishing cap is equally manifest from the first, since the spectator's attention is wholly taken up with the Tarnhelm and its magic when the theme is first pointedly uttered by the orchestra. The sword theme is introduced at the end of The Rhine Gold to express Wotan's hero inspiration; and I have already mentioned that Wagner, unable, when it came to practical stage management, to forgo the appeal to the eye as well as to the thought, here made Wotan pick up a sword and brandish it, though no such instruction appears in the printed score. When this sacrifice to Wagner's scepticism as to the reality of any appeal to an audience that is not made through their bodily sense is omitted the association of the theme with the sword is not formed until that point in the first act of The Valkyrie at which Siegmund is left alone by Hunding's hearth, weaponless, with the assurance that he will have to fight for his life at dawn with his host. He recalls then how his father promised him a sword for his hour of need; and as he does so, a flicker from the dying fire is caught by the golden hilt of the sword in the tree, when the theme immediately begins to gleam through the quiver of sound from the orchestra, and only dies out as the fire sinks and the sword is once more hidden by the darkness. Later on, this theme, which is never silent whilst Sieglinda is dwelling on the story of the sword, leaps out into the most dazzling splendor the band can give it when Siegmund triumphantly draws the weapon from the tree. As it consists of seven notes only, with a very marked measure, and a melody like a simple flourish on a trumpet or post horn, nobody capable of catching a tune can easily miss it.

The Valhalla theme, sounded with solemn grandeur as the home of the gods first appears to us and to Wotan at the beginning of the second scene of The Rhine Gold, also cannot be mistaken. It, too, has a memorable rhythm; and its majestic harmonies, far from presenting those novel or curious problems in polyphony of which Wagner still stands suspected by superstitious people, are just those three simple chords which festive students who vamp accompaniments to comic songs 'by ear' soon find sufficient for nearly all the popular tunes in the world.

On the other hand, the ring theme, when it begins to hurtle through the third scene of The Rhine Gold, cannot possibly be referred to any special feature in the general gloom and turmoil of the den of the dwarfs. It is not a melody, but merely the displaced metric accent which musicians call syncopation, rung on the notes of the familiar chord formed by piling three minor thirds on top of one another (technically, the chord of the minor ninth, *ci-devant* diminished seventh). One soon picks it up and identifies it; but it does not get introduced in the unequivocally clear fashion of the themes described above, or of that malignant monstrosity, the theme which denotes the curse on the gold. Consequently it cannot be said that the musical design of the work is perfectly clear at the first hearing as regards all the themes; but it is so as regards most of them, the main lines being laid down as emphatically and intelligibly as the dramatic motives in a Shakespearean play. As to the coyer subtleties of the score, their discovery provides fresh interest for repeated hearings, giving The Ring a Beethovenian inexhaustibility and toughness of wear.

The themes associated with the individual characters get stamped on the memory easily by the simple association of the sound of the theme with the appearance of the person indicated. Its appropriateness is generally pretty obvious. Thus, the entry of the giants is made to a vigorous stumping, tramping measure. Mimmy, being a quaint, weird old creature, has a quaint, weird theme of two thin chords that creep down eerily one to the other. Gutruna's theme is pretty and caressing: Gunther's bold, rough, and commonplace. It is a favorite trick of Wagner's, when one of his characters is killed on the stage, to make the theme attached to that character weaken, fail, and fade away with a broken echo into silence.

THE CHARACTERIZATION

All this, however, is the mere child's play of theme work. The more complex characters, instead of having a simple musical label attached to them, have their characteristic ideas and aspirations identified with special representative themes as they come into play in the drama; and the chief merit of the thematic structure of The Ring is the mastery with which the dramatic play of the ideas is reflected in the contrapuntal play of the themes. We do not find Wotan, like the dragon or the horse, or, for the matter of that, like the stage demon in Weber's Freischütz or Meyerbeer's Robert the Devil, with one fixed theme attached to him like a name plate to an umbrella, blaring unaltered from the orchestra whenever he steps on the stage. Sometimes we have the Valhalla theme used to express the greatness of the gods as an idea of Wotan's. Again, we have his spear, the symbol of his power, identified with another theme, on which Wagner finally exercises his favorite device by making it break and fail, cut through, as it were, by the tearing sound of the theme identified with the sword, when Siegfried shivers the spear with the stroke of Nothung. Yet another theme connected with Wotan is the Wanderer music which breaks with such a majestic reassurance on the nightmare terror of Mimmy when Wotan appears at the mouth of his cave in the scene of the three riddles. Thus not only are there several Wotan themes, but each varies in its inflexions and shades of tone color according to its dramatic circumstances. So, too, the merry horn tune of the young Siegfried changes its measure, loads itself with massive harmonies, and becomes an exordium of the most imposing splendor when it heralds his entry as full-fledged hero in the prologue to Night Falls on The Gods. Even Mimmy has his two or three themes: the weird one already described; the little one in triple measure imitating the tap of his hammer, and fiercely mocked in the savage laugh of Alberic at his death; and finally the crooning tune in which he details all his motherly kindnesses to the little foundling Siegfried. Besides this there are all manner of little musical blinkings and shamblings and whinings, the least hint of which from the orchestra at any moment instantly brings Mimmy to mind, whether he is on the stage at the time or not.

In truth, dramatic characterization in music cannot be carried very far by the use of representative themes. Mozart, the greatest of all masters of this art, never dreamt of employing them; and, extensively as they are used in The Ring, they do not enable Wagner to dispense with the Mozartian method. Apart from the themes, Siegfried and Mimmy are still as sharply distinguished from one another by the character of their music as Don Giovanni from Leporello, Wotan from Gutruna as Sarastro from Papagena. It is true that the themes attached to the characters have the same musical appropriateness as the rest of the music: for example, neither the Valhalla nor the spear themes could, without the most ludicrous incongruity, be used for the forest bird or the unstable, delusive Loki; but for all that the musical characterization must be regarded as independent of the specific themes, since the entire elimination of the thematic system from the score would leave the characters as well distinguished musically as they are at present.

One more illustration of the way in which the thematic system is worked. There are two themes connected with Loki. One is a rapid, sinuous, twisting, shifty semiquaver figure suggested by the unsubstantial, elusive logic-spinning of the clever one's braincraft. The other is the fire theme. In the first act of Siegfried, Mimmy makes his unavailing attempt to explain fear to Siegfried. With the horror fresh upon him of the sort of nightmare into which he has fallen after the departure of the Wanderer, and which has taken the form, at once fanciful and symbolic, of a delirious dread of light, he asks Siegfried whether he has never, whilst wandering in the forest, had his heart set hammering in frantic dread by the mysterious lights of the gloaming. To this, Siegfried, greatly astonished, replies that on such occasions his heart is altogether healthy and his sensations perfectly normal. Here Mimmy's question is accompanied by the tremulous sounding of the fire theme with its harmonies most oppressively disturbed and troubled; whereas with Siegfried's reply they become quite clear and straightforward, making the theme sound bold, brilliant, and serene. This is a typical instance of the way in which the themes are used.

The thematic system gives symphonic interest, reasonableness and unity to the music, enabling the composer to exhaust every aspect and quality of his melodic material, and, in Beethoven's manner, to work miracles of beauty, expression and significance with the briefest phrases. As a set-off against this, it has led Wagner to indulge in repetitions that would be intolerable in a purely dramatic work. Almost the first thing that a dramatist has to learn in constructing a play is that the persons must not come on the stage in the second act and tell one another at great length what the audience has already seen pass before its eyes in the first act. The extent to which Wagner has been seduced into violating this rule by his affection for his themes is startling to a practised playwright. Siegfried inherits from Wotan a mania for autobiography which leads him to inflict on everyone he meets the story of Mimmy and the dragon, although the audience have spent a whole evening witnessing the events he is narrating. Hagen tells the story to Gunther; and that same night Alberic's ghost tells it over again to Hagen, who knows it already as well as the audience. Siegfried tells the Rhine maidens as much of it as they will listen to, and then keeps telling it to his hunting companions until they kill him. Wotan's autobiography on the second evening becomes his biography in the mouths of the Norns on the fourth. The little that the Norns add to it is repeated an hour later by Valtrauta. How far all this repetition is tolerable is a matter of individual taste. A good story will bear repetition and if it has woven into it such pretty tunes as the Rhine maidens' yodel, Mimmy's tinkling anvil beat, the note of the forest bird, the call of Siegfried's horn, and so on, it will bear a good deal of rehearing. Those who have but newly learnt their way through The Ring will not readily admit that there is a bar too much repetition.

But how if you find some anti-Wagnerite raising the question whether the thematic system does not enable the composer to produce a music drama with much less musical fertility than was required from his predecessors for the composition of operas under the old system!

Such discussions are not within the scope of this little book. But as the book is now finished (for really nothing more need be said about The Ring), I am quite willing to add a few pages of ordinary musical criticism, partly to please the amateurs who enjoy that sort of reading, and partly for the guidance of those who wish to obtain some hints to help them through such critical small talk about Wagner and Bayreuth as may be forced upon them at the dinner table or between the acts.

THE OLD AND THE NEW MUSIC

In the old-fashioned opera every separate number involved the composition of a fresh melody; but it is quite a mistake to suppose that this creative effort extended continuously throughout the number from the first to the last bar. When a musician composes according to a set metrical pattern, the selection of the pattern and the composition of the first stave (a stave in music corresponds to a line in verse) generally completes the creative effort. All the rest follows more or less mechanically to fill up the pattern, an air being very like a wall-paper design in this respect. Thus the second stave is usually a perfectly obvious consequence of the first; and the third and fourth an exact or very slightly varied repetition of the first and second. For example, given the first line of Pop Goes the Weasel or Yankee Doodle, any musical cobbler could supply the remaining three. There is very little tune-turning of this kind in The Ring; and it is noteworthy that where it does occur, as in Siegmund's spring song and Mimmy's croon, 'Ein zullendes Kind', the effect of the symmetrical staves recurring as a mere matter of form, is perceptibly poor and platitudinous compared with the free flow of melody which prevails elsewhere.

The other and harder way of composing is to take a strain of free melody, and ring every variety of change of mood upon it as if it were a thought that sometimes brought hope, sometimes melancholy, sometimes exultation, sometimes raging despair and so on. To take several themes of this kind, and weave them together into a rich musical fabric passing panoramically before the ear with a continually varying flow of sentiment, is the highest feat of the musician: it is in this way that we get the fugue of Bach and the symphony of Beethoven. The admittedly inferior musician is the one who,

288

like Auber and Offenbach, not to mention our purveyors of drawing-room ballads, can produce an unlimited quantity of symmetrical tunes, but cannot weave themes symphonically.

When this is taken into account, it will be seen that the fact that there is a great deal of repetition in The Ring does not distinguish it from the old-fashioned operas. The real difference is that in them the repetition was used for the mechanical completion of conventional metric patterns, whereas in The Ring the recurrence of the theme is an intelligent and interesting consequence of the recurrence of the dramatic phenomenon which it denotes. It should be remembered also that the substitution of symphonically treated themes for tunes with symmetrical eight-bar staves and the like, has always been the rule in the highest forms of music. To describe it, or be affected by it, as an abandonment of melody, is to confess oneself an ignoramus conversant only with dance tunes and ballads.

The sort of stuff a purely dramatic musician produces when he hampers himself with metric patterns in composition is not unlike what might have resulted in literature if Carlyle (for example) had been compelled by convention to write his historical stories in rhymed stanzas. That is to say, it limits his fertility to an occasional phrase, and three quarters of the time exercises only his barren ingenuity in fitting rhymes and measures to it. In literature the great masters of the art have long emancipated themselves from metric patterns. Nobody claims that the hierarchy of modern impassioned prose writers, from Bunyan to Ruskin, should be placed below the writers of pretty lyrics, from Herrick to Mr Austin Dobson. Only in dramatic literature do we find the devastating tradition of blank verse still lingering, giving factitious prestige to the platitudes of dullards, and robbing the dramatic style of the genuine poet of its full natural endowment of variety, force and simplicity.

This state of things, as we have seen, finds its parallel in musical art, since music can be written in prose themes or in versified tunes; only here nobody dreams of disputing the greater difficulty of the prose forms and the comparative triviality of versification. Yet in dramatic music, as in dramatic literature, the tradition of versification clings with the same pernicious results; and the opera, like the tragedy, is conventionally made like a wall-paper. The theatre seems doomed to be in all things the last refuge of the hankering after cheap prettiness in art.

Unfortunately this confusion of the decorative with the dramatic element in both literature and music is maintained by the example of great masters in both arts. Very touching dramatic expression can be combined with decorative symmetry of versification when the artist happens to possess both the decorative and dramatic gifts, and to have cultivated both hand in hand. Shakespear and Shelley, for instance, far from being hampered by the conventional obligation to write their dramas in verse, found it much the easiest and cheapest way of producing them. But if Shakespear had been compelled by custom to write entirely in prose, all his ordinary dialogue might have been as good as the first scene of As You Like It, and all his lofty passages as fine as 'What a piece of work is Man!', thus sparing us a great deal of blank verse in which the thought is commonplace, and the expression, though catchingly turned, absurdly pompous. The Cenci might either have been a serious drama or might never have been written at all if Shelley had not been allowed to carry off its unreality by Elizabethan versification. Still, both poets have achieved many passages in which the decorative and dramatic qualities are not only reconciled, but seem to enhance one another to a pitch otherwise unattainable.

Just so in music. When we find, as in the case of Mozart, a prodigiously gifted and arduously trained musician who is also, by a happy accident, a dramatist comparable to Molière, the obligation to compose operas in versified numbers not only does not embarrass him, but actually saves him trouble and thought. No matter what his dramatic mood may be, he expresses it in exquisite musical verses more easily than a dramatist of ordinary singleness of talent can express it in prose. Accordingly, he too, like Shakespear and Shelley, leaves versified airs, like *Dalla sua pace*, or Gluck's *Che faro senza Euridice*, or Weber's *Leise, leise*, which are as dramatic from the first note to the last as the untrammelled themes of The Ring. In consequence, it used to be professorially demanded that all dramatic music should present the same double aspect. The demand was unreasonable, since symmetrical versification is no merit in dramatic music: one might as well stipulate that a dinner fork should be constructed so as to serve also as a tablecloth. It was an ignorant demand too, because it is not true that the composers of these exceptional examples were always, or even often, able to combine dramatic expression with symmetrical versification. Side by side with *Dalla sua pace* we have *Il mio tesoro* and *Non mi dir*, in which exquisitely expressive opening phrases lead to decorative passages which are as grotesque from the dramatic point of view as the music which Alberic sings when he is slipping and sneezing in the Rhine mud is from the decorative point of view. Further, there is to be considered the mass of shapeless 'dry recitative' which separates these symmetrical numbers, and which might have been raised to considerable dramatic and musical importance had it been incorporated into a continuous musical fabric by thematic treatment. Finally, Mozart's most dramatic finales and concerted numbers are more or less in sonata form, like symphonic movements, and must therefore be classed as musical prose. And sonata form dictates repetitions and recapitulations from which the perfectly unconventional form adopted by Wagner is free. On the whole, there is more scope for both repetition and convention in the old form than in the new; and the poorer a composer's musical gift is, the surer he is to resort to the eighteenth-century patterns to eke out his invention.

THE NINETEENTH CENTURY

When Wagner was born in 1813, music had newly become the most astonishing, the most fascinating, the most miraculous art in the world. Mozart's Don Giovanni had made all musical Europe conscious of the enchantments of the modern orchestra and of the perfect adaptability of music to the subtlest needs of the dramatist. Beethoven had shewn how those inarticulate mood-poems which surge through men who have, like himself, no exceptional command of words, can be written down in music as symphonies. Not that Mozart and Beethoven invented these applications of their art; but they were the first whose works made it clear that the dramatic and subjective powers of sound were enthralling enough to stand by themselves quite apart from the decorative musical structures of which they had hitherto been a mere feature. After the finales in Figaro and Don Giovanni, the possibility of the modern music drama lay bare. After the symphonies of Beethoven it was certain that the poetry that lies too deep for words does not lie too deep for music, and that the vicissitudes of the soul, from the roughest fun to the loftiest aspiration, can make symphonies without the aid of dance tunes. As much, perhaps, will be claimed for the preludes and fugues of Bach; but Bach's method was unattainable; his compositions were wonderful webs of exquisitely beautiful Gothic traceries in sound, quite beyond all ordinary human talent. Beethoven's far blunter craft was thoroughly popular and practicable; not to save his soul could he have drawn one long Gothic line in sound as Bach could, much less have woven several of them together with so apt a harmony that even when the composer is unmoved, its progressions saturate themselves with the emotion which (as modern critics are a little apt to forget) springs as warmly from our delicately touched admiration as from our sympathies, and sometimes makes us give a composer credit for pathetic intentions which he does not entertain, just as a boy imagines a treasure of tenderness and noble wisdom in the beauty of a woman. Besides, Bach set comic dialogue to music exactly as he set the recitatives of the Passion, there being for him, apparently, only one recitative possible, and that the musically best. He reserved the expression of his merry mood for the regular set numbers in which he could make one of his wonderful contrapuntal traceries of pure ornament with the requisite gaiety of line and movement. Beethoven bowed to no ideal of beauty; he only sought the expression for his feeling. To him a joke was a joke; and if it sounded funny in music he was satisfied. Until the old habit of judging all music by its decorative symmetry had worn out, musicians were shocked by his symphonies, and, misunderstanding his integrity, openly questioned his sanity. But to those who were not looking for pretty new sound patterns, but were longing for the expression of their moods in music, he achieved a revelation, because, being single in his aim to express his own moods, he anticipated with revolutionary courage and frankness all the moods of the rising generations of the nineteenth century.

The result was inevitable. In the nineteenth century it was no longer necessary to be a born pattern designer in sound to be a composer. One had but to be a dramatist or a poet completely susceptible to the dramatic and descriptive powers of sound. A race of literary and theatrical musicians appeared; and Meyerbeer, the first of them, made an extraordinary impression. The frankly delirious description of his Robert the Devil in Balzac's short story entitled Gambara, and Goethe's astonishingly mistaken notion that he could have composed music for Faust, shew how completely the enchantments of the new dramatic music upset the judgment of artists of eminent discernment. Meyerbeer was, people said (old gentlemen still say so in Paris), the successor of

Beethoven: he was, if a less perfect musician than Mozart, a profounder genius. Above all, he was original and daring. Wagner himself raved about the duet in the fourth act of Les Huguenots as wildly as anyone.

Yet all this effect of originality and profundity was produced by a quite limited talent for turning striking phrases, exploiting certain curious and rather catching rhythms and modulations, and devising suggestive or eccentric instrumentation. On its decorative side, it was the same phenomenon in music as the Baroque school in architecture: an energetic struggle to enliven organic decay by mechanical oddities and novelties. Meyerbeer was no symphonist. He could not apply the thematic system to his striking phrases, and so had to cobble them into metric patterns in the old style; and as he was no 'absolute musician' either, he hardly got his metric patterns beyond mere quadrille tunes, which were either wholly undistinguished, or else made remarkable by certain brusqueries which, in the true rococo manner, owed their singularity to their senselessness. He could produce neither a thorough music drama nor a charming opera. But with all this, and worse, Meyerbeer had some genuine dramatic energy, and even passion; and sometimes rose to the occasion in a manner which, whilst the imagination of his contemporaries remained on fire with the novelties of dramatic music, led them to overrate him with an extravagance which provoked Wagner to conduct a long critical campaign against his supremacy. In the eighteen-sixties this was inevitably ascribed to the professional jealousy of a disappointed rival. Nowadays young people cannot understand how anyone could ever have taken Meyerbeer's influence seriously. The few who remember the reputation he built on The Huguenots and The Prophet, and who now realize what a no-thoroughfare the path he opened proved to be, even to himself, know how invincible and how impersonal Wagner's attack was.

Wagner was the literary musician par excellence. He could

not, like Mozart and Beethoven, produce decorative tone structures independently of any dramatic or poetic subject matter, because, that craft being no longer necessary for his purpose, he did not cultivate it. As Shakespear, compared with Tennyson, appears to have an exclusively dramatic talent, so exactly does Wagner compared with Mendelssohn. On the other hand, he had not to go to third-rate literary hacks for 'librettos' to set to music: he produced his own dramatic poems, thus giving dramatic integrity to opera and making symphony articulate. A Beethoven symphony (except the articulate part of the ninth) expresses noble feeling, but not thought: it has moods, but no ideas. Wagner added thought and produced the music drama. Mozart's loftiest opera, his Ring, so to speak, The Magic Flute, has a libretto which, though none the worse for seeming, like The Rhine Gold, the merest Christmas tomfoolery to shallow spectators, is the product of a talent immeasurably inferior to Mozart's own. The libretto of Don Giovanni is coarse and trivial: its transfiguration by Mozart's music may be a marvel; but nobody will venture to contend that such transfigurations, however seductive, can be as satisfactory as tone poetry or drama in which the musician and the poet are at the same level. Here, then, we have the simple secret of Wagner's pre-eminence as a dramatic musician. He wrote the poems as well as composed the music of his 'stage festival plays', as he called them.

Up to a certain point in his career Wagner paid the penalty of undertaking two arts instead of one. Mozart had his trade as a musician at his fingers' ends when he was twenty, because he had served an arduous apprenticeship to that trade and no other. Wagner was very far from having attained equal mastery at thirty-five: indeed he himself has told us that not until he had passed the age at which Mozart died did he compose with that complete spontaneity of musical expression which can only be attained by winning entire freedom from all preoccupation with the difficulties of technical processes. But when that time came, he was not only a consummate musician, like Mozart, but a dramatic poet and a critical and philosophical essayist, exercising a considerable influence on his century. The sign of this consummation was his ability at last to play with his art, and thus to add to his already famous achievements in sentimental drama that lighthearted art of comedy of which the greatest masters, like Molière and Mozart, are so much rarer than the tragedians and sentimentalists. It was then that he composed the first two acts of Siegfried, and later on The Mastersingers, a professedly comedic work, and a quite Mozartian garden of melody, hardly credible as the work of the straining artificer of Tannhäuser. Only, as no man ever learns to do one thing by doing something else, however closely allied the two things may be, Wagner still produced no music independently of his poems. The overture to The Mastersingers is delightful when you know what it is all about; but only those to whom it came as a concert piece without any such clue, and who judged its reckless counterpoint by the standard of Bach and of Mozart's Magic Flute overture, can realize how atrocious it used to sound to musicians of the old school. When I first heard it, with the clear march of the polyphony in Bach's B minor Mass fresh in my memory, I confess I thought that the parts had got dislocated, and that some of the band were half a bar behind the others. Perhaps they were; but now that I am familiar with the work, and with Wagner's harmony, I can still quite understand certain passages producing that effect on an admirer of Bach even when performed with perfect accuracy.

THE MUSIC OF THE FUTURE

The ultimate success of Wagner was so prodigious that to his dazzled disciples it seemed that the age of what he called 'absolute' music must be at an end, and the musical future destined to be an exclusively Wagnerian one inaugurated at Bayreuth. All great geniuses produce this illusion. Wagner did not begin a movement: he consummated it. He was the summit of the nineteenth-century school of dramatic music in the same sense as Mozart was the summit (the word is Gounod's) of the eighteenth-century school. All those who attempted to carry on his Bayreuth tradition have shared the fate of the forgotten purveyors of second-hand Mozart a hundred years ago. As to the expected supersession of absolute music, Wagner's successors in European rank were Brahms, Elgar and Richard Strauss. The reputation of Brahms rests on his absolute music alone: such works as his German Requiem endear themselves to us as being musically great fun; but to take them quite seriously is to make them oppressively dull. Elgar followed Beethoven and Schumann: he owes nothing essential to Wagner, and secured his niche in the temple by his symphonies and his Enigma Variations, which are as absolutely musical as any modern music can be. Although Strauss produced works for the musical theatre which maintained it at the level to which Wagner had raised it, his new departure was a form of musical drama, comic epic and soul autobiography in which stage, singers and all the rest of the theatrical material of Bayreuth save only the orchestra are thrown overboard, and the work effected by instrumental music alone, even Beethoven's final innovation of a chorus being discarded. Just the same thing happened when Elgar took as his theme Shakespear's Henry IV, with Falstaff as its chief figure. He made the band do it all, and with such masterful success that one cannot bear to think of what would have been the result of a mere attempt to turn the play into an opera.

The Russian composers whose vogue succeeded that of Wagner were not in the least Wagnerian: they developed from the romantic school, from Weber and Meyerbeer, from Berlioz and Liszt, much as they might have done had Wagner never existed except as a propagandist of the importance of their art. A disparaging attitude towards Wagner resembling that of Chopin to Beethoven, and a very similar escape from his influence even in technique, was quite common among the composers whose early lives overlapped the last part of his. In England the composers who are the juniors of Elgar, but the seniors of (for example) Bax and Ireland, the most notable of whom are Mr Granville Bantock and Mr Rutland Boughton, were heavily Wagnerized in their youth, and began by Tristanizing and Götterdämmerunging heroically; but when they found themselves their Wagnerism vanished. The younger men do not begin with Wagner nor even with Strauss: they are mostly bent on producing curiosities of absolute music until they settle down into a serious style of their own. All that can be said for the Wagner tradition is that it finally killed the confusion between decorative pattern music and dramatic music which muddled Meyerbeer and imposed absurd repetitions on the heroes and heroines of Handel and Mozart. Even in absolute music, the post-Wagnerite sonata form has become so much less mechanical and thoughtless that the fact that it still persists in essentials is hardly worth asserting.

Writing before any of these developments had happened, I said in the first edition of this book that there was no more hope in attempts to out-Wagner Wagner in music drama than there had been in the old attempts to make Handel the starting point of a great school of oratorio. How true this was is now so obvious that my younger readers may wonder why I thought it worth while to say it. But if veterans did not indulge in these day-before-yesterdayisms Music would lose the thread of its history.

BAYREUTH

WHEN the Bayreuth Festival Playhouse was at last completed, and opened in 1876 with the first performance of The Ring, European society was compelled to admit that Wagner was 'a success'. Royal personages, detesting his music, sat out the performances in the row of boxes set apart for princes. They all complimented him on the astonishing 'push' with which, in the teeth of all obstacles, he had turned a fabulous and visionary project into a concrete commercial reality, patronized by the public at a pound a head. It is as well to know that these congratulations had no other effect upon Wagner than to open his eyes to the fact that the Bayreuth experiment, as an attempt to evade the ordinary social and commercial conditions of theatrical enterprise, was a failure. His own account of it contrasts the reality with his intentions in a vein which would be bitter if it were not so humorous. The precautions taken to keep the seats out of the hands of the frivolous public and in the hands of earnest disciples, banded together in little Wagner Societies throughout Europe, had ended in their forestalling by ticket speculators and their sale to just the sort of idle globe-trotting tourists against whom the temple was to have been strictly closed. The money, supposed to be contributed by the faithful, was begged by energetic subscription-hunting ladies from people who must have had the most grotesque misconceptions of the composer's aims: among others, the Khedive of Egypt and the Sultan of Turkey!

Since then, subscriptions are no longer needed; for the Festival Playhouse pays its own way now, and is commercially on the same footing as any other theatre. The only qualification required from the visitor is money. A Londoner spends twenty pounds on a visit: a native Bayreuther spends one pound. In either case 'the Folk', on whose behalf Wagner turned out in 1849, are effectually excluded; and the Festival Playhouse must therefore be classed as infinitely less Wagnerian in its character than Hampton Court Palace. Nobody knew this better than Wagner; and nothing can be further off the mark than to chatter about Bayreuth as if it had succeeded in escaping from the conditions of our modern civilization any more than the Grand Opera in Paris or London.

Within these conditions, however, it effected a new departure in that excellent German institution, the summer theatre. Unlike the old opera houses, which are constructed so that the audience may present a splendid pageant to the delighted manager, it was designed to secure an uninterrupted view of the stage, and an undisturbed hearing of the music, to the audience. The dramatic purpose of the performances was taken with entire and elaborate seriousness as the sole purpose of them; and the management was jealous for the reputation of Wagner. The sightseeing globe-trotter no longer crowds out the genuine disciple: the audiences are now as genuinely devoted as Wagner could have desired: the disconcerted, bewildered, bored followers of fashion have vanished with the sportsman on a holiday; the atmosphere is the right one for the work. There is, apparently, an effective demand for summer theatres of the highest class. There is no reason why the experiment should not be tried in England. If our enthusiasm for Handel can support Handel Festivals, laughably dull, stupid and anti-Handelian as these choral monstrosities are, as well as annual provincial festivals on the same model, there is no likelihood of a Wagner Festival failing. Suppose, for instance, a Wagner theatre were built at Hampton Court or on Richmond Hill, not to say Margate pier, so that we could have a delightful summer evening holiday, Bayreuth fashion, passing the hours between the acts in the park or on the river before sunset, is it seriously contended that there would be any lack of visitors? If a little of the money that is wasted on grandstands, Eiffel towers, and dismal Halls by the Sea, all as much tied to brief annual seasons as Bayreuth, were applied in this way, the profit would be far more certain and the social utility prodigiously greater. Any English enthusiasm for Bayreuth that does not take the form of clamor for a Festival playhouse in England may be set aside as mere pilgrimage mania.

Besides, the early Bayreuth performances were far from delectable. The singing was sometimes tolerable, and sometimes abominable. Some of the singers were mere animated beer casks, too lazy and conceited to practise the self-control and physical training that is expected as a matter of course from an acrobat, a jockey or a pugilist. The women's dresses were prudish and absurd. It is true that after some years Kundry no longer wore an early Victorian ball dress with 'ruchings', and that Freia was provided with a quaintly modish copy of the flowered gown of Spring in Botticelli's famous picture; but the mailclad Brynhild still climbed the mountains with her legs carefully hidden in a long white skirt, and looked so exactly like Mrs Leo Hunter as Minerva that it was quite impossible to feel a ray of illusion whilst looking at her. The ideal of womanly beauty aimed at reminded Englishmen of the barmaids of the seventies, when the craze for golden hair was at its worst. Further, while Wagner's stage directions were sometimes disregarded as unintelligently as at the old opera houses, Wagner's quaintly old-fashioned tradition of half rhetorical, half historical-pictorial attitude and gesture prevailed. The most striking moments of the drama were conceived as *tableaux vivants* with posed models, instead of as passages of action, motion and life.

I need hardly add that the supernatural powers of control attributed by credulous pilgrims to Wagner's widow, and later on to his son, did not exist. Prima donnas and tenors were as unmanageable at Bayreuth as anywhere else. Casts were capriciously changed; stage business was insufficiently rehearsed; the audience was compelled to listen to a Brynhild or Siegfried of fifty when they had carefully arranged to see one of twenty-five, much as in any ordinary opera house. Even the conductors upset the arrangements occasionally. On the other hand, we could always feel assured that in thoroughness of preparation of the chief work of the season, in strenuous artistic pretentiousness, in pious conviction that the work was of such enormous importance as to be worth doing well at all costs, the Bayreuth performances would deserve their reputation. Their example raised the quality of operatic performances throughout the world, even in apparently incorrigible centres of fashion and frivolity.

BAYREUTH IN ENGLAND

In 1898 I purposely dwelt on the early shortcomings of Bayreuth to shew that there was no reason in the world why as good and better performances of The Ring should not be given in England, and that neither Wagner's widow nor his son could pretend to handle them with greater authority than any artist who feels the impulse to interpret them. Nobody will ever know what Wagner himself thought of the artists who established the Bayreuth tradition; he was obviously not in a position to criticize them. For instance, had Rubini survived to create Siegmund, Wagner could hardly have written so amusing and vivid a description as he did of his Ottavio in the old Paris days. Wagner was under great obligations to the heroes and heroines of 1876; and he naturally said nothing to disparage their triumphs; but there is no reason to believe that all or indeed any of them satisfied him as Schnorr of Carolsfeld satisfied him as Tristan, or Schröder Devrient as Fidelio. It was just as likely that the next Schnorr or Schröder would arise in England. Nowadays it seems odd that anyone should need to be told all this. British and American singers have long since replaced the Bayreuth veterans to considerable advantage.

WAGNERIAN SINGERS

No nation need have any difficulty in producing a race of
Wagnerian singers. With the single exception of Handel, no
composer has written music so well calculated to make its
singers vocal athletes as Wagner. Abominably as the Germans
sang in Wagner's day, it was astonishing how they throve
physically on his leading parts. His secret is the Handelian
secret. Instead of specializing his vocal parts after the manner
of Verdi and Gounod for shrieking sopranos, goat-bleating
tenors and tremulous baritones with an effective compass of
about a fifth at the extreme tiptop of their ranges, and for
contraltos with chest registers forced all over their compass in
the manner of music-hall singers, he employs the entire range
of the human voice, demanding from everybody nearly two
effective octaves. The bulk of the work lies easily in the middle
of the voice, which is nevertheless well exercised all over, one
part of it relieving the other healthily and continually. He uses
the highest notes sparingly, and is ingeniously considerate in
the matter of instrumental accompaniment. Even when the
singer seems to dominate all the thunders of the full orchestra,
a glance at the score will shew that he is well heard, not because
of a stentorian voice, but because Wagner meant him to be
heard. The old lazy Italian style of orchestral accompaniment
as we find it in Rossini's Stabat or Verdi's Trovatore, where the
strings play a rum-tum accompaniment whilst the whole wind
band blares away, fortissimo, in unison with the singer, is
somehow not so brutally opaque in practice as it looks on paper;
but Wagner never condescends to it. Even in an ordinary opera
house, with the orchestra ranged directly between the singers
and the audience, his instrumentation is transparent to the
human voice.

On every point, then, a Wagner theatre and Wagner festivals
are much more generally practicable than the older and more
artificial forms of dramatic music. A presentable performance
of The Ring is a big undertaking only in the sense in which the

construction of a railway is a big undertaking: that is, it requires plenty of work and plenty of professional skill; but it does not, like the old operas and oratorios, require those extraordinary vocal gifts which only a few individuals scattered here and there throughout Europe are born with. Singers who could never execute the roulades of Semiramis, Assur, and Arsaces in Rossini's Semiramide, could sing the parts of Brynhild, Wotan and Erda without missing a note. Any Englishman can understand this if he considers for a moment the difference between a Cathedral service and an Italian opera at Covent Garden. The service is a much more serious matter than the opera. Yet provincial talent is sufficient for it, if the requisite industry and devotion are forthcoming. Even at the Opera I have seen lusty troopers and porters, without art or manners, accepted by fashion as principal tenors during the long interval between Mario and Jean de Reszke; and the two most extra-ordinary dramatic singers of the twentieth century, Chaliapin and Vladimir Rosing, are quite independent of the old metropolitan artificialities. Let us remember that Bayreuth has recruited its Parsifals from the peasantry, and that the artisans of a village in the Bavarian Alps are capable of a famous and elaborate Passion Play, and then consider whether any country is so poor in talent that its amateurs must journey to the centre of Europe to witness a Wagner Festival.

WAGNERISM WITH WAGNER LEFT OUT

In spite of the fact that my old suggestion of a Festival Play-house on Richmond Hill has now been proved perfectly feasi-ble as far as the availability of the necessary home talent is concerned, only one serious attempt to establish a Bayreuth in England has come to my knowledge; and that one, far from concerning itself with Wagner, owes its success to native Brit-ish music with some early ultra-classical assistance from Gluck. Mr Rutland Boughton, who began his career as a composer when the influence of Wagner was at its height, has attempted to do in Somerset what Wagner did in Thuringia, with the very material difference that Wagner had the King of Bavaria at his back, and Mr Boughton had nothing material at his back at all. He selected Glastonbury as his Bayreuth and has established an annual festival there which can already shew a remarkable record of work done. The very desperation of the enterprise has been its salvation. Had Mr Boughton been obsessed, as Wagner was, with the scale to which the Grand Operas of Paris, London and Berlin work, he would have had to wait for a king to help him; that is, he would have waited for ever. Fortunately he remembered that Wagner was not only the highly professionalized royal conductor of Dresden, brought up in the belief that the only success that can hallmark an opera is a Meyerbeerian success at the Paris Opera; he was also the author of the saying that music is kept alive, not by the triumphs of fashionable commercial professionalism, but on the cottage piano of the amateur. Mr Rutland Boughton began in ordinary village halls in Somerset, with a piano and his own fingers for orchestra, his wife as scene painter and costumier, and a fit-up for a stage. The singing and acting was done by the villagers and by anyone else who would come; and a surprising number of quite distinguished talents did come. On these terms, performances were achieved which in point of atmosphere and intimacy of interest were actually better than the performances at the enormously more pretentious Festival Playhouse in Bayreuth, or its copy the Prince Regent Theatre in Munich. There were friendly subscribers, not enough to prevent each festival from ruining Mr Boughton for six months or so, but enough to enable him to devote the remaining six months to preparation for another financial catastrophe, encouraged by the fact that the crashes were less and less disastrous as his enterprise became better and better known. His festival is now a yearly event in Avalon, once an island, now a city in a plain, Glastonbury, steeped in traditions which make it holy ground. But it still has no theatre, no electric light, no convenience for Wagnerian drama that every village does not possess. Yet it is here that the Wagnerist dream has been best realized in England.

That dream, truly interpreted, did not mean that the English soil should bring forth performances of Wagner's music copied from those at Bayreuth. It meant that the English soil should produce English music and English drama, and that English people should perform them in their own way. It is precisely because Mr Boughton has never performed a work of Wagner's, but, with the scholastic exception of an opera or two by Gluck, has composed his own music and had it and other English music sung in English ways, that he can claim to be a Perfect Wagnerite.

By this time there may be other and cognate experiments less known to me. During the twentieth century an important social development has transformed that costly and deleterious bore, the British holiday, into a genuinely recreative change. Under the title of Summer Schools, voluntary associations of artistically minded students of sociology, theosophy, science, history, and what not – shall we say people who take life, or some department of life, seriously, and cannot be happy unless they are using their brains and learning something in the intervals of dancing and singing for pure fun? – now appear in every autumn in the prettiest country districts. These Schools are open to everybody; they afford intimate glimpses of more or less celebrated people who come and lecture to them for the sake of propaganda; and they are very much jollier, as well as substantially cheaper and more genial, than the so-called pleasure resorts in which irritable and overworked professional entertainers hypnotize credulous Britons into believing that they are enjoying themselves when they are only paying through the nose for being worried and pillaged. Where there were formerly only one or two elderly congresses, like the meetings of the British Association, with no activity but that of elderly lecturers all lecturing at the same time in different rooms, there are now dozens of smaller but more youthful and vital gatherings in which, whatever the main subject to be studied may be, Art is continually breaking in in one form or another.

I myself, after a larger experience of professionally and commercially organized art than most men can afford (for I had to earn my living as a critic of such art in my early days), find that it is at such gatherings and from such voluntary enterprises that I can oftenest recapture something of that magic which music and drama had for me in my childhood, and which it is so utterly impossible to preserve under commercial conditions. Commerce in art can save me from many ridiculous blunders and makeshifts that do not matter; but it seldom achieves the things that do matter, never indeed except when they are forced on it in spite of its teeth by some individual artist, mostly one heavily persecuted by it as Wagner was.

Amateur art is discredited art in so far only as the amateur is known as the ape of commercial art. Persons who go to the theatre and opera house only to be smitten with an infatuate ambition to reproduce in their own untrained persons what they see the great professional artists doing there, are mostly foredoomed to failure and ridicule. Here and there one of them succeeds, only to be absorbed by the commercial profession. But the countryside is full of stout characters with no such folly and no such ambition, who will do as much for any really gifted artistic leader as they have done for Mr Boughton and for the organizers of our provincial choirs and brass bands. If Little Bethel has raised the miners of England in a few generations from troglodyte savagery to pious respectability, Little Bayreuth may as easily raise them from pious respectability to a happy consciousness of and interest in fine art, without which all their piety and respectability will not save their children from resorting to cruel sports and squalid sensualities in their natural need for enjoyment. And so, good luck to Little Bayreuth; and may it be as successful as Little Bethel in demonstrating that the laughter of fools is as the crackling of thorns under a pot!

THE SANITY OF ART

AN EXPOSURE OF THE CURRENT NONSENSE ABOUT
ARTISTS BEING DEGENERATE

PREFACE

THE re-publication of this open letter to Mr Benjamin Tucker places me, not for the first time, in the difficulty of the journalist whose work survives the day on which it was written. What the journalist writes about is what everybody is thinking about (or ought to be thinking about) at the moment of writing. To revive his utterances when everybody is thinking about something else; when the tide of public thought and imagination has turned; when the front of the stage is filled with new actors; when many lusty crowers have either survived their vogue or perished with it; when the little men you patronized have become great, and the great men you attacked have been sanctified and pardoned by popular sentiment in the tomb: all these inevitables test the quality of your journalism very severely. Nevertheless, journalism can claim to be the highest form of literature; for all the highest literature is journalism. The writer who aims at producing the platitudes which are 'not for an age, but for all time' has his reward in being unreadable in all ages; whilst Plato and Aristophanes trying to knock some sense into the Athens of their day, Shakespear peopling that same Athens with Elizabethan mechanics and Warwickshire hunts, Ibsen photographing the local doctors and vestrymen of a Norwegian parish, Carpaccio painting the life of St Ursula exactly as if she were a lady living in the next street to him, are still alive and at home everywhere among the dust and ashes of many thousands of academic, punctilious, most archaeologically correct men of letters and art who spent their lives haughtily avoiding the journalist's vulgar obsession with the ephemeral. I also am a journalist, proud of it, deliberately cutting out of my works all that is not journalism, convinced that nothing that is not journalism will live long as literature,

311

or be of any use whilst it does live. I deal with all periods; but I never study any period but the present, which I have not yet mastered and never shall; and as a dramatist I have no clue to any historical or other personage save that part of him which is also myself, and which may be nine tenths of him or ninety-nine hundredths, as the case may be (if, indeed, I do not transcend the creature), but which, anyhow, is all that can ever come within my knowledge of his soul. The man who writes about himself and his own time is the only man who writes about all people and about all time. The other sort of man, who believes that he and his period are so distinct from all other men and periods that it would be immodest and irrelevant to allude to them or assume that they could illustrate anything but his own private circumstances, is the most infatuated of all the egotists, and consequently the most unreadable and negligible of all the authors. And so, let others cultivate what they call literature: journalism for me!

The following remnant of the journalism of 1895 will, I hope, bear out these preliminary remarks, which are none the less valid because they are dragged in here to dismount the critics who ride the high horse of Letters at me. It was undertaken under the following circumstances. In 1893 Doctor Max Nordau, one of those remarkable cosmopolitan Jews who go forth against modern civilization as David went against the Philistines or Charles Martel against the Saracens, smiting it hip and thigh without any sense of common humanity with it, trumped up an indictment of its men of genius as depraved lunatics, and pled it (in German) before the bar of Europe under the title Entartung. It was soon translated for England and America as Degeneration. Like all rigorous and thorough-going sallies of special pleading, it had its value; for the way to get at the merits of a case is not to listen to the fool who imagines himself impartial, but to get it argued with reckless bias for and against. To understand a saint, you must hear the devil's advocate; and the same is true of the artist. Nordau had briefed himself as devil's advocate against the great artistic reputations

312

of the nineteenth century; and he did his duty as well as it could be done at the price, incidentally saying many more true and important things than most of the counsel on the other side were capable of.

Indeed counsel on the other side mostly threw up their briefs in consternation, and began to protest that they entirely agreed with Dr Nordau, and that though they had perhaps dallied a little with Rossetti, Wagner, Ibsen, Tolstoy, Nietzsche and the rest of the degenerates before their true character had been exposed, yet they had never really approved of them. Even those who stood to their guns had not sufficient variety of culture to contradict the cosmopolitan doctor on more than one or two points, being often not champions of Art at large, but merely jealous fanciers of some particular artist. Thus the Wagnerians were ready to give up Ibsen; the Ibsenites were equally suspicious of Wagner; the Tolstoyans gave up both; the Nietzscheans were only too glad to see Tolstoy catching it; and the connoisseurs of Impressionism in painting, though fairly impartial in music and literature, could not handle the technics of the case for the defence. Yet Dr Nordau knew so little, and his technical handling of painting and music was so like Captain Lemuel Gulliver's nautical observations, that I, being familiar with all the arts, and as accustomed as any Jew to the revolutionary cosmopolitan climate, looked on at his triumph much as Napoleon looked on at the massacre of the Swiss, thinking how easy it would be to change the rout into the cheapest of victories. However, none of our silly editors had the gumption to offer me the command; so, like Napoleon, I went home and left them to be cut to pieces.

But Destiny will not allow her offers to be completely overlooked. In the Easter of 1895, when Nordau was master of the field, and the newspaper champions of modern Literature and Art were on their knees before him, weeping and protesting their innocence, I was staying in the wooden hotel

313

on Beachy Head, with a select party of Fabians, politicians and philosophers, diligently trying to ride a bicycle for the first time in my life. My efforts set the coastguards laughing as no audience had ever laughed at my plays. I made myself ridiculous with such success that I felt quite ready to laugh at somebody else. Just then there arrived a proposal from Mr Benjamin Tucker, philosophic Anarchist, and Editor of an American paper called Liberty, which, as it was written valiantly up to its title, was having a desperate struggle for existence in a country where every citizen is free to suppress liberty, and usually does so in such moments as he cares to spare from the pursuit of money. Mr Tucker, seeing that nobody had answered Dr Nordau, and perceiving with the penetration of an unterrified commonsense that a doctor who had written manifest nonsense must be answerable technically by anybody who could handle his weapons, was of opinion that I was the man to do it. Accordingly, said Mr Tucker, I invite you, Shaw, to ascertain the highest price that has ever been paid to any man, even to Gladstone, for a magazine article; and I will pay you that price for a review of Degeneration in the columns of Liberty.

This was really great editing. Mr Tucker got his review, as he deserved, and sent a copy of the number of Liberty containing it (now a collector's treasure), to every paper in the United States. There was a brisk and quick sale of copies in London among the cognoscenti. And Degeneration was never heard of again. It is open to the envious to contend that this was a mere coincidence – that the Degeneration boom was exhausted at that moment; but I naturally prefer to believe that Mr Tucker and I slew it. I may add that the slaughter incidentally ruined Mr Tucker, as a circulation among cognoscenti does not repay the cost of a free distribution to the Philistines; but Mr Tucker was always ruining himself for Liberty and always retrieving the situation by his business ability. I saw him this year in London, as prosperous

314

looking a man as I could desire to dine with, thirsting for fresh struggles with the courts and public departments of the United States.

It may now be asked why, if the work of my essay be done, I need revive it after twelve years of peaceful burial. I should answer: partly because Mr Tucker wishes to reproduce his editorial success in a more permanent form, and is strongly seconded by Messrs Holbrook Jackson and A. R. Orage in England, who have piously preserved a copy of Liberty and desire to make it the beginning of their series of pamphlets in connection with their paper The New Age, and their pet organization The Arts Group of the Fabian Society; partly because on looking through it myself again, I find that as far as it goes it is still readable and likely to be helpful to those who are confused by the eternal strife between the artist-philosophers and the Philistines.

I have left the essay substantially as it first appeared, the main alteration being an expansion of the section dealing with the importance of that mass of law which lies completely outside morals and religion, and is really pure invention: the point being, not that the course prescribed by such law is ethically right, or indeed better in any sense than its direct opposite (as in the rule of the road, for example), but that it is absolutely necessary for economy and smoothness of social action that everybody should do the same thing and be able to count on everybody else doing it. I have appropriated this from Mr Aylmer Maude's criticism of Tolstoyan Anarchism, on which I am unable to improve.

I have also, with the squeamishness of advancing years, softened one or two expressions which now shock me as uncivil to Dr Nordau. In doing so I am not offering him the insult of an attempt to spare his feelings: I am simply trying to mend my own manners.

Finally, let me say that though I think this essay of mine

did dispose of Dr Nordau's special pleadings, neither the pleadings nor the criticism dispose of the main question as to how far genius is a morbid symptom. I should rather like Dr Nordau to try again; for I do not see how any observant student of genius from the life can deny that the Arts have their criminals and lunatics as well as their sane and honest men (they are more or less the same men too, just as our ordinary criminals are in the dock by the accident of a single transaction and not by a difference in nature between them and the judge and jury), and that the gratuitous delusion that the great poet and artist can do no wrong is much more mischievous than the necessary convention that the King can do no wrong and that the Pope is infallible.

In my play called The Doctor's Dilemma I have recognized this by dramatizing a rascally genius, with the disquieting result that several highly intelligent and sensitive persons have passionately defended him, on the ground, apparently, that high artistic faculty and an ardent artistic imagination entitle a man to be recklessly dishonest about money and recklessly selfish about women, just as kingship in an African tribe entitles a man to kill whom he pleases on the most trifling provocation. I know no harder practical question than how much selfishness one ought to stand from a gifted person for the sake of his gifts or on the chance of his being right in the long run. The Superman will certainly come like a thief in the night and be shot at accordingly; but we cannot leave our property wholly undefended on that account. On the other hand, we cannot ask the Superman simply to add a higher set of virtues to current respectable morals; for he is undoubtedly going to empty a good deal of respectable morality out like so much dirty water, and replace it by new and strange customs, shedding old obligations and accepting new and heavier ones. Every step of his progress must horrify conventional people; and if it were possible for even the most superior man to march ahead all the time, every pioneer of the march towards the Superman would be crucified. Fortunately what actually happens is that your geniuses are for the most part keeping step and marking time with the rest, an occasional stumble forward being the utmost they can accomplish, often visibly against their own notions of propriety. The greatest possible difference in conduct between a genius and his contemporaries is so small that it is always difficult to persuade the people who are in daily contact with the gifted one that he is anybody in particular, all the instances to the contrary (Gorki scandalizing New York, for example) being cases in which the genius is in conflict, not with contemporary feeling in his own class, but with some institution which is far behind the times, like the institution of marriage in Russia (to put it no nearer home). In really contemporary situations, your genius is ever 1 part genius and 99 parts Tory.

Still, especially when we turn from conduct to the expression of opinion – from what the man of genius dares do to what he dares advocate – it is necessary for the welfare of society that genius should be privileged to utter sedition, to blaspheme, to outrage good taste, to corrupt the youthful mind, and, generally, to scandalize one's uncles. But such license is accordable only on the assumption that men of genius are saner, sounder, farther sighted and deeper fathoming than the uncles; and it is idle to demand unlimited toleration of apparently outrageous conduct on the plea that the offender is a genius, even if by the abnormal development of some specific talent he may be highly skilled as an artist. Andrea del Sarto was a better draughtsman and fresco painter than Raphael; but he was a swindler all the same; and no honorable artist would plead on his behalf that misappropriating trust money is one of the superiorities of that very loosely defined diathesis which we call the artistic temperament. If Dr Nordau would make a serious attempt to shew us exactly where we are in this matter by ascertaining the real stigmata of genius; so that we may know whom to crucify

317

and whom to put above the law, he would place the civilization he attacks under an obligation which would wipe out the marks of all the wounds (mostly thoroughly deserved) he has dealt it.

LONDON, July 1907

My dear Tucker,

I have read Max Nordau's Degeneration at your request: two hundred and sixty thousand mortal words, saying the same thing over and over again. That is the proper way to drive a thing into the mind of the world, though Nordau considers it a symptom of insane 'obsession' on the part of writers who do not share his own opinions. His message to the world is that all our characteristically modern works of art are symptoms of disease in the artists, and that these diseased artists are themselves symptoms of the nervous exhaustion of the race by overwork.

To me, who am a professional critic of art, and have for many successive London seasons had to watch the grand march past of books, of pictures, of concerts and operas, and of stage plays, there is nothing new in Dr Nordau's outburst. I have heard it all before. At every new wave of energy in art the same alarm has been raised; and as these alarms always had their public, like prophecies of the end of the world, there is nothing surprising in the fact that a book which might have been produced by playing the resurrection man in the old newspaper rooms of our public libraries, and collecting all the exploded bogey-criticisms of the last half-century into a huge volume, should have a considerable success. To give you an idea of the heap of material ready to hand for such a compilation, let me lay before you a sketch of one or two of the Reformations I have myself witnessed in the fine arts.

IMPRESSIONISM

When I was engaged chiefly in the criticism of pictures, the Impressionist movement was struggling for life in London; and I supported it vigorously because, being the outcome of heightened attention and quickened consciousness on the part of its disciples, it was evidently destined to improve pictures greatly by substituting a natural, observant, real style for a conventional, taken-for-granted, ideal one. The result has entirely justified my choice of sides. I can remember when Whistler, bent on forcing the public to observe the qualities he was introducing into pictorial work, had to exhibit a fine drawing of a girl with the head deliberately crossed out with a few rough pencil strokes, knowing perfectly well that if he left a woman's face discernible the British philistine would simply look to see whether she was a pretty girl or not, or whether she represented some of his pet characters in fiction, and pass on without having seen any of the qualities of artistic execution which made the drawing valuable. But it was easier for the critics to resent the obliteration of the face as an insolent eccentricity, and to shew their own good manners by writing of Mr Whistler as Jimmy, than to think out what he meant. It took several years of 'propaganda by deed' before the qualities which the Impressionists insisted on came to be looked for as matters of course in pictures; so that at last the keen picture-gallery frequenter, when he came face to face with Bouguereau's 'Girl in a Cornfield', could no longer accept it as a window-glimpse of nature, because he saw at once that the girl is really standing in a studio with what the house agents call a good north light, and that the cornfield is a conventional sham. This advance in the education of our art fanciers was effected by persistently exhibiting pictures which, like Whistler's girl with her head scratched out, were propagandist samples of workmanship rather than complete works of art. But the moment Whistler and his party forced the dealers and the societies of painters to exhibit these studies, and, by doing so, to accustom the public to tolerate what appeared to it at first to be absurdities, the door was necessarily opened to real absurdities. Artists of doubtful or incomplete vocation find it difficult to draw or paint well; but it is easy for them to smudge paper or canvas so as to suggest a picture just as the stains on an old ceiling or the dark spots in a glowing coal-fire do. Plenty of rubbish of this kind was produced, exhibited and tolerated at the time when people could not see the difference between any daub in which there were aniline shadows and a landscape by Monet. Not that they thought the daub as good as the Monet: they thought the Monet as ridiculous as the daub; but they were afraid to say so, because they had discovered that people who were good judges did not think Monet ridiculous.

Then, beside the mere impostors, there were certain unaffected and conscientious painters who produced abnormal pictures because they saw abnormally. My own sight happened to be 'normal' in the oculist's sense; that is, I saw things with the naked eye as most people can only be made to see them by the aid of spectacles. Once I had a discussion with an artist who was shewing me a clever picture of his in which the parted lips in a pretty woman's face revealed what seemed to me like a mouthful of virgin snow. The painter lectured me for not consulting my eyes instead of my knowledge of facts. 'You dont see the divisions in a set of teeth when you look at a person's mouth,' he said, 'all you see is a strip of white, or yellow, or pearl, as the case may be. But because you know, as a matter of anatomic fact, that there are divisions there, you want to have them represented by strokes in a drawing. That is just like you art critics, etc., etc.' I do not think he believed me when I told him that when I looked at a row of teeth, I saw, not only the divisions between them, but their exact shape, both in contour and in modelling, just as well as I saw their general color. Some of the most able of the Impressionists evidently did not see forms as definitely as they appreciated color relationship; and, since there is always a great deal of imitation in the arts, we soon had young painters with perfectly good sight looking at landscapes or at their models with their eyes half closed and a little asquint, until what they saw looked to them like one of their favorite master's pictures.

Further, the Impressionist movement led to a busy study of the atmosphere, conventionally supposed to be invisible, but seldom really completely so, and of what were called values: that is, the relation of light and dark between the various objects depicted, on the correctness of which relation truth of effect largely depends. This, though very difficult in full outdoor light with the various colors brilliantly visible, was comparatively easy in gloomy rooms where the absence of light reduced all colors to masses of brown or grey of varying depth. Whistler's portrait of Sarasate, a masterpiece in its way, would look like a study in monochrome if hung beside a portrait by Holbein; and the little bouquets of color with which he sometimes decorates his female sitters, exquisite as the best of them are, have the character of enamel, of mosaic, of jewellery, never of primitive nature. His disciples could paint dark interiors, or figures placed apparently in coal cellars, with admirable truth and delicacy of values whilst they were still helplessly unable to represent a green tree or a blue sky, much less paint an interior with the light and local color as clear as they are in the works of Peter de Hooghe. Naturally the public eye, with its utilitarian familiarity with local color, and its Philistine insensibility to values and atmosphere, did not at first see what the Impressionists were driving at, and dismissed them as mere perverse, notoriety-hunting cranks.

Here, then, you had a movement wholly beneficial and progressive, and in no sense insane or decadent. Nevertheless

322

it led to the public exhibition of daubs which even the authors themselves would never have presumed to offer for exhibition before; it betrayed aberrations of vision in painters who, on the old academic lines, would have hidden their defects by drawing objects (teeth for instance) as they knew them to exist, and not as they saw them; it set clear-sighted students practising optical distortion, so as to see things myopically and astigmatically; and it substituted canvases which looked like enlargements of under-exposed photographs for the familiar portraits of masters of the hounds in cheerfully unmistakable pink coats, mounted on bright chestnut horses. All of which, and much else, to a man who looked on without any sense of the deficiencies in conventional painting, necessarily suggested that the Impressionists and their contemporaries were much less sane than their fathers.

WAGNERISM

Again, my duties as a musical critic compelled me to ascertain very carefully the exact bearings of the controversy which has raged round Wagner's music-dramas since the middle of the century. When you and I last met, we were basking in the sun between the acts of Parsifal at Bayreuth; but experience has taught me that an American may appear at Bayreuth without being necessarily fonder than most men of a technical discussion on music. Let me therefore put the case to you in a mercifully intelligible way. Music is like drawing, in that it can be purely decorative, or purely dramatic, or anything between the two. A draughtsman may be a pattern-designer like William Morris, or he may be a delineator of life and character, like Ford Madox Brown. Or he may come between these two extremes, and treat scenes of life and character in a decorative way, like Walter Crane or Burne-Jones: both of them consummate pattern-designers, whose subject-pictures and illustrations are also fundamentally figure-patterns, prettier than Madox Brown's, but much less convincingly alive.

Do you realize that in music we have these same alternative applications of the art to drama and decoration? You can compose a graceful, symmetrical sound-pattern that exists solely for the sake of its own grace and symmetry. Or you can compose music to heighten the expression of human emotion; and such music will be intensely affecting in the presence of that emotion and utter nonsense apart from it. For examples of pure pattern-designing in music I should have to go back to the old music of the thirteenth, fourteenth, and fifteenth centuries, before the operatic movement gained the upper hand; but I am afraid my assertions that much of this music is very beautiful, and hugely superior to the stuff our music publishers turn out today, would not be believed in America; for when I hinted at something of the kind lately in the American Musical Courier, and pointed out also the beauty of the instruments for which this old music was written (viols, virginals and so on), one of your leading musical critics rebuked me with an expatiation on the superiority (meaning apparently the greater loudness) of the modern concert grand pianoforte, and contemptuously ordered the Middle Ages out from the majestic presence of the nineteenth century.[1] You must take my word for it that in England alone a long line of composers, from Henry VIII to Lawes and Purcell, have left us quantities of instrumental music which was neither dramatic music nor descriptive music, but was designed to affect the hearer solely by its beauty of sound and grace and ingenuity of pattern. This is the art which Wagner called absolute music. It is represented today by the formal sonata and symphony; and we are coming back to it in something like its old integrity by a post-Wagnerian reaction led by that greatly gifted absolute musician and hopelessly commonplace and tedious homilist, Johannes Brahms.

To understand the present muddle, you must know that modern dramatic music did not appear as an independent branch of musical art, but as an adulteration of decorative music. The first modern dramatic composers accepted as binding on them the rules of good pattern-designing in sound; and this absurdity was made to appear practicable by the fact that Mozart had such an extraordinary command of his art that his operas contain numbers which, though they seem to follow that dramatic play of emotion and character without reference to any other consideration whatever, are seen, on examining them from the point of view of the absolute musician, to be symmetrical sound-patterns. But these *tours de force* were no real justification for imposing the laws of pattern-designing on other dramatic musicians; and even Mozart himself broke away from them in all directions, and was violently attacked by his contemporaries for doing so, the accusations levelled at him (absence of melody, illegitimate and discordant harmonic progressions and monstrous abuse of the orchestra) being exactly those with which the opponents of Wagner so often pester ourselves. Wagner, whose leading lay characteristic was his enormous commonsense, completed the emancipation of the dramatic musician from these laws of pattern-designing; and we now have operas, and very good ones too, written by composers like Bruneau, who are not musicians in the old sense at all: that is, they are not pattern-designers; they do not compose music apart from drama; and when they have to furnish their operas with dances, instrumental intermezzos or the like, they either take themes from the dramatic part of their operas and rhapsodize on them, or else they turn out some perfectly simple song or dance tune, at the cheapness of which Haydn would have laughed, and give it an air of momentousness by orchestral and harmonic fineries.

If I add now that music in the academic, professorial, Conservative, respectable sense always means decorative music, and that students are taught that the laws of pattern-designing are binding on all musicians, and that violations of them are absolutely 'wrong'; and if I mention incidentally that these laws are themselves confused by the survivals from a still older tradition based on the Church art, technically very highly specialized, of writing perfectly smooth and beautiful vocal harmony for unaccompanied voices, worthy to be sung by angelic doctors round the throne of God (this was Palestrina's art), you will understand why all the professional musicians who could not see beyond the routine they were taught, and all the men and women (and there are many of them) who have little or no sense of drama, but a very keen sense of beauty of sound and prettiness of pattern in music, regarded Wagner as a madman who was reducing music to chaos, perversely introducing ugly and brutal sounds into a region where beauty and grace had reigned alone, and substituting an incoherent, aimless, formless, endless meandering for the old familiar symmetrical tunes like Pop Goes the Weasel, in which the second and third lines repeat, or nearly repeat, the pattern of the first and second; so that anyone can remember and treasure them like nursery rhymes. It was the unprofessional, 'unmusical' public which caught the dramatic clue, and saw order and power, strength and sanity, in the supposed Wagner chaos; and now, his battle being won and overwon, the professors, to avert the ridicule of their pupils, are compelled to explain (quite truly) that Wagner's technical procedure in music is almost pedantically logical and grammatical; that the Lohengrin and Tristan preludes are masterpieces of the form proper to their aim; and that his disregard of 'false relations', and his free use of the most extreme discords without 'preparation', are straight and sensible instances of that natural development of harmony which has proceeded continuously from the days when common six-four chords were considered 'wrong', and such free use of unprepared dominant sevenths and minor ninths as had become common in Mozart's time would have seemed the maddest cacophony.[2]

The dramatic development also touched purely instrumental music. Liszt tried hard to extricate himself from pianoforte arabesques, and become a tone poet like his friend Wagner. He wanted his symphonic poems to express emotions and their development. And he defined the emotion by connecting it with some known story, poem or even picture: Mazeppa, Victor Hugo's Les Préludes, Kaulbach's Die Hunnenschlacht, or the like. But the moment you try to make an instrumental composition follow a story, you are forced to abandon the decorative pattern forms, since all patterns consist of some form which is repeated over and over again, and which generally consists in itself of a repetition of two similar halves. For example, if you take a playing-card (say the five of diamonds) as a simple example of a pattern, you find not only that the diamond figure is repeated five times, but that each side of each pip is a reversed duplicate of the other. Now, the established form for a symphony is essentially a pattern form involving just such symmetrical repetitions; and, since a story does not repeat itself, but pursues a continuous chain of fresh incident and correspondingly varied emotions, Liszt had either to find a new musical form for his musical poems, or else face the intolerable anomalies and absurdities which spoil the many attempts made by Mendelssohn, Raff and others, to handcuff the old form to the new matter. Consequently he invented the symphonic poem, a perfectly simple and fitting commonsense form for his purpose, and one which makes Les Préludes much plainer sailing for the ordinary hearer than Mendelssohn's Melusine overture or Raff's Lenore or Im Walde symphonies, in both of which the formal repetitions would stamp Raff as a madman if we did not know that they were mere superstitions, which he had not the strength of mind to shake off as Liszt did. But still, to the people who would not read Liszt's explanations and cared nothing for his purpose, who had no taste for symphonic poetry, and consequently insisted on judging the symphonic poems as sound-patterns, Liszt must needs appear, like Wagner, a perverse egotist with something fundamentally disordered in his intellect; in short, a lunatic.

The sequel was the same as in the Impressionist movement. Wagner, Berlioz, and Liszt, in securing tolerance for their own works, secured it for what sounded to many people absurd; and this tolerance necessarily extended to a great deal of stuff which was really absurd, but which the secretly bewildered critics dared not denounce, lest it, too, should turn out to be great, like the music of Wagner, over which they had made the most ludicrous exhibition of their incompetence. Even at such stupidly conservative concerts as those of the London Philharmonic Society I have seen ultra-modern composers, supposed to be representatives of the Wagnerian movement, conducting pretentious rubbish in no essential superior to Jullien's British Army Quadrilles. And then, of course, there are the young imitators, who are corrupted by the desire to make their harmonies sound like those of the masters whose purposes and principles of work they are too young to understand, and who fall between the old forms and the new into simple incoherence.

Here, again, you see, you have a progressive, intelligent, wholesome and thoroughly sane movement in art, producing plenty of evidence to prove the case of any clever man who does not understand music, but who has a theory which involves the proposition that all the leaders of the art movements of our time are degenerate and, consequently, retrogressive lunatics.

IBSENISM

There is no need for me to go at any great length into the grounds on which any development in our moral views must at first appear insane and blasphemous to people who are satisfied, or more than satisfied, with the current morality. Perhaps you remember the opening chapters of my Quintessence of Ibsenism, in which I shewed why the London press, now abjectly polite to Ibsen, received him four years ago with a shriek of horror. Every step in morals is made by challenging the validity of the existing conception of perfect propriety of conduct; and when a man does that, he must look out for a very different reception from the painter who has ventured to paint a shadow brilliant lilac, or the composer who ends his symphony with an unresolved discord. Heterodoxy in art is at worst rated as eccentricity or folly: heterodoxy in morals is at once rated as scoundrelism, and, what is worse, propagandist scoundrelism, which must, if successful, undermine society and bring us back to barbarism after a period of decadence like that which brought imperialist Rome to its downfall. Your function as a philosophic Anarchist in American society is to combat the attempts that are constantly being made to arrest development by using the force of the State to suppress all departures from those habits of the majority which it pretentiously calls its morals. You must find the modern democratic voter a very troublesome person, chicken-heartedly diffident as to the value of his opinions on the technics of art or science, about which he can learn all that there is to be known, but cocksure about right and wrong in morals, politics and religion, about which he can at best only guess at the depth and danger of his ignorance. Happily, this cocksureness is not confined to the Conservatives. Shelley was as cocksure as the dons who expelled him from Oxford. It is true that the revolutionist of twenty-five, who sees nothing for it but a clean sweep of all our institutions, finds himself, at forty, accepting and even clinging to them on condition of a few reforms to bring them up to date. But he does not wait patiently for this reconciliation. He expresses his (or her) early dissatisfaction with the wisdom of his elders loudly and irreverently, and formulates his heresy as a faith. He demands the abolition of marriage, of the State, of the Church; he preaches the divinity of love and the heroism of the man who believes in himself and dares do the thing he wills; he contemns the slavery to duty and discipline which has left so many soured old people with nothing but envious regrets for a virtuous youth. He recognizes his gospel in such utterances as that quoted by Nordau from Brandes: 'To obey one's senses is to have character. He who allows himself to be guided by his passions has individuality.' For my part, I am not at all afraid of this doctrine, either in Brandes's form or in the older form: 'He that is unjust, let him be unjust still; and he which is filthy, let him be filthy still; and he that is righteous, let him be righteous still; and he that is holy, let him be holy still.' But Nordau expresses his horror of Brandes with all the epithets he can command: 'debauchery, dissoluteness, depravity disguised as modernity, bestial instincts, *maître de plaisir*, egomaniacal Anarchist', and such sentences as the following:

It is comprehensible that an educator who turns the schoolroom into a tavern and a brothel should have success and a crowd of followers. He certainly runs the risk of being slain by the parents if they come to know what he is teaching their children; but the pupils will hardly complain and will be eager to attend the lessons of so agreeable a teacher. This is the explanation of the influence Brandes gained over the youth of his country, such as his writings, with their emptiness of thought and unending tattle, would certainly never have procured for him.

To appreciate this spluttering, you must know that it is immediately followed by an attack on Ibsen for the weakness of 'obsession by the doctrine of original sin'. Yet what would the passage I have just quoted be without the doctrine of original sin as a postulate? If 'the heart of man is deceitful above all things, and desperately wicked', then, truly, the man who allows himself to be guided by his passions must needs be a scoundrel; and his teacher might well be slain by his parents. But how if the youth thrown helpless on his passions found that honesty, that self-respect, that hatred of cruelty and injustice, that the desire for soundness and health and efficiency, were master passions; nay, that their excess is so dangerous to youth that it is part of the wisdom of age to say to the young: 'Be not righteous overmuch: why shouldst thou destroy thyself?' I am sure, my dear Tucker, your friends have paraphrased that in vernacular American often enough in remonstrating with you for your Anarchism, which defies not only God, but even the wisdom of the United States Congress. On the other hand, the people who profess to renounce and abjure their own passions, and ostentatiously regulate their conduct by the most convenient interpretation of what the Bible means, or, worse still, by their ability to find reasons for it (as if there were not excellent reasons to be found for every conceivable course of conduct, from dynamiting and vivisection to martyrdom), seldom need a warning against being righteous overmuch, their attention, indeed, often needing a rather pressing jog in the opposite direction.

Passion is the steam in the engine of all religious and moral systems. In so far as it is malevolent, the religious are malevolent too, and insist on human sacrifices, on hell, wrath, and vengeance. You cannot read Browning's Caliban upon Setebos (Natural Theology in The Island) without admitting that all our religions have been made as Caliban made his, and that the difference between Caliban and Prospero is not that Prospero has killed passion in himself whilst Caliban has yielded to it, but that Prospero is mastered by holier passions than Caliban's. Abstract principles of conduct break down in practice because kindness and truth and justice are not duties founded on abstract principles external to man, but human passions, which have, in their time, conflicted with higher passions as well as with lower ones. If a young woman, in a mood of strong reaction against the preaching of duty and self-sacrifice and the rest of it, were to tell me that she was determined not to murder her own instincts and throw away her life in obedience to a mouthful of empty phrases, I should say to her 'By all means do as you propose. Try how wicked you can be: it is precisely the same experiment as trying how good you can be. At worst you will only find out the sort of person you really are. At best you will find that your passions, if you really and honestly let them all loose impartially, will discipline you with a severity which your conventional friends, abandoning themselves to the mechanical routine of fashion, could not stand for a day.' As a matter of fact, we have seen over and over again this comedy of the 'emancipated' young enthusiast flinging duty and religion, convention and parental authority, to the winds, only to find herself, for the first time in her life, plunged into duties, responsibilities, and sacrifices from which she is often glad to retreat, after a few years' wearing down of her enthusiasm, into the comparatively loose life of an ordinary respectable woman of fashion.

WHY LAW IS INDISPENSABLE

The truth is, laws, religions, creeds and systems of ethics, instead of making society better than its best unit, make it worse than its average unit, because they are never up to date. You will ask me: 'Why have them at all?' I will tell you. They are made necessary, though we all secretly detest them, by the fact that the number of people who can think out a line of conduct for themselves even on one point is very small, and the number who can afford the time for it still smaller. Nobody can afford the time to do it on all points. The professional thinker may on occasion make his own morality and philosophy as the cobbler may make his own boots; but the ordinary man of business must buy at the shop, so to speak, and put up with what he finds on sale there, whether it exactly suits him or not, because he can neither make a morality for himself nor do without one. This typewriter with which I am writing is the best I can get; but it is by no means a perfect instrument; and I have not the smallest doubt that in fifty years' time authors will wonder how men could have put up with so clumsy a contrivance. When a better one is invented I shall buy it; until then, not being myself an inventor, I must make the best of it, just as my Protestant and Roman Catholic and Agnostic friends make the best of their imperfect creeds and systems. Oh, Father Tucker, worshipper of Liberty, where shall we find a land where the thinking and moralizing can be done without division of labor?

Besides, what have deep thinking and moralizing to do with the most necessary and least questionable side of law? Just consider how much we need law in matters which have absolutely no moral bearing at all. Is there anything more aggravating than to be told, when you are socially promoted, and are not quite sure how to behave yourself in the circles you enter for the first time, that good manners are merely a matter of good sense, and that rank is but the guinea's stamp: the man's the gowd for a' that? Imagine taking the field with an army which knew nothing except that the soldier's duty is to defend his country bravely, and think, not of his own safety, nor of home and beauty, but of ENGLAND! Or of leaving the traffic of Piccadilly or Broadway to proceed on the understanding that every driver should keep to that side of the road which seemed to him to promote the greatest happiness of the greatest number! Or of stage-managing Hamlet by assuring the Ghost that whether he entered from the right or the left could make no difference to the greatness of Shakespear's play, and that all he need concern himself about was holding the mirror up to nature! Law is never so necessary as when it has no ethical significance whatever, and is pure law for the sake of law. The law that compels me to keep to the left when driving along Oxford Street is ethically senseless, as is shewn by the fact that keeping to the right answers equally well in Paris; and it certainly destroys my freedom to choose my side; but by enabling me to count on everyone else keeping to the left also, thus making traffic possible and safe, it enlarges my life and sets my mind free for nobler issues. Most laws, in short, are not the expression of the ethical verdicts of the community, but pure etiquet and nothing else. What they do express is the fact that over most of the field of social life there are wide limits within which it does not matter what people do, though it matters enormously whether under given circumstances you can depend on their all doing the same thing. The wasp, who can be depended on absolutely to sting you if you squeeze him, is less of a nuisance than the man who tries to do business with you not according to the customs of business, but according to the Sermon on the Mount, or than the lady who dines with you and refuses, on republican and dietetic principles, to allow precedence to a duchess or to partake of food which contains uric acid. The ordinary man cannot get through the world without being told what to do at every turn, and basing such calculations as he is capable of on the assumption that everyone else will calculate on the same assumptions. Even your man of genius accepts a hundred rules for every one he challenges; and you may lodge in the same house with an Anarchist for ten years without noticing anything exceptional about him. Martin Luther, the priest, horrified the greater half of Christendom by marrying a nun, yet was a submissive conformist in countless ways, living orderly as a husband and father, wearing what his bootmaker and tailor made for him, and dwelling in what the builder built for him, although he would have died rather than take his Church from the Pope. And when he got a Church made by himself to his liking, generations of men calling themselves Lutherans took that Church from him just as unquestioningly as he took the fashion of his clothes from his tailor. As the race evolves, many a convention which recommends itself by its obvious utility to everyone passes into an automatic habit, like breathing. Doubtless also an improvement in our nerves and judgment may enlarge the list of emergencies which individuals may be trusted to deal with on the spur of the moment without reference to regulations; but a ready-made code of conduct for general use will always be needed as a matter of overwhelming convenience by all members of communities.

The continual danger to liberty created by law arises, not from the encroachments of Governments, which are always regarded with suspicion, but from the immense utility and consequent popularity of law, and the terrifying danger

334

and obvious inconvenience of anarchy; so that even pirates appoint and obey a captain. Law soon acquires such a good character that people will believe no evil of it; and at this point it becomes possible for priests and rulers to commit the most pernicious crimes in the name of law and order. Creeds and laws come to be regarded as applications to human conduct of eternal and immutable principles of good and evil; and breakers of the law are abhorred as sacrilegious scoundrels to whom nothing is sacred. Now this, I need not tell you, is a very serious error. No law is so independent of circumstances that the time never comes for breaking it, changing it, scrapping it as obsolete, and even making its observance a crime. In a developing civilization nothing can make laws tolerable unless their changes and modifications are kept as closely as possible on the heels of the changes and modifications in social conditions which development involves. Also there is a bad side to the very convenience of law. It deadens the conscience of individuals by relieving them of the ethical responsibility of their own actions. When this relief is made as complete as possible, it reduces a man to a condition in which his very virtues are contemptible. Military discipline, for example, aims at destroying the individuality and initiative of the soldier whilst increasing his mechanical efficiency, until he is simply a weapon with the power of hearing and obeying orders. In him you have legality, duty, obedience, self-denial, submission to external authority, carried as far as it can be carried; and the result is that in England, where military service is voluntary, the common soldier is less respected than any other serviceable worker in the community. The police constable, who is a civilian and has to use his own judgment and act on his own responsibility in innumerable petty emergencies, is by comparison a popular and esteemed citizen. The Roman Catholic peasant who consults his parish priest instead of his conscience, and submits wholly to the authority of his Church, is mastered and governed either by statesmen and cardinals who despise his superstition, or by Protestants who are at least allowed to persuade themselves that they have arrived at their religious opinions through the exercise of their private judgment. The moral evolution of the social individual is from submission and obedience as economizers of effort and responsibility, and safeguards against panic and incontinence, to wilfulness and self-assertion made safe by reason and self-control, just as plainly as his physical growth leads from the perambulator and the nurse's apron-string to the power of walking alone, and from the tutelage of the boy to the responsibility of the man. But it is useless for impatient spirits (you and I, for instance) to call on people to walk before they can stand. Without high gifts of reason and self-control, that is, without strong common-sense, no man dares yet trust himself out of the school of authority. What he does is to claim gradual relaxations of the discipline, so as to have as much liberty as he thinks is good for him, and as much government as he thinks he needs to keep him straight. If he goes too fast he soon finds himself asking helplessly 'What ought I to do?' and so, after running to the doctor, the lawyer, the expert, the old friend and all the other quacks for advice, he runs back to the law again to save him from all these and from himself. The law may be wrong; but anyhow it spares him the responsibility of choosing, and will either punish those who make him look ridiculous by exposing its folly, or, when the constitution is too democratic for this, at least guarantee that the majority is on his side.

PROTESTANT ANARCHISM

We see this in the history of British-American Christianity. Man, as the hero of that history, starts by accepting as binding on him the revelation of God's will as interpreted by the Church. Finding his confidence, or rather his intellectual laziness, grossly abused by the Church, he claims a right to exercise his own judgment, which the Reformed Church, competing with the Unreformed for clients, grants him on condition that he arrive at the same conclusions as itself. Later on he violates this condition in certain particulars, and dissents, flying to America in the Mayflower from the prison of Conformity, but promptly building a new jail, suited to the needs of his sect, in his adopted country. In all these mutinies he finds excellent arguments to prove that he is exchanging a false authority for *the* true one, never daring even to think of brazenly admitting that what he is really doing is substituting his own will, bit by bit, for what he calls the will of God or the laws of Nature. These arguments so accustom the world to submit authority to the test of discussion that he is at last emboldened to claim the right to do anything he can find good arguments for, even to the extent of questioning the scientific accuracy of the Book of Genesis, and the validity of the popular conception of God as an omniscient, omnipotent and frightfully jealous and vindictive old gentleman sitting on a throne above the clouds. This seems a giant stride towards emancipation; but it leaves our hero, as Rationalist and Materialist, regarding Reason as a creative dynamic motor, independent of and superior to his erring passions, at which point it is easy for the churches to suggest that if Reason is to decide the matter, perhaps the conclusions of an Ecumenical Council of learned and skilled churchmen might be more trustworthy than the first crop of cheap syllogisms excogitated by a handful of raw Rationalistists in their sects of 'Freethinkers' and 'Secularists' and 'Positivists' or 'Don't Knowists' (Agnostics).

Yet it was not the churches but that very freethinking philosopher Schopenhauer who re-established the old theological doctrine that reason is no motive power; that the true motive power in the world is will (otherwise Life); and that the setting-up of reason above will is a damnable error. But the theologians could not open their arms to Schopenhauer, because he led gloomily disposed thinkers into the Rationalist-Mercantilist error of valuing life according to its individual profits in pleasure, with its idiotic pessimist conclusion that life is not worth living, and that the will which urges us to live in spite of this is necessarily a malign torturer, or at least a bad hand at business, the desirable end of all things being the cessation of the will and the consequent setting of life's sun 'into the blind cave of eternal night'. Further, the will of the theologians was the will of a God standing outside man and in authority above him, whereas the Schopenhauer-ian will is a purely secular force of nature, attaining various degrees of organization, here as a jelly-fish, there as a cabbage, more complexly as an ape or a tiger, and attaining its highest (and sometimes most mischievous) form so far in the human being. As to the Rationalists, they approved of Schopen-hauer's secularism and pessimism, but of course could not stomach his metaphysical method nor his dethronement of reason by will. Accordingly, his turn for popularity did not come until after Darwin's, and then mostly through the influence of two great artists, Richard Wagner and Ibsen, whose Tristan and Isolde, and Emperor Or Galilean, shew that Schopenhauer was a true pioneer in the forward march of the human spirit. We can now, as soon as we are strong-minded enough, drop the pessimism, the rationalism, the supernatural theology, and all the other subterfuges to which we cling because we are afraid to look life straight in the face and see in it, not the fulfilment of a moral law or of the deductions of reason, but the satisfaction of a passion in us of which we can give no rational account whatever.

It is natural for man to shrink from the terrible responsi-bility thrown on him by this inexorable fact. All his stock excuses vanish before it: 'The woman tempted me', 'The serpent tempted me', 'I was not myself at the time', 'I meant well', 'My passion got the better of my reason', 'It was my duty to do it', 'The Bible says that we should do it', 'Everybody does it', and so on. Nothing is left but the frank avowal: 'I did it because I am built that way'. Every man hates to say that.

He wants to believe that his generous actions are characteristic of him, and that his meannesses are aberrations or concessions to the force of circumstances. Our murderers, with the assistance of the jail chaplain, square accounts with the devil and with God, never with themselves. The convict gives every reason for his having stolen something except the reason that he is a thief. Cruel people flog their children for their children's good, or offer the information that a guinea-pig expires under atrocious torture as an affectionate contribution to science. Lynched negroes are riddled by dozens of superfluous bullets, every one of which is offered as the expression of a sense of outraged justice and chastity in the scamp and libertine who fires it. And such is the desire of men to keep one another in countenance that they positively demand such excuses from one another as a matter of public decency. An uncle of mine, who made it a rule to offer tramps a job when they begged from him, naturally very soon became familiar with every excuse that human ingenuity can invent for not working. But he lost his temper only once; and that was with a tramp who frankly replied that he was too lazy. This my uncle described with disgust as 'cynicism'. And yet our family arms bear the motto, in Latin, 'Know thyself'.

As you know, the true trend of this movement has been mistaken by many of its supporters as well as by its opponents. The ingrained habit of thinking of the propensities of which we are ashamed as 'our passions', and our shame of them and our propensities to noble conduct as a negative and inhibitory department called generally our conscience, leads us to conclude that to accept the guidance of our passions is to plunge recklessly into the insupportable tedium of what is called a life of pleasure. Reactionists against the almost equally insupportable slavery of what is called a life of duty are nevertheless willing to venture on these terms. The revolted daughter, exasperated at being systematically lied to by her parents on every subject of vital importance to an eager and intensely curious young student of life, allies herself with really vicious people and with humorists who like to shock the pious with gay paradoxes, in claiming an impossible licence in personal conduct. No great harm is done beyond the inevitable and temporary excesses produced by all reactions; for, as I have said, the would-be wicked ones find, when they come to the point, that the indispensable qualification for a wicked life is not freedom but wickedness. But the misunderstanding supports the clamor of the opponents of the newest opinions, who naturally shriek as Nordau shrieks in the passages about Brandes, quoted above. Thus you have here again a movement which is thoroughly beneficial and progressive presenting a hideous appearance of moral corruption and decay, not only to our old-fashioned religious folk, but to our comparatively modern scientific Rationalists as well. And here again, because the press and the gossips have found out that this apparent corruption and decay is considered the right thing in some influential quarters, and must be spoken of with respect, and patronized and published and sold and read, we have a certain number of pitiful imitators taking advantage of their tolerance to bring out really silly and vicious stuff, which the reviewers are afraid to expose, lest it, too, should turn out to be the correct thing.

NORDAU'S BOOK

After this long preamble, you will have no difficulty in understanding the sort of book Nordau has written. Imagine a huge volume, stuffed with the most slashing of the criticisms which were hurled at the Impressionists, the Tone Poets, and the philosophers and dramatists of the Schopenhauerian revival, before these movements had reached the point at which it began to require some real courage to attack them. Imagine a rehash not only of the newspaper criticisms of this period, but of all its little parasitic paragraphs of small-talk and scandal, from the long-forgotten jibes against Oscar

Wilde's momentary attempt to bring knee-breeches into fashion years ago, to the latest scurrilities about 'the New Woman'. Imagine the general staleness and occasional putrescence of this mess disguised by a dressing of the terminology invented by Krafft-Ebing, Lombroso, and all the latest specialists in madness and crime, to describe the artistic faculties and propensities as they operate in the insane. Imagine all this done by a man who is a vigorous and capable journalist, shrewd enough to see that there is a good opening for a big reactionary book as a relief to the Wagner and Ibsen booms, bold enough to let himself go without respect to persons or reputations, lucky enough to be a stronger, clearer-headed man than ninety-nine out of a hundred of his critics, besides having a keener interest in science: a born theorist, reasoner and busybody; therefore able, without insight, or even any very remarkable intensive industry (he is, like most Germans, *ex*tensively industrious to an appalling degree), to produce a book which has made a very considerable impression on the artistic ignorance of Europe and America. For he says a thing as if he meant it; he holds superficial ideas obstinately, and sees them clearly; and his mind works so impetuously that it is a pleasure to watch it – for a while. All the same, he is the dupe of a theory which would hardly impose even on the gamblers who have a system or martingale founded on a solid rock of algebra, by which they can infallibly break the bank at Monte Carlo. 'Psychiatry' takes the place of algebra in Nordau's martingale.

This theory of his is, at bottom, nothing but the familiar delusion of the used-up man that the world is going to the dogs. But Nordau is too clever to be driven back on ready-made mistakes – he makes them for himself in his own way. He appeals to the prodigious extension of the quantity of business a single man can transact through the modern machinery of social intercourse: the railway, the telegraph and telephone, the post and so forth. He gives appalling statistics of the increase of railway mileage and shipping, of the number of letters written per head of the population,[3] of the newspapers which tell us things (mostly lies) of which we used to know nothing. 'In the last fifty years,' he says, 'the population of Europe has not doubled, whereas the sum of its labors has increased tenfold; in part, even fifty-fold. Every civilized man furnishes, at the present time, from five to twenty-five times as much work as was demanded of him half a century ago.'[4] Then follow more statistics of 'the constant increase of crime, madness and suicide', of increases in the mortality from diseases of the nerves and heart, of increased consumption of stimulants, of new nervous diseases like 'railway spine and railway brain', with the general moral that we are all suffering from exhaustion, and that symptoms of degeneracy are visible in all directions, culminating at various points in Wagner's music, Ibsen's dramas, Manet's pictures, Tolstoy's novels, Whitman's poetry, Dr Jaeger's woollen clothing, vegetarianism, scepticism as to vivisection and vaccination, Anarchism and Humanitarianism, and, in short, everything that Dr Nordau does not happen to approve of.

You will at once see that such a case, if well got up and argued, is worth hearing, even though its advocate has no chance of a verdict, because it is sure to bring out a certain number of interesting and important facts. It is, I take it, quite true that with our railways and our postal services many of us are for the moment very like a pedestrian converted to bicycling, who, instead of using his machine to go twenty miles with less labor than he used to walk seven, proceeds to do a hundred miles instead, with the result that the 'labor-saving' contrivance acts as a means of working its user to exhaustion. It is also true that, under our existing industrial system, machinery in industrial processes is regarded solely as a means of extracting a larger product from the unremitted toil of the actual wage-worker. And I do not think any person who is in touch with the artistic professions will deny that they are recruited largely by persons who become actors, or painters, or journalists and authors because they are incapable of steady work and regular habits, or that the attraction which the patrons of the stage, music, and literature find in their favorite arts has often little or nothing to do with the need which nerves great artists to the heavy travail of creation. The claim of art to our respect must stand or fall with the validity of its pretension to cultivate and refine our senses and faculties until seeing, hearing, feeling, smelling and tasting become highly conscious and critical acts with us, protesting vehemently against ugliness, noise, discordant speech, frowzy clothing and re-breathed air, and taking keen interest and pleasure in beauty, in music and in nature, besides making us insist, as necessary for comfort and decency, on clean, wholesome, handsome fabrics to wear and utensils of fine material and elegant workmanship to handle. Further, art should refine our sense of character and conduct, of justice and sympathy, greatly heightening our self-knowledge, self-control, precision of action, and considerateness, and making us intolerant of baseness, cruelty, injustice and intellectual superficiality or vulgarity. The worthy artist or craftsman is he who serves the physical and moral senses by feeding them with pictures, musical compositions, pleasant houses and gardens, good clothes and fine implements, poems, fictions, essays and dramas which call the heightened senses and ennobled faculties into pleasurable activity. The great artist is he who goes a step beyond the demand, and, by supplying works of a higher beauty and a higher interest than have yet been perceived, succeeds after a brief struggle with its strangeness, in adding this fresh extension of sense to the heritage of the race. This is why we value art; this is why we feel that the iconoclast and the Philistine are attacking something made holier, by solid usefulness, than their own theories of purity and practicality; this is why art has won the privileges of religion; so that London shopkeepers who would fiercely resent a compulsory church rate, who do not know 'Yankee Doodle' from Luther's hymn, and who are more interested in photographs of the latest celebrities than in the Velasquez portraits in the National Gallery, tamely allow the London County Council to spend their money on bands, on municipal art inspectors and on plaster casts from the antique.

But the business of responding to the demand for the gratification of the senses has many grades. The confectioner who makes unwholesome sweets, the bull-fighter, the women whose advertisements in the American papers are so astounding to English people, are examples ready to hand to shew what the art and trade of pleasing may be, not at its lowest, but at the lowest that we can speak of without intolerable shame. We have dramatists who write their lines in such a way as to enable low comedians of a certain class to give them an indecorous turn; we have painters who aim no higher than Giulio Romano did when he decorated the Palazzo Te in Mantua; we have poets who have nothing to versify but the commonplaces of amorous infatuation; and, worse than all the rest put together, we have journalists who openly profess that it is their duty to 'reflect' what they believe to be the ignorance and prejudice of their readers, instead of leading and enlightening them to the best of their ability; an excuse for cowardice and time-serving which is also becoming well worn in political circles as 'the duty of a democratic statesman'. In short, the artist can be a prostitute, a pander and a flatterer more easily, as far as external pressure goes, than a faithful servant of the community, much less the founder of a school or the father of a church. Even an artist who is doing the best he can may be doing a very low class of work; for instance, many performers at the rougher music-halls, who get their living by singing coarse songs in the rowdiest possible way, do so to the utmost of their ability in that direction in the most conscientious spirit of earning their money honestly and being a credit to their profession. And the exaltation of the greatest artists is not continuous: you cannot defend every line of Shakespear or every stroke of

Titian. Since the artist is a man and his patron a man, all human moods and grades of development are reflected in art; consequently the iconoclast's or the Philistine's indictments of art have as many counts as the misanthrope's indictment of humanity. And this is the Achilles heel of art at which Nordau has struck. He has piled the iconoclast on the Philistine, the Philistine on the misanthrope, in order to make out his case.

ECHOLALIA

Let me describe to you one or two of his artifices as a special pleader making the most of the eddies at the sides of the stream of progress. Take as a first specimen the old and effective trick of pointing out, as 'stigmata of degeneration' in the person he is abusing, features which are common to the whole human race. The drawing-room palmist astonishes ladies by telling them 'secrets' about themselves which are nothing but the inevitable experiences of ninety-nine people out of every hundred, though each individual is vain enough to suppose that they are peculiar to herself. Nordau turns the trick inside out by trusting to the fact that people are in the habit of assuming that uniformity and symmetry are laws of nature: for example, that every normal person's face is precisely symmetrical, that all persons have the same number of bones in their bodies, and so on. He takes advantage of this popular error to claim asymmetry as a stigma of degeneration. As a matter of fact, perfect symmetry or uniformity does not exist in nature. My two profiles, when photographed, are hardly recognizable as belonging to the same person by those who do not know me; so that the camera would prove me an utter degenerate if my case were exceptional. Probably, however, you would not object to testify that my face is as symmetrical as faces are ordinarily made. Another unfailing trick is the common one of having two names for the same thing, one abusive, the other complimentary, for use according to circumstances. You know how it is done: 'We trust the Government will be firm' in one paper and 'We hope the obstinate elements in the Cabinet will take warning in time' in another. The powers of Empires armed to the teeth to impose their will by fire and sword on weaker communities are called simply Sanctions. Repudiations of national debts are called stabilizations of the currency. The following is a typical specimen of Nordau's use of this device. First, let me explain that when a man with a turn for rhyming goes mad, he repeats rhymes as if he were quoting a rhyming dictionary. You say 'Come' to him, and he starts away with 'Dumb, plum, sum, rum, numb, gum' and so on. This the doctors call echolalia. Dickens gives a specimen of it in Great Expectations, where Mr Jaggers's Jewish client expresses his rapture of admiration for the lawyer by exclaiming, 'Oh, Jaggerth, Jaggerth, Jaggerth! all otherth ith Cag-Maggerth: give me Jaggerth!' There are some well-known verses by Swinburne, beginning, 'If love were what the rose is', which, rhyming and tripping along very prettily, express a sentiment without making any intelligible statement whatsoever; and we have plenty of nonsensically inconsequent nursery rhymes, like 'Ba, Ba, Black Sheep', or 'Old Daddy Long Legs', which please sane children just as Mr Swinburne's verses please sane adults, simply as funny or pretty little word-patterns. People do not write such things for the sake of conveying information, but for the sake of amusing and pleasing, just as people do not eat strawberries and cream to nourish their bones and muscles, but to enjoy the taste of a toothsome dish. A lunatic may plead that he eats kitchen soap and tin tacks on the same ground; and as far as I can see the lunatic would completely shut up Nordau by this answer; for Nordau is absurd enough, in the case of rhyming, to claim that every rhyme made for its own sake, as proved by the fact that it does not convey an intelligible statement of fact of any kind, convicts the rhymer of echolalia. He can thus convict any poet whom he dislikes of being a degenerate by simply picking out a rhyme which exists for its own sake, or a pun, or what is called a burden in a ballad, and claiming them as symptoms of echolalia, supporting this diagnosis by carefully examining the poem for contradictions and inconsistencies as to time, place, description, or the like. It will occur to you probably that by this means he must bring out Shakespear as the champion instance of poetic degeneracy, since Shakespear was an incorrigible punster; delighted in burdens (for instance, 'With hey, ho, the wind and the rain,' which exactly fulfils all the conditions accepted by Nordau as symptomatic of insanity in Rossetti's case); and rhymed for the sake of rhyming in a quite childish fashion; whilst, as to contradictions and inconsistencies, A Midsummer Night's Dream, as to which Shakespear never made up his mind whether the action covered a week or a single night, is only one of a dozen instances of his slips. But no: Shakespear, not being a nineteenth-century poet, would have spoiled the case for modern degeneration by shewing that its symptoms existed before the telegraph and the railway were dreamt of; and besides, Nordau likes Shakespear, just as he likes Goethe, and holds him up as a model of sanity in contrast to the nineteenth-century poets. Thus Wagner is a degenerate because he made puns; and Shakespear, who made worse ones, is a great poet. Swinburne, with his 'unmeaning' refrains of 'Small red leaves in the mill water' and 'Apples of gold for the King's daughter' is a diseased madman; but Shakespear, with his 'In spring time, the only merry ring time, when birds do sing hey ding a ding ding' (if this is not the worst case of echolalia in the world, what *is* echolalia?), is a sober master mind. Rossetti, with his Blessed Damozel leaning out from the gold bar of heaven; weeping though she is in paradise, which is a happy place; describing the dead in one line as 'dressed in white' and in another as 'mounting like thin flames'; and calculating days and years quite otherwise than commercial almanacks do, is that dangerous and cranky thing, a mystic; whilst Goethe (the author of the second part of Faust, if you please)

347

is a hard-headed, accurate, sound, scientific poet. As to the list of inconsistencies of which poor Ibsen is convicted, it is too long to be dealt with in detail. But I assure you I am not doing Nordau less than justice when I say that if he had accused Shakespear of inconsistency on the ground that Othello is represented in the first act as loving his wife, and in the last as strangling her, the demonstration would have left you with more respect for his good sense than his pages on Ibsen, the folly of which goes beyond all patience.[5]

When Nordau deals with painting and music, he is less irritating, because he errs through ignorance, and ignorance, too, of a sort that is now perfectly well recognized and understood. We all know what the old-fashioned critic of literature and science who cultivated his detective logic without ever dreaming of cultivating his eyes and ears, can be relied upon to say when painters and composers are under discussion. Nordau gives himself away with laughable punctuality. He celebrates 'the most glorious period of the Renaissance' and 'the rosy dawn of the new thought' with all the gravity of the older editions of Murray's Guides to Italy. He tells us that 'to copy Cimabue and Giotto is comparatively easy: to imitate Raphael it is necessary to be able to draw and paint to perfection.' He lumps Fra Angelico with Giotto and Cimabue, as if they represented the same stage in the development of technical execution, and Pollaiuolo with Ghirlandaio. 'Here,' he says, speaking of the great Florentine painters, from Giotto to Masaccio, 'were paintings bad in drawing, faded or smoked, their coloring either originally feeble or impaired by the action of centuries, pictures *executed with the awkwardness of a learner* . . . easy of imitation, since, in painting pictures in the style of the early masters, faulty drawing, deficient sense of color, and *general artistic incapacity*, are so many advantages.' To make any comment on these howlers would be to hit a man when he is down. Poor Nordau offers them as a demonstration that Ruskin, who gave this sort of ignorant nonsense its death-blow in England, was a delirious mystic. Also that Millais and Holman Hunt, in the days of the pre-Raphaelite brotherhood, strove to acquire the qualities of the early Florentine masters because the Florentine easel pictures were so much easier to imitate than those of the apprentices in Raphael's Roman fresco factory.

In music we find Nordau equally content with the theories as to how music is composed which were current among literary men fifty years ago. He tells us of 'the severe discipline and fixed rules of the theory of composition, which gave a grammar to the musical babbling of primeval times, and made of it a worthy medium for the expression of the emotions of civilized men', and describes Wagner as breaking these fixed rules and rebelling against this severe discipline because he was 'an inattentive mystic, abandoned to amorphous dreams'. This notion that there are certain rules, derived from a science of counterpoint, by the application of which pieces of music can be constructed just as an equilateral triangle can be constructed on a given straight line by anyone who has mastered Euclid's first proposition, is highly characteristic of the generation of blind and deaf critics to which Nordau belongs. It is evident that if there were fixed rules by which Wagner or anyone else could have composed good music, there could have been no more severe discipline in the work of composition than in the work of arranging a list of names in alphabetical order. The severity of artistic discipline is produced by the fact that in creative art no ready-made rules can help you. There is nothing to guide you to the right expression for your thought except your own sense of beauty and fitness; and, as you advance upon those who went before you, that sense of beauty and fitness is necessarily often in conflict, not with fixed rules, because there are no rules, but with precedents, which are what Nordau means by fixed rules, as far as he knows what he is talking about enough to mean anything at all. If Wagner had composed the prelude to Das Rheingold with a half close at the end of the eighth bar and a full close at the end of the sixteenth, he would undoubtedly have followed the precedent of Mozart and other great composers, and complied with the requirements of Messrs Hanslick, Nordau and Company. Only, as it happened, that was not what he wanted to do. His purpose was to produce a tone picture of the mighty flood in the depths of the Rhine; and, as the poetic imagination does not conceive the Rhine as stopping at every eight feet to take off its hat to the author of Degeneration, the closes and half closes are omitted, and Nordau, huffed at being passed by as if he were a person of no consequence, complains that the composer is 'an inattentive mystic, abandoned to amorphous dreams'. But, even if Wagner's descriptive purpose is left out of the question, Nordau's general criticism of him is an ignorant one; for the truth is that Wagner, like most artists who have great intellectual power, was dominated in the technical work of his gigantic scores by so strong a regard for system, order, logic, symmetry and syntax, that when in the course of time his melody and harmony become perfectly familiar to us, he will be ranked with Handel as a composer whose extreme regularity of procedure must make his work appear drily mechanical to those who cannot catch its dramatic inspiration. In this very fluminous Rheingold prelude which I have cited there is a four-bar rhythm of Mozartian symmetry which may yet serve as the text of such a reproach. If Nordau had said: 'This fellow, whom you all imagine to be the creator of a new heaven and a new earth in music out of a chaos of poetic emotion, is really an arrant pedant and formalist,' I should have pricked up my ears and listened to him with some curiosity, knowing how good a case a really keen technical critic could make out for that view. As it is, I have only to expose him as having picked up a vulgar error under the influence of a vulgar literary superstition. For the rest, you will hardly need any prompting of mine to appreciate the absurdity of dismissing as 'inattentive' the Paris journalist, the Dresden conductor, the designer and founder of the Bayreuth enterprise, the humorous and practical author of

On Conducting, and the man who scored and stage-managed the four evenings of The Niblung's Ring. I purposely leave out the composer, the poet, the philosopher, the reformer, since Nordau cannot be compelled to admit that Wagner's eminence in these departments was real. Striking them all out accordingly, there remain the indisputable objective facts of Wagner's practical professional ability and organizing power to put Nordau's diagnosis of Wagner as an amorphous, inattentive person out of the question. If Nordau had one hundredth part of the truly terrific power of attention which Wagner must have maintained all his life almost as easily as a common man breathes, he would not now be so deplorable an example of the truth of his own saying that the power of attention may be taken as the measure of mental strength.

Nordau's trick of calling rhyme echolalia when he happens not to like the rhymer is reapplied in the case of authorship, which he calls graphomania when he happens not to like the author. He insists that Wagner, who was a voluminous author as well as a composer, was a graphomaniac; and his proof is that in his books we find 'the restless repetition of one and the same strain of thought . . . Opera and Drama, Judaism in Music, Religion and the State, Art and Religion, and the Vocation of Opera are nothing more than the amplification of single passages in The Art-Work of the Future'. This is a capital example of Nordau's limited power of attention. The moment that limited power is concentrated on his theory of degeneration, he loses sight of everything else, and drives his one borrowed horse into every obstacle on the road. To those of us who can attend to more than one thing at a time, there is no observation more familiar and more frequently confirmed than that this growth of pregnant single sentences into whole books which Nordau discovers in Wagner, balanced as it always is by the contraction of whole boyish chapters into single epigrams, is the process by which all great writers, speakers, artists and thinkers elaborate their life-work. Let me take a writer after Nordau's own heart, a shrewd Yorkshireman, one whom he quotes as a trustworthy example of what he calls 'the clear, mentally sane author, who, feeling himself impelled to say something, once for all expresses himself as distinctly and impressively as it is possible for him to do, and has done with it', namely, Dr Henry Maudsley. Dr Maudsley is a clever and cultivated specialist in insanity, who has written several interesting books, consisting of repetitions, amplifications and historical illustrations of the same idea, which is, if I may put it rather more bluntly than the urbane author, nothing less than the identification of religious with sexual ecstasy. And the upshot of it is the conventional scientific pessimism, from which Dr Maudsley never gets away; so that his last book repeats his first book, instead of leaving it far behind, as Wagner's State and Religion leaves his Art and Revolution behind. But now that I have prepared the way by quoting Dr Maudsley, why should I not ask Max Nordau himself to step before the looking-glass and tell us frankly whether, even in the ranks of his 'psychiatrists' and lunacy doctors, he can pick out a crank more hopelessly obsessed with one idea than himself? If you want an example of echolalia, can you find a more shocking one than this gentleman who, when you say 'mania', immediately begins to gabble Egomania, Graphomania, Megalomania, Onomatomania, Pyromania, Kleptomania, Dipsomania, Erotomania, Arithmomania, Oniomania, and is started off by the termination 'phobia' with a string of Agoraphobia, Claustrophobia, Rupophobia, Iophobia, Nosophobia, Aichmophobia, Belenophobia, Cremnophobia, and Trichophobia? After which he suddenly observes, 'This is simply philologico-medical trifling,' a remark which looks like returning sanity until he follows it up by clasping his temples in the true bedlamite manner, and complaining that 'psychiatry is being stuffed with useless and disturbing designations', whereas, if the psychiatrists would only listen to him, they would see that there is only one phobia and one mania, namely, degeneracy. That is, the philologico-medical triflers are not crazy enough for him. He is so utterly mad on the subject of degeneration that he finds the symptoms of it in the loftiest geniuses as plainly as in the lowest jailbirds, the exceptions being himself, Lombroso, Krafft-Ebing, Dr Maudsley, Goethe, Shakespear, and Beethoven. Perhaps he would have dwelt on a case so convenient in many ways for his theory as Coleridge but that it would spoil the connection between degeneration and 'railway spine'. If a man's senses are acute, he is degenerate, hyperaesthesia having been observed in asylums. If they are dull, he is degenerate, anaesthesia being the stigma of the craziness which made old women confess to witchcraft. If he is particular as to what he wears, he is degenerate: silk dressing-gowns and knee-breeches are grave symptoms and woollen shirts conclusive. If he is negligent in these matters, clearly he is inattentive, and therefore degenerate. If he drinks, he is neurotic: if he is a vegetarian and teetotaller, let him be locked up at once. If he lives an evil life, that fact condemns him without further words; if, on the other hand, his conduct is irreproachable, he is a wretched 'mattoid', incapable of the will and courage to realize his vicious propensities in action. If he writes verse, he is afflicted with echolalia; if he writes prose, he is a graphomaniac; if in his books he is tenacious of his ideas, he is obsessed; if not, he is 'amorphous' and 'inattentive'. Wagner, as we have seen, contrived to be both obsessed and inattentive, as might be expected from one who was 'himself alone charged with a greater abundance of degeneration than all the other degenerates put together'. And so on and so forth.

There is, however, one sort of mental weakness, common among men who take to science, as so many people take to art, without the necessary brain power, which Nordau, with amusing unconsciousness of himself, has omitted. I mean the weakness of a man who, when his theory works out into a flagrant contradiction of the facts, concludes 'So much the worse for the facts: let them be altered', instead of 'So much the worse for my theory'. What in the name of common-sense is the value of a theory which identifies Ibsen, Wagner, Tolstoy, Ruskin and Victor Hugo with the refuse of our prisons and lunatic asylums? What is to be said of the state of mind of an inveterate pamphleteer and journalist who, instead of accepting that identification as a *reductio ad absurdum* of the theory, desperately sets to work to prove it by pointing out that there are numerous resemblances; that they all have heads and bodies, appetites, aberrations, whims, weaknesses, asymmetrical features, erotic impulses, fallible judgments, and the like common properties, not merely of all human beings, but all vertebrate organisms. Take Nordau's own list: 'vague and incoherent thought, the tyranny of the association of ideas, the presence of obsessions, erotic excitability, religious enthusiasm, feebleness of perception, will, memory and judgment, as well as inattention and instability'. Is there a single man capable of understanding these terms who will not plead guilty to some experience of all of them, especially when he is accused vaguely and unscientifically, without any statement of the subject, or the moment, or the circumstances to which the accusation refers, or any attempt to fix a standard of sanity? I could prove Nordau to be an elephant on more evidence than he has brought to prove that our greatest men are degenerate lunatics. The papers in which Swift, having predicted the death of the sham prophet Bickerstaff on a certain date, did, after that date, immediately prove that he was dead, are much more closely and fairly reasoned than any of Nordau's chapters. And Swift, though he afterwards died in a madhouse, was too sane to be the dupe of his own logic. At that rate, where will Nordau die? Probably in a highly respectable suburban villa.

Nordau's most likeable point is the freedom and boldness with which he expresses himself. Speaking of Peladan (of whose works I know nothing), he says, whilst holding him up as a typical degenerate of the mystical variety: 'His moral ideal is high and noble. He pursues with ardent hatred all that is base and vulgar, every form of egoism, falsehood and thirst for pleasure; and his characters are thoroughly aristocratic souls, whose thoughts are concerned only with the worthiest, if somewhat exclusively artistic, interests of society.' On the other hand, Maeterlinck is a 'poor devil of an idiot'; Mr W. D. O'Connor, for describing Whitman as 'the good grey poet', is politely introduced as 'an American driveller'; Nietzsche 'belongs, body and soul, to the flock of the mangy sheep'; Ibsen is 'a malignant, anti-social simpleton'; and so on. Only occasionally is he Pharisaical in his tone, as, for instance, when he becomes virtuously indignant over Wagner's dramas, and plays to Mrs Grundy by exclaiming ironically, 'How unperverted must wives and readers be, when they are in a state of mind to witness these pieces without blushing crimson and sinking into the earth for shame!' This, to do him justice, is only an exceptional lapse: a far more characteristic comment of his on Wagner's love-scenes is 'The lovers in his pieces behave like tom cats gone mad, rolling in contortions and convulsions over a root of valerian.' And he is not always on the side of the police, so to speak; for he is as careless of the feelings of the 'beer-drinking' German *bourgeoisie* as of those of the aesthetes. Thus, though on one page he is pointing out that socialism and all other forms of discontent with the existing social order are 'stigmata of degeneration', on the next he is talking pure Karl Marx. For example, taking the two sides in their order:

Ibsen's egomania assumes the form of Anarchism. He is in a state of constant revolt against all that exists ... The psychological roots of his anti-social impulses are well known. They are the degenerate's incapacity for self-adaptation, and the resultant discomfort in the midst of circumstances to which, in consequence of his organic deficiencies, he cannot accommodate himself. 'The criminal,' says Lombroso, 'through his neurotic and impulsive nature, and his hatred of the institutions which have punished or imprisoned him, is a perpetual latent political rebel, who finds in insurrection the means, not only of satisfying his passions, but of even having them countenanced for the first time by a numerous public.'

Wagner is a declared Anarchist . . . He betrays that mental condition which the degenerate shares with enlightened reformers, born criminals with the martyrs of human progress, namely, deep, devouring discontent with existing facts . . . He would like to crush 'political and criminal civilization,' as he calls it.

Now for Nordau speaking for himself:

Is it not the duty of intelligent philanthropy and justice, without destroying civilization, to adopt a better system of economy and transform the artisan from a factory convict, condemned to misery and ill-health, into a free producer of wealth, who enjoys the fruits of his labor himself, and works no more than is compatible with his health and his claims on life?

Every gift that a man receives from some other man without work, without reciprocal service, is an alms, and as such is deeply immoral.

Not in the impossible 'return to nature' lies healing for human misery, but in the reasonable organization of our struggle with nature – I might say, in universal and obligatory service against it, from which only the crippled should be exempted.

In England it was Tolstoy's sexual morality that excited the greatest interest; for in that country economic reasons condemn a formidable number of girls, particularly of the educated classes, to forgo marriage; and, from a theory which honored chastity as the highest dignity and noblest human destiny, and branded marriage with gloomy wrath as abominable depravity, these poor creatures would naturally derive rich consolation for their lonely, empty lives and their cruel exclusion from the possibility of fulfilling their natural calling.

So it appears that Nordau, too, shares 'the degenerate's incapacity for self-adaptation, and the resultant discomfort in the midst of circumstances to which, in consequence of his organic deficiencies, he cannot accommodate himself'. Is he not, indeed, the author of Conventional Lies of Civilization? But he has his usual easy way out of the dilemma. If Ibsen and Wagner are dissatisfied with the world, that is because the world is too good for them; but, if Max Nordau is dissatisfied, it is because Max is too good for the world. His modesty does not permit him to draw the distinction in these exact terms. Here is his statement of it:

Discontent shews itself otherwise in the degenerate than in reformers. The latter grow angry over real evils only and make rational proposals for their remedy which are in advance of the time these remedies may presuppose a better and wiser humanity than actually exists, but at least they are capable of being defended on reasonable grounds. The degenerate, on the other hand, selects among the arrangements of civilization such as are either immaterial or distinctly suitable, in order to rebel against them. His fury has either ridiculously insignificant aims, or simply beats the air. He either gives no earnest thought to improvement, or hatches astoundingly mad projects for making the world happy. His fundamental frame of mind is persistent rage against everything and everyone, which he displays in venomous phrases, savage threats, and the destructive mania of wild beasts. *Wagner is a good specimen of this species.*

Wagner was named because the passage occurs in the almost incredibly foolish chapter which is headed with his name. In another chapter it might have been Ibsen, or Tolstoy, or Ruskin, or William Morris, or any other eminent artist who shares Nordau's objection, and yours and mine, to our existing social arrangements. In the face of this, it is really impossible to deny oneself the fun of asking Nordau, with all possible good humor, who he is and what he is, that he should rail in this fashion at great men. Wagner was discontented with the condition of musical art in Europe. In essay after essay he pointed out with the most laborious exactitude what it was he complained of, and how it might be remedied. He not only shewed, in the teeth of the most envenomed opposition from all the dunderheads, pedants and vested interests in Europe, what the musical drama ought to be as a work of art, but how theatres for its proper performance should be managed – nay, how they should be built, down to the arrangement of the seats and the position of the instruments in the orchestra. And he not only shewed this on paper, but he successfully composed the music dramas, built a model theatre, gave the model performances, *did* the impossible; so that there is now nobody left, not even Hanslick, who cares to stultify himself by repeating the old anti-Wagner cry of craziness and Impossibilism – nobody, save only Max Nordau, who, like a true journalist, is fact-proof. William Morris objected to the abominable ugliness of early Victorian decoration and furniture, to the rhymed rhetoric which did duty for poetry from the Renaissance to the nineteenth century, to kamptulicon-stained glass, and, later on, to the shiny commercial gentility of typography according to the American ideal, spread through England by Harper's Magazine and The Century. Well, did he sit down, as Nordau suggests, to rail helplessly at the men who were at all events getting the work of the world done, however inartistically? Not a bit of it: he designed and manufactured the decorations he wanted, and furnished and decorated houses with them; he put into public halls and churches tapestries and picture-windows which cultivated people now travel to see as they travel to see first-rate fifteenth-century work in that kind; the books from his Kelmscott Press, printed with type designed by his own hand, are pounced on by collectors like the treasures of our national museums: all this work, remember, involving the successful conduction of a large business establishment and factory, and being relieved by the incidental production of a series of poems and prose romances which placed their author in the position of the greatest living English poet. Now let me repeat the terms in which Nordau describes this kind of activity. 'Ridiculously insignificant aims – beating the air – no earnest thought to improvement – astoundingly mad projects for making the world happy – persistent rage against everything and everyone, displayed in venomous phrases, savage threats and destructive mania of wild beasts.' Is there not something deliciously ironical in the ease with which a splenetic pamphleteer, with nothing to shew for himself except a bookful of blunders tacked on to a mock scientific theory picked up at second hand from a few lunacy doctors with a literary turn, should be able to create a European scandal by declaring that the greatest creative artists of the century are barren and hysterical madmen? I do not know what the American critics have said about Nordau; but here the tone has been that there is much in what he says, and that he is evidently an authority on the subjects with which he deals. And yet I assure you, on my credit as a man who lives by art criticism, that from his preliminary description of a Morris design as one 'on which strange birds flit among crazily ramping branches, and blowzy flowers coquet with vain butterflies' (which is about as sensible as a description of the Norman chapel in the Tower of London as a characteristic specimen of Baroque architecture would be) to his coupling of Cimabue and Fra Angelico as primitive Florentine masters – from his unashamed bounce about 'the conscientious observance of the laws of counterpoint' by Beethoven and other masters celebrated for breaking them to his unlucky shot about 'a pedal bass with correct harmonization' (a pedal bass happening to be the particular instance in which even the professor-made rules of 'correct harmonization' are suspended), Nordau exposes his sciolism time after time as an authority upon the fine arts. But his critics, being for the most part ignorant literary men like himself, with sharpened wits and neglected eyes and ears, have swallowed Cimabue and Ghirlandaio and the pedal bass like so many gulls. Here an Ibsen admirer may maintain that Ibsen is an exception to the degenerate theory and should be classed with Goethe; there a Wagnerite may plead that Wagner is entitled to the honors of Beethoven; els_where one may find a champion of Rossetti venturing cautiously to suggest a suspicion of the glaringly obvious fact that Nordau has read only the two or three popular ballads like The Blessed Damozel, Eden Bower, Sister Helen and so on, which every smatterer reads, and that his knowledge of the mass of pictorial, dramatic, and decorative work turned out by Rossetti, Burne-Jones, Ford Madox Brown, William Morris and Holman Hunt, without a large knowledge and careful study of which no man can possibly speak with any critical authority of the pre-Raphaelite movement, is apparently limited to a glance at Holman Hunt's Shadow of the Cross or possibly an engraving thereof. But in the main he is received as a serious authority on his subjects; and that is why we two, without malice and solely as a matter of public duty, are compelled to take all this trouble to destroy him.

And now, my dear Tucker, I have told you as much about Nordau's book as it is worth. In a country where art was really known to the people, instead of being merely read about, it would not be necessary to spend three lines on such a work. But in England, where nothing but superstitious awe and self-mistrust prevents most men from thinking about art as Nordau boldly speaks about it; where to have a sense of art is to be one in a thousand, the other nine hundred and ninety-nine being either Philistine voluptuaries or Calvinistic anti-voluptuaries, it is useless to pretend that Nordau's errors will be self-evident. Already we have native writers, without half his cleverness or energy of expression, clumsily imitating his sham-scientific vivisection in their attacks on artists whose work they happen to dislike. Therefore, in riveting his book to the counter, I have used a nail long enough to go through a few pages by other people as well; and that must be my excuse for my disregard of the familiar editorial stigma of degeneracy which Nordau calls Agoraphobia, or Fear of Space.

THE QUINTESSENCE OF IBSENISM

THE TWO PIONEERS

1. The curious persistence of this proposition in the higher poetry of the nineteenth century is not easy to account for now that it sounds both unimportant and old-fashioned. It is as if one said, 'It is not wrong to stand on one's head.' The reply is: 'You may be very right; but as nobody wants to, why bother about it?' Yet I think this sensible way of treating the matter – obviously more healthy than the old morbid horror – has been produced largely by the refusal of poets like Shelley and Wagner to accept the theory of natural antipathy as the basis of the tables of consanguinity, and by the subsequent publication of masses of evidence by sociologists, from Herbert Spencer to Westermarck, showing that such tables are entirely conventional and that all our prohibitions have been either ignored or actually turned into positive obligations at one time or another without any shock to human instincts. The consequence is that our eyes are now opened to the practical social reasons for barring marriage between Laon and Cythna, Siegmund and Sieglinda; and the preaching of incest as something poetic in itself has lost all its morbid interest and ceased. Also we are beginning to recognize the important fact that the absence of romantic illusion as between persons brought up together, which undoubtedly exists, and which used to be mistaken for natural antipathy, cannot be depended on as between strangers, however close their consanguinity, and that any domestic or educational system which segregates the sexes produces romantic illusion, no matter how undesirable it may be. It

will be seen later on in the chapter dealing with the play called Ghosts, that Ibsen took this modern view that consanguinity does not count between strangers. I have accepted it myself in my play Mrs Warren's Profession (1912).

2. I had better here warn students of philosophy that I am speaking of rationalism, not as classified in the books, but as apparent in men.

3. I say the moderns, because the will is our old friend the soul or spirit of man; and the doctrine of justification, not by works, but by faith, clearly derives its validity from the consideration that no action, taken apart from the will behind it, has any moral character: for example, the acts which make the murderer and incendiary infamous are exactly similar to those which make the patriotic hero famous. 'Original sin' is the will doing mischief. 'Divine grace' is the will doing good. Our fathers, unversed in the Hegelian dialectic, could not conceive that these two, each the negation of the other, were the same. Schopenhauer's philosophy, like that of all pessimists, is really based on the old view of the will as original sin, and on the 1750–1850 view that the intellect is the divine grace that is to save us from it. It is as well to warn those who fancy that Schopenhauerism is one and indivisible, that acceptance of its metaphysics by no means involves endorsement of its philosophy.

4. The correlation between Rationalism and Materialism in this process has some immediate practical importance. Those who give up Materialism whilst clinging to Rationalism generally either relapse into abject submission to the most paternal of the Churches, or are caught by the attempts, constantly renewed, of mystics to found a new faith by rationalizing on the hollowness of materialism. The hollowness has nothing in it; and if you have come to grief as a materialist by reasoning about something, you are not likely, as a mystic, to improve matters by reasoning about nothing.

5. This is not precisely true. Voltaire was what we should now call an advanced Congregationalist: in fact, modern

362

Dissent, on its educated side, is sound Voltaireanism. Voltaire was for some time on very friendly terms with the Genevese pastors. But what with his jests at the expense of Bible worship, and the fact that he could not formally cut himself off from the Established Church of France without placing himself in its power, the pastors had finally to conceal their agreement with him (1912).

IDEALS AND IDEALISTS

1. The following are examples of the two stages of Shelley criticism:

We feel as if one of the darkest of the fiends had been clothed with a human body to enable him to gratify his enmity against the human race, and as if the supernatural atrocity of his hate were only heightened by his power to do injury. So strongly has this impression dwelt upon our minds that we absolutely asked a friend, who had seen this individual, to describe him to us – as if a cloven hoof, or horn, or flame from the mouth, must have marked the external appearance of so bitter an enemy of mankind. (*Literary Gazette*, 19 May 1821.)

A beautiful and ineffectual angel, beating in the void his luminous wings in vain. (Matthew Arnold, in the preface to his selection of poems by Byron, dated 1881.)

The 1881 opinion is much sillier than the 1821 opinion. Further samples will be found in the articles of Henry Salt, one of the few writers on Shelley who understand his true position as a social pioneer.

2. The above was written in 1890, ten years before Ibsen, in When We Dead Awaken, fully adopted its metaphor without, as far as I know, having any knowledge of my essay. Such an anticipation is a better proof than any mere argument that I found the right track of Ibsen's thought (1912).

THE WOMANLY WOMAN

1. It was to force the Government to take steps to suppress child prostitution that Stead resorted to the desperate expedient already alluded to. He succeeded.

2. Shortly after the publication of this passage, a German lady told me that she knew 'where I had got it from', evidently not meaning from Ibsen. She added, 'You have been reading Nietzsche's Through Good and Evil and Out at the other Side.' That was the first I ever heard of Nietzsche. I mention this fact, not with the ridiculous object of vindicating my 'originality' in nineteenth-century fashion, but because I attach great importance to the evidence that the movement voiced by Schopenhauer, Wagner, Ibsen, Nietzsche and Strindberg, was a world movement, and would have found expression if every one of these writers had perished in his cradle. I have dealt with this question in the preface to my play Major Barbara. The movement is alive today in the philosophy of Bergson and the plays of Gorki, Tchekov and the post-Ibsen English drama (1912).

3. A dissertation on the anomalies and impossibilities of the marriage law at its present stage would be too far out of the main course of my argument to be introduced in the text above; but it may be well to point out in passing to those who regard marriage as an inviolable and inviolate institution, that necessity has already forced us to tamper with it to such an extent that at this moment (1891) the highest court in the kingdom is face to face with a husband and wife, the one demanding whether a woman may saddle him with all the responsibilities of a husband and then refuse to live with him, and the other asking whether the law allows her husband to commit abduction, imprisonment and rape upon her. If the court says 'Yes' to the husband, indissoluble marriage is made intolerable for women; and as this exhausts the possible alternatives, it is clear that provision must be made for the dissolution of such marriages if the institution is to be

maintained at all, which it must be until its social function is otherwise provided for. Marriage is thus, by force of circumstances, compelled to buy extension of life by extension of divorce, much as if a fugitive should try to delay a pursuing wolf by throwing portions of his own heart to it. (The court decided against the man; but England still lags behind the rest of Protestant Europe in the necessary readjustment of the law of divorce. See the preface to my play Getting Married, which supplies the dissertation crowded out of the foregoing note [1912].)

4. I should have warned my male readers to be very careful how they presume on this position. In actual practice marriage reduces the man to a greater dependence on the woman than is good for either party. But the woman can tyrannize only by misconduct or threats of misconduct, whilst the man can tyrannize legally, though it must be added that a good deal of the makeshift law that has been set up to restrain this tyranny is very unfair to the man. The writings of Belfort Bax are instructive on this point (1912).

THE PLAYS

Peer Gynt

1. Miss Pagan, who has produced scenes from Peer Gynt in Edinburgh and London (which, to its shame, has not yet seen a complete public performance of Peer Gynt), regards the death of Peer as occurring in the scene where all the wasted possibilities of his life drift about him as withered leaves and fluffs of bog-cotton. He picks up an onion, and, playing with the idea that it is himself, and that its skins are the phases of his own career wrapped round the kernel of his real self, strips them off one after another, only to discover that there is no kernel. 'Nature is ironical,' says Peer bitterly; and that discovery of his own nothingness is taken by Miss Pagan as his death, the subsequent adventures being those of his soul.

It is impossible to demur to so poetic an interpretation; though it assumes, in spite of the onion, that Peer had not wholly destroyed his soul. Still, as the button moulder (who might be Brand's ghost) does respite Peer 'until the next crossroads', it cannot be said that Ibsen leaves Peer definitely scrapped (1912).

Emperor and Galilean

2. As such misgivings seldom arise except when the conscience revolts against the contemplated action, an appeal to Scripture to justify a point of conduct is generally found in practice to be an attempt to excuse a crime.

3. Or, as we should now say, the 'Superman' (1912).

THE OBJECTIVE ANTI-IDEALIST PLAYS

Ghosts

1. A forgotten production, published in the English Illustrated Magazine for January 1890. Besant makes the moneylender, as a reformed man, and a pattern of all the virtues, hold a forged bill *in terrorem* over Nora's grown-up daughter, engaged to his son. The bill has been forged by her brother, who has inherited a tendency to forge from his mother. Helmer having taken to drink after the departure of his wife, and forfeited his social position, the moneylender tells the girl that if she persists in disgracing him by marrying his son, he will send her brother to gaol. She evades the dilemma by drowning herself. The moral is that if Nora had never run away from her husband her daughter would never have drowned herself. Note that the moneylender does over again what he did in Ibsen's play, with the difference that, having become eminently respectable, he has also become a remorseless scoundrel. Ibsen shows him as a good-natured fellow at bottom. I wrote a sequel to this sequel. Another sequel was

written by Eleanor, the youngest daughter of Karl Marx. I forget where they appeared.

Descriptions of Ibsen's Admirers

2. Outrageous as the above extracts now seem, I could make them appear quite moderate by setting beside them the hue and cry raised in New York in 1905 against a play of my own entitled Mrs Warren's Profession. But there was a commercial reason for that. My play exposed what has since become known as the 'white slave traffic'; that is the organization of prostitution as a regular commercial industry yielding huge profits to capital invested in it, directly or indirectly, by 'pillars of society'. The attack on the play was so corrupt that the newspaper that took the lead in it was heavily fined shortly afterwards for trading in advertisements of the traffic. But the attack on Ghosts was, I believe, really disinterested and sincere on its moral side. No doubt Ibsen was virulently hated by some of the writers quoted, as all great and original artists are hated by contemporary mediocrity, which needs must hate the highest when it sees it. Our own mediocrities would abuse Ibsen as heartily as their fathers did if they were not young enough to have started with an entirely inculcated and unintelligent assumption that he is a classic, like Shakespear and Goethe, and therefore must not be abused and need not be understood. But we have only to compare the frantic and indecent vituperation quoted above with the mere disparagement and dislike expressed towards Ibsen's other plays at the same period to perceive that here Ibsen struck at something much deeper than the fancies of critics as to the proper way to write plays. An ordinary farcical comedy ridiculing Pastor Manders and making Alving out to be a good fellow would have enlisted their sympathy at once, as their tradition was distinctly Bohemian. Their horror at Ghosts is a striking proof of the worthlessness of mere Bohemianism, which has all the idle sentimentality and

idolatry of conventionality without any of its backbone of contract and law (1912).

THE LESSON OF THE PLAYS

1. The common-sense solution of the ethical problem has often been delivered by acclamation in the theatre. Many years ago, I witnessed a performance of a melodrama founded on this story. After the painful trial scene, in which Jeanie Deans condemns her sister to death by refusing to swear to a perfectly innocent fiction, came a scene in the prison. 'If it had been me,' said the gaoler, 'I wad ha sworn a hole through an iron pot.' The roar of applause which burst from the pit and gallery was thoroughly Ibsenist in sentiment. The speech, by the way, must have been a gag of the actor's: at all events, I cannot find it in the acting edition of the play.

2. The warning implied in this sentence is less needed now than it was twenty years ago. The association of Bohemianism with the artistic professions and with revolutionary political views has been weakened by the revolt of the children of the Bohemians against its domestic squalor and social outlawry. Bohemianism is now rather one of the stigmata of the highly conservative 'smart sets' of the idle rich than of the studio, the stage and the socialist organizations (1912).

NOTES

THE PERFECT WAGNERITE

SIEGFRIED AS PROTESTANT

1. The necessity for breeding the governing class from a selected stock has always been recognized by Aristocrats, however erroneous their methods of selection. We have changed our system from Aristocracy to Democracy, without considering that we were at the same time changing, as regards our governing class, from Selection to Promiscuity. Those who have taken a practical part in modern politics best know how farcical the result is.

NIGHT FALLS ON THE GODS

1. 'We must learn to die, and to die in the fullest sense of the word. The fear of the end is the source of all lovelessness; and this fear is generated only when love begins to wane. How came it that this love, the highest blessedness to all things living, was so far lost sight of by the human race that at last it came to this – all that mankind did, ordered and established, was conceived only in fear of the end? My poem sets this forth.' (Wagner to Roeckel, 25th Jan. 1854).
2. Die Götterdämmerung means literally Godsgloaming. The English versions of the opera are usually called The Dusk of the Gods or The Twilight of the Gods. I have purposely introduced the ordinary title in the sentence above for the reader's information.

THE SANITY OF ART

1. Perhaps by this time, however, Mr Arnold Dolmetsch has educated America in this matter, as he educated London and educated me.

2. As I spent the first twenty years of my life in Ireland I am, for the purposes of this survey of musical art, at least a century and a half old. I can remember the sensation given by the opening chord of Beethoven's youthful Prometheus overture. It sounded strangely strong and momentous, because the use of the third inversion of the chord of the dominant seventh without preparation was unexpected in those days. As to exploding undiminished chords of the ninth and thirteenth on the unsuspecting ear in the same way (everybody does it nowadays), one might as well have sat down on the keyboard and called it music. The very name of the thirteenth was inconceivable; a discreetly prepared and resolved suspension of 'four to three' was the only form in which that discord was known. I can remember, too, the indignation with which Macfarren, after correcting his pupils for unintentional consecutive fifths all his life, found himself expected to write an analytic program for the performance at a Philharmonic concert of an overture by a composer (Goetz) who actually wrote consecutive sevenths intentionally because he liked them.

However, I do not insert this note for the sake of my reminiscences, but because, since writing the text above, a composer of the first order (Richard Strauss) has become known in London, and has been attacked, just as Wagner was, by the very men who lived through the huge blunder of anti-Wagnerism. This cannot be accounted for by the superstitions of the age of decorative music. Every critic nowadays is thoroughly inured to descriptive and dramatic music which is not only as independent of the old decorative forms as Strauss's, but a good deal more so; for Strauss lives on the verge of a barcarolle and seldom resists a nursery tune for long. The hostility to him may be partly due to the fact that by his great achievement of rescuing music from the realm of tights and wigs and stage armor in which Wagner, with all his genius, dwelt to the last, and bringing it into direct contact with modern life, he was enabled in his Heldenleben to give

370

an orchestral caricature of his critics which comes much closer home than Wagner's medievally disguised Beckmesser. But Strauss is denounced by men who are quite capable of laughing at themselves, who are sincere advocates of modern realism in other arts, and who are sufficiently good judges to know, for instance, that the greater popularity of Tchaikowsky is like the greater popularity of Rossini as compared with Beethoven nearly a century ago; that is, the vogue of a musical voluptuary, who, though very pleasant in his lighter vein, very strenuous in his energetic vein, and at least grandiose in his sublime vein, never attains, nor desires to attain, the elevation at which the great modern musicians from Bach to Strauss maintain themselves. Anti-Straussism is therefore accounted for neither by the old anti-Wagnerian confusion nor by the petulance of the critic who is beaten by his job.

I conclude that the disagreeable effect which an unaccustomed discord produces on people who cannot divine its resolution is to blame for most of the nonsense now written about Strauss. Strauss's technical procedure involves a profusion of such shocks. But the disagreeable effect will not last. There is no longer a single discord used by Wagner of which the resolution is not already as much a platitude as the resolution of the simple sevenths of Mozart and Meyerbeer. Strauss not only goes from discord to discord, leaving the implied resolutions to be inferred by people who never heard them before, but actually makes a feature of unresolved discords, just as Wagner made a feature of unprepared ones. Men who were reconciled quite late in life to compositions beginning with dominant thirteenths *fortissimo*, find themselves disquieted now by compositions ending with unresolved tonic sevenths.

I think this phase of protest will soon pass. I think so because I find myself able to follow Strauss's harmonic procedure; to divining the destination of his most discordant passing phrases (it is too late now to talk of mere 'passing notes'); and to tolerate his most off-hand ellipses and most unceremonious omissions of final concords, with enjoyment, though my musical endowment is none of the acutest. In twenty years the complaints about his music will be as unintelligible as the similar complaints about Handel, Mozart, Beethoven and Wagner in the past.

I must apologize for the technical jargon I have had to use in this note. Probably it is all obsolete by this time; but I know nothing newer. Stainer would have understood it thirty years ago. If nobody understands it today, my knowledge will seem all the more profound.

3. Perhaps I had better remark in passing that unless it were true – which it is not – that the length of the modern penny letter or halfpenny post-card is the same as that of the eighteenth-century letter, and that the number of persons who know how to read and write has not increased, there is no reason whatever to draw Nordau's conclusion from the postal statistics.

4. Here again we have a statement which means nothing unless it be compared with statistics as to the multiplication of the civilized man's power of production by machinery, which in some industries has multiplied a single man's output by hundreds and in others by thousands whilst actually lightening his labor. As to crimes and disease, Nordau should state whether convictions under modern laws – for offences against the Joint Stock Company Acts, for instance – prove that we have degenerated since those Acts were passed, and whether the invention of new names for a dozen varieties of fever which were formerly counted as one single disease is any evidence of decaying health in the face of the increasing duration of life.

5. Perhaps I had better give one example. Nordau first quotes a couple of speeches from An Enemy of the People and The Wild Duck:

STOCKMANN: I love my native town so well that I had rather ruin it than see it flourishing on a lie. All men who live on

372

lies must be exterminated like vermin. (An Enemy of the People.)

RELLING: Yes: I said illusion [lie]. For illusion, you know, is the stimulating principle. Rob the average man of his life illusion and you rob him of his happiness at the same time. (The Wild Duck.)

Nordau proceeds to comment as follows: 'Now, what is Ibsen's real opinion? Is a man to strive for truth or to swelter in deceit? Is Ibsen with Stockmann or with Relling? Ibsen owes us an answer to these questions or, rather, he replies to them affirmatively and negatively with equal ardor and equal poetic power.'

FOR THE BEST IN PAPERBACKS, LOOK FOR THE

In every corner of the world, on every subject under the sun, Penguin represents quality and variety – the very best in publishing today.

For complete information about books available from Penguin – including Puffins, Penguin Classics and Arkana – and how to order them, write to us at the appropriate address below. Please note that for copyright reasons the selection of books varies from country to country.

In the United Kingdom: Please write to *Dept E.P., Penguin Books Ltd, Harmondsworth, Middlesex, UB7 0DA.*

If you have any difficulty in obtaining a title, please send your order with the correct money, plus ten per cent for postage and packaging, to *PO Box No 11, West Drayton, Middlesex*

In the United States: Please write to *Dept BA, Penguin, 299 Murray Hill Parkway, East Rutherford, New Jersey 07073*

In Canada: Please write to *Penguin Books Canada Ltd, 2801 John Street, Markham, Ontario L3R 1B4*

In Australia: Please write to the *Marketing Department, Penguin Books Australia Ltd, P.O. Box 257, Ringwood, Victoria 3134*

In New Zealand: Please write to the *Marketing Department, Penguin Books (NZ) Ltd, Private Bag, Takapuna, Auckland 9*

In India: Please write to *Penguin Overseas Ltd, 706 Eros Apartments, 56 Nehru Place, New Delhi, 110019*

In the Netherlands: Please write to *Penguin Books Netherlands B.V., Postbus 195, NL–1380AD Weesp*

In West Germany: Please write to *Penguin Books Ltd, Friedrichstrasse 10–12, D–6000 Frankfurt/Main 1*

In Spain: Please write to *Longman Penguin España, Calle San Nicolas 15, E–28013 Madrid*

In Italy: Please write to *Penguin Italia s.r.l., Via Como 4, I-20096 Pioltello (Milano)*

In France: Please write to *Penguin Books Ltd, 39 Rue de Montmorency, F-75003 Paris*

In Japan: Please write to *Longman Penguin Japan Co Ltd, Yamaguchi Building, 2–12–9 Kanda Jimbocho, Chiyoda-Ku, Tokyo 101*

FOR THE BEST IN PAPERBACKS, LOOK FOR THE 🐧

PLAYS IN PENGUIN

Edward Albee **Who's Afraid of Virginia Woolf?**

Alan Ayckbourn **The Norman Conquests**

Bertolt Brecht **Parables for the Theatre (The Good Woman of Setzuan/The Caucasian Chalk Circle)**

Anton Chekhov **Plays (The Cherry Orchard/Three Sisters/Ivanov/The Seagull/Uncle Vanya)**

Henrik Ibsen **Hedda Gabler/The Pillars of the Community/The Wild Duck**

Eugène Ionesco **Absurd Drama (Rhinoceros/The Chair/The Lesson)**

Ben Jonson **Three Comedies (Volpone/The Alchemist/Bartholomew Fair)**

D. H. Lawrence **Three Plays (The Collier's Friday Night/ The Daughter-in-Law/The Widowing of Mrs Holroyd)**

Arthur Miller **Death of a Salesman**

John Mortimer **A Voyage Round My Father/What Shall We Tell Caroline?/ The Dock Brief**

J. B. Priestley **Time and the Conways/I Have Been Here Before/An Inspector Calls/The Linden Tree**

Peter Shaffer **Lettice and Lovage/Yonadab**

Bernard Shaw **Plays Pleasant (Arms and the Man/Candida/The Man of Destiny/You Never Can Tell)**

Sophocles **Three Theban Plays (Oedipus the King/Antigone/Oedipus at Colonus)**

Arnold Wesker **Plays, Volume 1: The Wesker Trilogy (Chicken Soup with Barley/Roots/I'm Talking about Jerusalem)**

Oscar Wilde **Plays (Lady Windermere's Fan/A Woman of No Importance/ An Ideal Husband/The Importance of Being Earnest/Salome)**

Thornton Wilder **Our Town/The Skin of Our Teeth/The Matchmaker**

Tennessee Williams **Sweet Bird of Youth/A Streetcar Named Desire/The Glass Menagerie**

FOR THE BEST IN PAPERBACKS, LOOK FOR THE 🐧

PENGUIN CLASSICS

Matthew Arnold	**Selected Prose**
Jane Austen	**Emma**
	Lady Susan, The Watsons, Sanditon
	Mansfield Park
	Northanger Abbey
	Persuasion
	Pride and Prejudice
	Sense and Sensibility
Anne Brontë	**Agnes Grey**
	The Tenant of Wildfell Hall
Charlotte Brontë	**Jane Eyre**
	Shirley
	Villette
Emily Brontë	**Wuthering Heights**
Samuel Butler	**Erewhon**
	The Way of All Flesh
Thomas Carlyle	**Selected Writings**
Wilkie Collins	**The Moonstone**
	The Woman in White
Charles Darwin	**The Origin of Species**
	The Voyage of the Beagle
Benjamin Disraeli	**Sybil**
George Eliot	**Adam Bede**
	Daniel Deronda
	Felix Holt
	Middlemarch
	The Mill on the Floss
	Romola
	Scenes of Clerical Life
	Silas Marner
Elizabeth Gaskell	**Cranford** and **Cousin Phillis**
	The Life of Charlotte Brontë
	Mary Barton
	North and South
	Wives and Daughters

Charles Dickens	**American Notes for General Circulation**
	Barnaby Rudge
	Bleak House
	The Christmas Books
	David Copperfield
	Dombey and Son
	Great Expectations
	Hard Times
	Little Dorrit
	Martin Chuzzlewit
	The Mystery of Edwin Drood
	Nicholas Nickleby
	The Old Curiosity Shop
	Oliver Twist
	Our Mutual Friend
	The Pickwick Papers
	Selected Short Fiction
	A Tale of Two Cities
Edward Gibbon	**The Decline and Fall of the Roman Empire**
George Gissing	**New Grub Street**
William Godwin	**Caleb Williams**
Edmund Gosse	**Father and Son**
Thomas Hardy	**The Distracted Preacher and Other Tales**
	Far From the Madding Crowd
	Jude the Obscure
	The Mayor of Casterbridge
	The Return of the Native
	Tess of the d'Urbervilles
	The Trumpet Major
	Under the Greenwood Tree
	The Woodlanders

FOR THE BEST IN PAPERBACKS, LOOK FOR THE 🐧

PENGUIN CLASSICS

Richard Jefferies	**Landscape with Figures**
Thomas Macaulay	**The History of England**
Henry Mayhew	**Selections from London Labour** and **The London Poor**
John Stuart Mill	**On Liberty**
William Morris	**News from Nowhere** and **Selected Writings and Designs**
Walter Pater	**Marius the Epicurean**
John Ruskin	**'Unto This Last' and Other Writings**
Sir Walter Scott	**Ivanhoe**
Robert Louis Stevenson	**Dr Jekyll and Mr Hyde**
William Makepeace Thackeray	**The History of Henry Esmond**
	Vanity Fair
Anthony Trollope	**Barchester Towers**
	Framley Parsonage
	Phineas Finn
	The Warden
Mrs Humphrey Ward	**Helbeck of Bannisdale**
Mary Wollstonecraft	**Vindication of the Rights of Woman**
Dorothy and William Wordsworth	**Home at Grasmere**

FOR THE BEST IN PAPERBACKS, LOOK FOR THE 🐧

PENGUIN CLASSICS

Arnold Bennett	**The Old Wives' Tale**
Joseph Conrad	**Heart of Darkness**
	Nostromo
	The Secret Agent
	The Shadow-Line
	Twixt Land and Sea
	Under Western Eyes
E. M. Forster	**Howard's End**
	The Longest Journey
	A Passage to India
	A Room With a View
	Where Angels Fear to Tread
Henry James	**The Aspern Papers** and **The Turn of the Screw**
	The Bostonians
	Daisy Miller
	The Europeans
	The Golden Bowl
	Portrait of a Lady
	Roderick Hudson
	Washington Square
	What Maisie Knew
	The Wings of the Dove
Rudyard Kipling	**The Day's Work**
	The Light That Failed
	Wee Willie Winkie
D. H. Lawrence	**The Plumed Serpent**
	The Rainbow
	Selected Short Stories
	Sons and Lovers
	The White Peacock
	Women in Love

FOR THE BEST IN PAPERBACKS, LOOK FOR THE 🐧

PENGUIN PASSNOTES

This comprehensive series, designed to help GCSE students, includes:

SUBJECTS
Biology
Chemistry
Economics
English Language
Geography
Human Biology
Mathematics
Nursing
Oral English
Physics

SHAKESPEARE
As You Like It
Henry IV Part I
Henry V
Julius Caesar
Macbeth
The Merchant of Venice
A Midsummer Night's Dream
Romeo and Juliet
Twelfth Night

LITERATURE
Across the Barricades
The Catcher in the Rye
Cider with Rosie
The Crucible
Death of a Salesman
Far From the Madding Crowd
Great Expectations
Gregory's Girl
I am the Cheese
I'm the King of the Castle
The Importance of Being Earnest
Jane Eyre
Joby
Journey's End
Kes
Lord of the Flies
A Man for All Seasons
The Mayor of Casterbridge
My Family and Other Animals
Oliver Twist
The Pardoner's Tale
Pride and Prejudice
The Prologue to the Canterbury
   Tales
Pygmalion
Roots
The Royal Hunt of the Sun
Silas Marner
A Taste of Honey
To Kill a Mockingbird
Wuthering Heights
Z for Zachariah